G000056689

Lyric Encounters

Lyric Encounters

Essays on American Poetry from Lazarus and Frost to Ortiz Cofer and Alexie

Daniel Morris

B L O O M S B U R Y

NEW YORK • LONDON • NEW DELHI • SYDNEY

Bloomsbury Academic

An imprint of Bloomsbury Publishing Plc

175 Fifth Avenue	50 Bedford Square
New York	London
NY 10010	WC1B 3DP
USA	UK

www.bloomsbury.com

First published 2013

© Daniel Morris, 2013

All rights reserved. No part of this publication may be reproduced or transmitted in any form or by any means, electronic or mechanical, including photocopying, recording, or any information storage or retrieval system, without prior permission in writing from the publishers.

No responsibility for loss caused to any individual or organization acting on or refraining from action as a result of the material in this publication can be accepted by Bloomsbury Academic or the author.

ISBN PB: 978-1-4411-5156-8
HB: 978-1-4411-9442-8
ePub: 978-1-4411-1017-6
ePDF: 978-1-4411-5994-6

Library of Congress Cataloging-in-Publication Data
Morris, Daniel, 1962-
Lyric encounters : essays on American poetry from Lazarus and Frost to Ortiz Cofer and Alexie / by Daniel Morris.
pages cm
Includes bibliographical references and index.
ISBN 978-1-4411-9442-8 (hardcover : alk. paper) – ISBN 978-1-4411-5156-8 (pbk. : alk. paper) 1. American poetry–20th century–History and criticism. 2. Lyric poetry–History and criticism. I. Title.
PS323.5.M66 2013
811'.509–dc23
2012049675

Typeset by Fakenham Prepress Solutions, Fakenham, Norfolk NR21 8NN
Printed and bound in the United States of America

CONTENTS

ACKNOWLEDGMENTS

I am grateful to the many persons who have discussed aspects of this book with me. I am sure I will not remember everybody. I thank Purdue colleagues: Marlo David, Wendy Flory, Christian Knoeller, Matthew Kroll, Walter Moore, Bill Mullen, Venetria Patton, Nancy Peterson, Donald Platt, Amy Pommerening, Charles Ross, Jimmy Saunders, Mike Yetman. At conferences and through correspondences: David Epstein, Tom Fink, Norman Finkelstein, Eugene Goodheart, Allen Grossman, Trudier Harris, Michael Heller, Glen MacLeod, R. Baxter Miller, Stephen Paul Miller, Ranen Omer-Sherman, Donald E. Pease, Margaret Scanlan, Daniel R. Schwarz, Siobhan Somerville. A very special thank you to Ethan Goffman. Ethan has read, commented upon, and edited my work – on this project and others – for several years. His knowledge of literature, politics, and culture is extensive. He pushes me to refine my thoughts and do my best work. Bloomsbury has been a fabulous publisher. I am grateful to Susan Dunsmore, Ally Jane Grossan, Haaris Naqvi, Kim Storry. Purdue has offered significant financial and staff support. I thank Liberal Arts Dean Irwin Weiser, Jewish Studies director Daniel Frank, and English department Head Nancy Peterson for providing research support. I thank Sheila Featherstone and Erica Cox of the English department staff for their support. Purdue libraries have provided great access to materials, including through the Interlibrary Loan service. My greatest thank you goes to my family. I am so very grateful to my wife Joy and children Isaac, Aaron, and Hannah. You make every day special.

Some of the chapters in this book originally appeared in somewhat different form in the following journals. I thank the editors and referees for these journals. Their efforts have improved the current versions.

"The Erotics of Close Reading: Williams, Demuth, and 'The Crimson Cyclamen'." *William Carlos Williams Review* 27. 1 (2007 Spring): 57–68.

"'The Word Gets Around': Silko's Theory of Narrative Survival in The Delicacy and Strength of Lace." *Western American Literature* 34. 1 (1999 Spring): 48–67.

"'Go Home and Write a Page Tonight': Subversive Irony and Resistant Reading in "Theme for English B." *The Langston Hughes Review*. Volume 24–25. Winter/Fall 2010/2011: 20–30.

"'Mending Wall': The Case for the Humanities Classroom." *Tikkun* 26(1): 2011. Online exclusive.

"Active and Passive Citizenship in Emma Lazarus's 'The New Colossus' and Judith Ortiz Cofer's 'The Latin Deli: An Ars Poetica.'" *Papers on Language and Literature*. 287–301. Volume 48, Number 3, Summer 2012.

"On the Amtrak from Boston to New York City" from *First Indian on the Moon* (c) 1993 by Sherman Alexie. Reprinted by permission of Hanging Loose Press.

"Dear John, Dear Coltrane" from *Songlines in Michaeltree: New and Collected Poems* by Michael S. Harper. Reprinted by permission of the University of Illinois Press.

"Ellen West" from *In The Western Night: Collected Poems 1965–1990* by Frank Bidart. Copyright © 1990 by Frank Bidart. Reprinted by permission of Farrar, Straus and Giroux, LLC. and Carcanet Press Limited.

"Theme for English B" from *The Collected Poems of Langston Hughes* by Langston Hughes, edited by Arnold Rampersad with

David Roessel, Associate Editor, copyright © 1994 by the Estate of Langston Hughes. Used by permission of Alfred A. Knopf, a division of Random House, Inc. Any third party use of this material, outside of this publication, is prohibited. Interested parties must apply directly to Random House, Inc. for permission.

"The Crimson Cyclamen" from *The Collected Poems of William Carlos Williams, Vol. 1: 1909–1939*. Copyright by New Directions Publishing Corporation. Copyright © 1982, 1986 by William Eric Williams and Paul H. Williams.

"The Latin Deli: An Ars Poetica" by Judith Ortiz Cofer. Reprinted by permission of the University of Houston and Arte Publico Press.

"America" from *Collected Poems 1947-1980* by Allen Ginsberg. Copyright (c) 1956, 1959 by Allen Ginsberg. Reprinted by Permission of HarperCollins Publishers.

For additional territory. The Estate of Allen Ginsberg, as successor in interest to the rights of Allen Ginsberg, c/o The Wylie Agency, Inc., 250 West 57th Street, New York, NY 10107.

1

Introduction

In their popular textbook, *An Introduction to Poetry*, X. J. Kennedy and Dana Gioia define lyric as "a short poem expressing the thoughts and feelings of a single speaker" (2009, p. 10). Contrasting lyric with what she calls the "social genres"—epic, fiction, and drama—that "make us look at the wide panorama of a social group" (1997, p. xl), Harvard's influential poetry critic Helen Vendler, like Kennedy and Gioia, emphasizes the genre's monologic nature: "Lyric is the genre of private life: it is what we say to ourselves when we are alone" (p. xl). Reading lyric as a representation of the speaker's innermost thoughts and feelings, Vendler compares the form to a private diary. She admits lyric takes the reader into account, but only to the point where the reader can identify his or her experience with the lyric speaker's:

> [A] lyric is meant to be spoken by its reader as if the reader were the one uttering the words. A lyric poem is a script for performance by its reader. It is, then, the most intimate of genres, constructing a twinship between writer and reader. And it is the most universal of genres, because it presumes that the reader resembles the writer enough to step into the writer's shoes and speak the lines the writer has written as though they were the reader's own.
>
> (pp. xl–xli)

Vendler's conception of speaker and reader as twins disallows the element of resistance to a redundant interpretation of the relationship between self and other that, I will argue, is crucial to the interpersonal and pedagogic conception of twentieth-century American lyric poetry that I will be stressing in this book.

Since the early 1990s, I have taught twentieth-century American poetry to undergraduates at Purdue, a Land Grant Midwestern university better known as the "cradle of astronauts" and the "cradle of quarterbacks" than as the "cradle of literary critics." In my courses I often adopt Helen Vendler's *Poems, Poets, and Poetry*, which emphasizes the formal dimensions of verse, but I do so with reservations that require the critical interventions apparent throughout this book. In her introductory textbook, Vendler treats "the poem as arranged life." In a chapter devoted to "poems as pleasure," she divides the lyric into formal elements such as "rhyme," "structure," "images," and "argument." Unquestionably, undergraduate readers need to be reminded that while poems may originate in life, they are made objects. Observing a poem's "tone," "genre," "form," "rhythm," and "spatial arrangement," Vendler provides students with the vocabulary and the critical skills necessary to transcend impressionistic responses in class discussion and, we hope, to read poetry for pleasure long after the final bell of their college days has echoed:

> The important thing is to be accustomed to looking, in any poem, at several levels – the sound, the rhythms and rhymes, the grammar, the images, the sentences, the plot, the assertions, the allusions, the self-contradictions. Somewhere the energy of the poem awaits you. The moment you see the main and subordinate patterns, you smile, and it "all makes sense."
>
> (p. 81)

Vendler's program for reading lyrics has become popular with students and teachers alike because it turns interpretation into a game with a clear end game. The objective of reading a poem is to solve an intriguing and dynamic formal puzzle through attention to what she calls "the internal structure of the poem" (p. 114). However challenging the lyric, Vendler assures us, if the teacher follows her lead by recognizing, for example, a lyric's "fault lines," "the logic of argument," and changes "in tense or speech act" (p. 114), the student will then have found the skeleton key to unlock a formal mystery. The result of the transaction is a happy one: "you smile" with appreciation at a poem's fundamental intelligibility: "it all makes sense."

Vendler is not a hardcore formalist. She devotes her first chapter to what she calls "the poem as life." And she *does* include chapters on "Poetry and Social Identity" and "History and Regionality." In teaching with her book over many years, however, I have found her readings in these less formal chapters lack the depth, exuberance, and sensitivity to nuance that are evident in her discussion of poems organized under chapter headings such as "The Poem as Arranged Life."

Her lead-in to Sherman Alexie's "On the Amtrak from Boston to New York City" (1990 in journal, 1993 in a book), a poem I analyze in depth in my penultimate chapter on the acclaimed Wellpinit Indian author from Spokane, WA, in her section on "Regionality" is a case in point.

> Though European colonizers thought the New World bare of culture, Native Americans had already consecrated certain lands and mountains as sacred, and had composed poetry about them. This first acculturation of space in the United States has been in great part lost, with many of the Indian languages and their oral literatures fallen into extinction. But an imaginative claim to American territory is now being repeated by Native American poets like Sherman Alexie, who recalls, in his poem "On the Amtrak from Boston to New York City," a well-meaning woman whose ideas of American history, American landscape, and American literature start with the Revolutionary period and end with Thoreau.
>
> (p. 247)

Vendler regards Alexie's poem as a latter-day revision of the conventional (and modern formalist) category of what she calls a "spatial context." By situating "On the Amtrak" within the category of the "power of imagination to clothe a landscape in powerful allusive images" (p. 246), she removes the poem from the interpersonal, multicultural, and gendered tensions that, I argue, animate this lyric.

Even when focusing on history and place, Vendler limits her discussion of the exchange between lyric and landscape in her "Regionality" chapter to a technical problem involving the spatial issue of lyric compression:

In thinking about history poems, the main thing to remember is that there is always a tension between the copiousness of history and the brevity of lyric. To see how a structure as brief as lyric can present, speculate on, and judge history is to see a form straining against its own limits. When it succeeds, it strikes us as a triumph of style over difficulty.

(p. 251)

In contrast to Vendler's strict attention to the poet's spatial dilemma when dealing with "the copiousness of history," I contextualize Alexie's thinking about his status as a terrorist and resident alien in "On the Amtrak." I do so by comparing his understanding of the interpersonal in the poem from 1990 with Alexie's works written after the terrorist attacks on 11 September, 2001. I discuss Alexie's *Time* magazine essay on Sacagawea, his semi-autobiographical, young adult novel *The Absolutely True Diary of a Part-Time Indian* (2007), his visionary historical novel *Flight* (2007), and poems from *Face* (2009) to historicize "On the Amtrak."

The title of this book, *Lyric Encounters*, signals my emphasis on poems that represent dialogues between a lyric speaker—such as Alexie's young native American male from the Pacific Northwest – and another character—such as the "white woman" he meets on the Amtrak from Boston to New York. But my extensive commentary on Alexie novels and other writings in a chapter that begins with a close reading of "On the Amtrak" speaks to a second meaning of my title—the encounter between lyric poetry and other texts. I believe that literary criticism should attend to what Vendler calls the arrangement of life through analysis of a poem's form and style. By placing "On the Amtrak" in the context of prose and poetry he published in a post-9/11 environment, however, we can also notice how Alexie has put his writings in conversation with each other. Acts of creative revision of his prior texts, Alexie's later work refreshes his thinking about nation, history, ethnicity, multiculturalism, identity, and especially of interpersonal relationships. He has come to regard the binary thinking about self and other as well as Native American and White European citizenry evident in "On the Amtrak" as politically toxic. Read as a revisionary encounter with the terrorist conceit evident in "On the Amtrak," the later works may be interpreted, in terms Freud set forth in his classic paper "Mourning and Melancholia" (1917) as a "working through," rather than as an "acting out" of personal upset and historical traumas. Overall, Alexie takes an individualist journey of self-creation that accounts for, but is not superseded by, a multiplicity of more fixed, nationalist identities.

As in "On the Amtrak," other poems I discuss in this study foreground relationships between a lyric speaker and another character in the poem who represents a primary intended figure of address. Contra the once New Criticism, therefore, poems in this book illustrate literary theorist William Waters's point that post-Romantic lyric poetry may be considered less a "monologic genre" than one that highlights the "ways a poem resembles ordinary communication" (2003, p. 3). At the same time, however, I point out places where Waters's "ordinary communication" is blocked or deferred, as when Alexie's persona in "On the Amtrak" turns inward and avoids a confrontation with the white woman. I thus attend to interpersonal lyrics in which social discourse fails, and the speaker withdraws from Waters's "ordinary communication," and thus re-enters the Romantic lyric mode in which, as J. S. Mill theorized, the poem represents "feeling confessing itself to itself, in moments of solitude" (quoted in Waters, p. 4).

American poet and theorist Allen R. Grossman has emphasized the social elements of lyric poetry. In *The Sighted Singer: Two Works on Poetry for Readers and Writers* (1992), Grossman engages in a series of conversations about poetry with his former student, the poet Mark Halliday. In this appropriately interpersonal format, Grossman argues that lyric poetry functions to make "persons acknowledgeable" to each other (p. 3). Grossman believes that lyric poetry can and should express an interest in the presence, truth claims, and visibility of other persons besides the lyric speaker. Lyric poetry, he states, is not merely "an instrument of private self-legitimation" (p. 10). Instead, "[p]oetry is situated upon the central question of our civilization—how do we know a *person* is present?—and suffers all of the strains which we feel when we contemplate the precariousness of our visibility to others in this Postmodern world" (p. 10). Following Grossman, my study focuses on poems that imagine conversation, teaching, and debate, often, as in the Alexie works, involving a strong-willed lyric speaker and another self, bent on resisting how the speaker imagines the world. Demonstrating how lyric is an interactive endeavor, I describe how the speaker and an answerer, sometimes successfully, sometimes less so, find the terms to mark each other's respect for differing ways of seeing the world. In my reading of "queer" lyrics by William Carlos Williams, Allen Ginsberg, and Michael S. Harper, I notice how the speaker's relation to an other (Charles Demuth, Ginsberg's conservative self in a Cold War imaginary, John Coltrane), challenges the foundations of the self/other distinction by questioning rigid formulations of masculinity, heteronormativity, and a monolithic (as well as monologic) perspective on identity.[1]

In *After the Fall*, a study of post-9/11 literature, Richard Gray critiques texts that withdraw "into the domestic and the security fortress of America" (2011, p. 17). Privileging what Homi K. Bhaba calls an "interstitial perspective" (quoted in Gray, p. 64), Gray applauds writers who "get it right ... thanks to a strategy of convergence, rooted in the conviction that the hybrid is the only space in which the location of cultures and the bearing witness to trauma can really occur" (p. 17). Gray's prescription for a post-9/11 literature that foregrounds the interpersonal and hybridity is apparent in the poetry I treat in this book. Given the contemporary sociopolitical context addressed by Gray, this book argues that we need to expand our understanding of lyric poetry by twentieth-century U.S. poets to emphasize the themes of dialogue, responsibility, resistance, and pedagogy. The aforementioned themes characterize the intertextual aesthetics and interpersonal ethics that are more typically associated, as in Bakhtin, with non-lyric genres such as drama and prose fiction. Concerned with authors who hail from different backgrounds and practice varying stylistics, I demonstrate, through close and yet contextualized readings of signature poems such as Robert Frost's "Mending Wall" (1914), William Carlos Williams's "The Crimson Cyclamen" (1936), Langston Hughes's "Theme for English B" (1949), Allen Ginsberg's "America" (1956), Michael S. Harper's "Dear John, Dear Coltrane" (1970), Frank Bidart's "Ellen West" (1977), and Judith Ortiz Cofer's "The Latin

---

[1]My understanding of "queer theory" relies on Rosemary Hennessy's definition: "Queer theory calls into question obvious categories (man, woman, latina, jew, butch, femme), oppositions (man vs. woman, heterosexual), or equations (gender=sex) upon which conventional notions of sexuality and identity rely" (1993, p. 964).

Deli: An Ars Poetica" (1993), how each author imagines his or her text as an unsettling and often contested site of meeting between a lyric self and an interlocutor. Illustrating a constructive element of dialogue, the exchange between self and other has the capacity to alter the attitudes, values, beliefs, and judgments of both participants in the conversation.

Overview of the book

I have sequenced my chapters, roughly speaking, along chronological lines. I begin with essays on Langston Hughes and Williams Carlos Williams—Modernists whose prolific careers stretched well into contemporary times (Chapters 2 and 3). Locating dialogue in a pedagogical context inside a traditional classroom, I analyze how the theme of poetry as a form of teaching appears in Langston Hughes's "Theme for English B." The chapter on Hughes points to the theme of pedagogy as dialogue. It concerns an unruly and brilliant student and an insensitive teacher who fails to acknowledge how the student's unique subject position influences his uncertainty about how to respond to a writing prompt that assumes terms such as "you" and "home" are stable concepts. The chapter on Williams's interarts dialogue with his friend Charles Demuth's "The Crimson Cyclamen" watercolor from 1936 makes evident my own experience of interpretation as a response to a complex encounter with a poem or visual work that reveals as much about the respondent's attitudes, beliefs, judgments, and desires as it does about the formal contours of the object under scrutiny. In Williams's creative encounter with "The Crimson Cyclamen," I notice how the speaker's way of seeing the flower Demuth has rendered (microscopically, cubistically, imaginatively) becomes a form of active engagement with the visual object to the point where the differences between seeing—as a figure for reading and writing—and actively creating, between witnessing and cocreating, marks Williams's efforts as a transgressive or "queer" poetic act. The poet both courts and rejects his imaginative entrance into the visual space through the language of formal restraint.

Following two chapters on Modernists, I offer two that pivot between modern and postmodern times. Each foregrounds the social, political, and public issue of American citizenship in a multi-cultural, historically-inflected environment. In Chapter 4 on Allen Ginsberg's "America," I address the dialogue between poetry and mass culture, illustrated through the poet's ambivalent response to *Time* magazine. Ginsberg imagines himself as at once a Queer countercultural figure *and* an adherent to mainstream social values through the instruction of *Time* magazine, Henry Luce's notoriously conservative weekly. I also read "America" as an internal debate, situated in the context of a Cold War binary, in which Ginsberg deconstructs the "Us/Them" thinking that characterized what Alan Nadel has described as the "containment culture" of the Atomic Age (1995). Following my analysis of Ginsberg, a seminal mid-century poet, I place a classic sonnet written on the cusp of modernism—Emma Lazarus's "The New Colossus" (1883)—in conversation with an *ars poetica* by contemporary Puerto Rican author Judith Ortiz Cofer from about one century later, in Chapter 5. Contra Lazarus, Ortiz Cofer casts Lady Liberty as the proprietor of a Latin Deli that caters to exiled American citizens who long for tastes, smells, companionship, and language reminiscent of their Latin American heritage.

After Chapter 5 on Lazarus and Ortiz Cofer, which bridges modern and postmodern approaches to citizenship in the context of immigration, I move to the contemporary scene with chapters on how the themes of dialogue, responsibility, resistance, and pedagogy play out in many forms.

I begin by exploring the interarts dialogue that occurs in the jazz-influenced poetry of Michael S. Harper, which incorporates the life story and improvisational stylings of legendary sax man John Coltrane (Chapter 6). Focusing on how Harper puts forward a High Modernist collage aesthetic reminiscent of T. S. Eliot's *The Waste Land* (1922) in order to sublimate his lyric's expression of queer desire, my essay on Harper's signature expression of a poetry/jazz dialogue from 1970 recalls how the age-old verbal-visual controversy that manifested itself in Williams's "The Crimson Cyclamen" was also a veiled expression of queer desire.

In my essay on Frank Bidart's long poem "Ellen West" (Chapter 7), I hone in on the ethical implications of the intertextual dialogue between self and other that has been an implicit subject in prior essays. In "Ellen West," Bidart includes "found" prose from the English translation of Lionel Binswanger's case history to lend historical veracity to lyric passages spoken by West, a Swiss Jewish woman who suffered from a severe eating disorder that eventually led to her suicide. In his representation of Binswanger's text, however, Bidart excludes key points that connect West's disgust with her "Jewish" body type to her internalization of an anti-Semitic discourse. Bidart omits Binswanger's speculation that West privileged the blond, thin, "Aryan type" because she associated it with control that was assigned the value of transcendence over physical desires. Instead of focusing on the anti-Semitic discourse that animates West's body hatred, Bidart reads West's devaluation of the body and her wish for its erasure as in line with German Idealism and an aesthetic sublime. This chapter thus explores the ethical implications of Bidart's invocation of Ellen West *as a historical figure*.

Then, in Chapter 8, I explore the literal epistolary exchange between Native American female poet, Leslie Marmon Silko and white, Midwestern, male poet James Wright in *The Delicacy and Strength of Lace* (1986). For Wright and Silko, the use-function of poetry and story had to do with how texts translate voice, body, and the personality of the writer into artifacts. From Silko's point of view, artifactual appearance is the residence of personal identity. Her project in the correspondence, her gift to Wright, was to articulate his visibility within her Laguna (Navajo) tradition of stories—an alternative narrative reality that contains within it the personal experiences of all members of the Laguna people, and maybe somehow all persons, because Silko presents sharing narratives in poetry as a way of making sense or at least making bearable the inevitable pain and loss of all personal life.

It is important for me to stress that *Lyric Encounters* is designed as a series of interrelated essays that have been written over several years, and in response to my own development as a teacher, thinker, reader, and person. As an interdisciplinarian, I contextualize classroom poems by introducing students to the visual art, music, prose writings (letters, memoirs, prose statements, even fictions), and to precursor poems that influenced the poet's composition and thus should make a difference to our reception of the poem. My interests in modern art and jazz music inspire my discussions of Williams Carlos Williams and Michael S. Harper. Chapters in this book also reflect an increasing awareness on my part—informed by readings in "Queer Theory," poststructuralist approaches to identity such as are found in the writings of Judith Butler, and exposure to criticism by champions and practitioners of Language Poetry such as Marjorie Perloff, Charles Bernstein, and Lyn Hejinian—that stable notions of self and other, and therefore, of conceptions of the interpersonal, are tricky and worthy of scrutiny because of the intertextual and performative qualities of identity. Sounding like a latter-day Whitman in terms of imagining the self as plural, contradictory, and open to textual revision, Hejinian remarks in "The Person in Description":

> The "personal" is already a plural condition. Perhaps one feels that it is located somewhere within, somewhere inside the body – in the stomach? the genitals? the throat? the head? One can look for it, and already one is not oneself, one is several, incomplete, and subject to dispersal.
>
> (1991, p. 170)[2]

My essays on Ginsberg and Cold War America, Williams's relationship to Demuth, Harper and Coltrane, Bidart and Ellen West, and the post-9/11 Alexie poetry from *Face* have benefited from readings such as Hejinian's, which have taught me to challenge pat definitions of identity, selfhood, and otherness.

My essay on Ginsberg's "America," for example, is not interpersonal in the obvious sense of conversation between one persona and another, but rather takes Hejinian's understanding of the "personal" as already a "plural condition." I interpret Ginsberg's seminal Cold War lyric as an expression of the poet's ambivalent musings about his fragmented relation to the repressive national paradigm that, ironically, animates Ginsberg's famously countercultural persona in works from the 1950s such as "America," "Howl," "A Supermarket in California," and "Sunflower Sutra." I join other scholars and poets in situating Ginsberg's mid-century lyrics in the context of the Manichean ethics of a Cold War imaginary. My reading of "America" differs from these other Cold War readings, however, in that I argue Ginsberg's conservatism

---

[2]In "The Poetics of Everyday Life," ed. Barrett Watten and Lyn Hejinian, *Poetics Journal*, vol. 9, 1991.

authorizes what I am calling a "queer" form of lyric dialogue.[3] By "queer" form of lyric dialogism, I mean to say that Ginsberg's semiosis deconstructs Cold War discourse on a deep structural level. Ginsberg's expression of conservative impulses, however parodic, upsets the binary (us/them) mindset characteristic of that period's emphasis on containment of the Unruly/Other (queer, progressive) dimensions of post-war America, and is implicated in and critical of the "America" that Ginsberg's persona at times talks to as if it were a national imaginary outside the self and at other times represents the apostrophic "you" as a desublimated projection of his own mimicry of the status quo.

After the audaciously lengthy and wide-ranging penultimate essay on Alexie, which I described in my remarks at the start of this chapter, I conclude the book with a (mercifully!) brief and personal reflection that I originally wrote for *Tikkun*, a popular Jewish periodical, upon being asked by Rabbi Michael Lerner, the editor, to be included among a group of scholars, poets, clergy, and intellectuals to celebrate *Tikkun*'s Twenty-Fifth Anniversary by offering what "they would give future Tikkunistas, or what their own work for tikkun olam had consisted of." Given that Tikkun Olam means World Mending, I immediately thought of Frost's poem. My reading of "Mending Wall" returns to the theme of pedagogy as dialogue that animated my first chapter on Hughes's "Theme for English B." Now middle-aged, tenured, a father of three, and, I hope, a tad less concerned about publication as a form of self-promotion, I notice that it has become increasingly important for me to relate my scholarship to my teaching. Further, I have come to understand teaching poetry to be a rare form of popular culture that fosters deep thinking, critical reflection, close

---

[3] By "queer relationship to identity," I am thinking of how Ginsberg consistently, in the definition of "queer" set forth by E. Patrick Johnson and Mae G. Henderson in *Black Queer Studies*, "disrupts dominant and hegemonic discourses by consistently destabilizing fixed notions of identity by deconstructing binaries such as heterosexual/homosexual, gay/lesbian, and masculine/feminine as well as the concept of heteronormativity in general (2005, p. 5). I would add the political binary "conservative mainstream/radical progressive," which is the significant Cold War binary that I would like to address in my reading of "America" and the one that has received less attention than the other distinctions that scholars such as Johnson and Henderson focus upon.

reading, and, perhaps that rarest of things, a genuinely interpersonal experience in which flesh and blood human beings, teachers and students, share a text in the same space, and at the same time, with no mediation other than a poem on a page. As my *Tikkun* piece makes clear, I feel a sense of urgency concerning the contested value of the project of discussing poetry in the classroom, which has been my life's work, and, I believe, where I am my best self. As in my reading of "Mending Wall," all of the chapters in this book reflect my belief that poetry, often considered the most elitist and private of arts, comes alive in various contexts of engagement with other texts and other lives, including the mysterious otherness of our selves. My hope is that the essays I have collected here could contribute in a small way to the continuing conversation about the value of an art that is best received in a social environment.

2

"Go Home and Write a Page Tonight": Subversive Irony and Resistant Reading in "Theme for English B"

In the summer of 1948, Langston Hughes, 46 years old and arguably the preeminent poet of the African-American experience for over two decades, became, for the first time in his distinguished, but peripatetic and impoverished existence, a homeowner. A decade after his flirtations with radical socialism following his visit to the Soviet Union in 1932 to take part in a film regarding race relations there, Hughes was now what he might himself have referred to, with not a little self-effacement, as a card-carrying member of "the black bourgeoisie." Paid for with the accumulated savings of decades on the grueling lecture circuit, a stint teaching in Atlanta, profits from a hit Broadway musical, consultancies for radio and television networks, newspaper columns for the *Chicago Defender*, and royalties from children's books and other commercially driven publications, Hughes had purchased a "two-room suite" on the third floor of the home of long-time friends Toy and Emerson Harper at 20 East 127th Street in Harlem. "Here, at last, Langston had ample space for his growing library of books, his manuscripts, clippings, photographs, memorabilia, and correspondence, and work tables for himself and his helpers," reports Arnold Rampersad in "On Solid Ground," a chapter of his magisterial two-volume biography of the poet (2002, p. 146).

Hughes, however, had paid a high price to achieve the status of homeowner. In contrast to younger competitors for the mantle of foremost interpreter of the African-American experience such as Ralph Ellison, who concentrated his efforts on completing one definitive literary masterpiece, by the late 1940s it was clear to many observers that Hughes had sapped his creative strength for financial gain. A self-described "literary sharecropper," Rampersad writes that by 1950 "in many ways he was not working as a serious artist" (p. 187). It is into the context of his enjoyment of "the sweet, familial confinement that life with the Harpers brought" (p. 149), but also as a poet whom many believed had lost his touch because of his felt need to compromise his radicalism in order to facilitate his commercial viability in the midst of Cold War Red Baiting, that Hughes recalled a scene of literary composition undertaken by a younger, far less well-established, and yet more daring version of himself. Replacing the contemporary scene of authorship that included "work tables for himself and his helpers" in the late 1940s, Hughes rehearses a literary performance that occurred in the early 1920s at the writing desk of another, far less bourgeois, upper-deck Harlem dwelling. I am referring, of course, to "Theme for English B," the much-anthologized poem set, in large part, at the student's writing desk in his boarding room at the Harlem "Y."[1] In a somewhat historicist vein, I have inquired initially into the personal state of commerce that produced the poetic text. In

---

[1]Although often anthologized, "Theme" has received scant critical attention. Exceptions include a one-paragraph analysis by Onwuchekwa Jemie. In "Jazz, Jive, and Jam," Jemie argues the poem suggests "American identity of necessity embraces equally the white and the black experience" (1989, p. 73). In a two-page essay on "Theme," Tracy J. Prince Ferrell argues the poem "can be viewed as an explanation to those who criticized his use of the common vernacular and as a poignant summarization of the disparity between the stereotyped American Dream and the deferred dreams of Harlem" (1995, p. 36). An early reference to "Theme" appears in James A. Emanuel's Twayne Series study on Hughes. Comparing the ending of "Theme" to the ending of "Madam and Her Madam," Emanuel writes, "the ending ... reveals Hughes's tendency to turn both sides of the racial coin. In both poems the Negro camp denies that the feelings of white people have any more significance that those of Negroes" (1967, p. 55).

what follows, I will discuss the structural techniques that enable the reversal of two figures and roles in "Theme," collapsing a hierarchy of pedagogical power, and, finally, the way that the more formal inquiry reveals, in a return to history, a steady transition from the radical 1930s to the Cold War of the 1950s.

First published in 1949 in *Common Ground* (Spring 1949, pp. 89–90) and then collected in 1951 in *Montage of a Dream Deferred,* Hughes's thirteenth book of poetry, "Theme for English B" is Hughes's witty free verse representation of a young black student's response to a white college teacher's rather thoughtless assignment to "go home and write a page tonight." [2] In my reading of this poem, I will demonstrate how Hughes uses irony and subversive humor to challenge the teacher's assumptions about what it means for a young, diasporic black man living at the Harlem "Y" to experience the kind of unproblematic sense of "self," "home," and "truth" implied by the teacher's prompt. By noting the contingent nature of the speaker's identity—where he lives, where he was born and raised, his age, the color of his skin, his musical tastes—Hughes challenges the association of a universal speaker with the lyric "I" that inevitably represents a limited subset of potential speakers whose experiences are inflected by their subject position. A British Romantic poet such as John Keats, famous for the concept of "negative capability" that he felt enabled Shakespeare to imagine the lives of others with insight and to endure "uncertainties, mysteries, doubts," is, however, unself-conscious about applying the lyric "I" to an identity he presumes to be universal in "When I have fears that I may cease to be" (1818). [3] Hughes, by contrast to Keats, uses irony, humor, and resistant reading strategies to deconstruct universal notions of lyric subjectivity. At the same time, he challenges his teacher's assumptions about what it means for the older white instructor and the younger

---

[2] In an essay on "Mulatto" from *Fine Clothes to the Jew* (1927), Robert Paul Lamb argues that Hughes employs the traditional African-American cultural aesthetics of "call and response" and "signifying" to represent a mulatto son's protest of his white father's disavowal of paternity. In "Theme," Hughes similarly employs "call and response" and "signifying" to engage a white authority figure, the class instructor.

[3] For a discussion of Keats and "Negative Capability," see *A Modern Lexicon of Literary Terms* (Liberman & Foster, 1968, pp. 76–7).

black student to share space as fellow American citizens as well as dialogic interlocutors in a primary scene of the dissemination of cultural norms and values, the college classroom. Transforming his response to the teacher's bland assignment—ironically recast in the form of an atavistically formal rhymed quatrain—into a free verse poem that highlights function over form, Hughes illustrates that the middle-aged homeowner and professional author has remained in touch with a youthful, witty, risk-taking version of himself.[4]

Although set in the 1920s, "Theme for English B" reveals how the poet's sense of creative play can be put into the service of a critical reading of the American social text in the Cold War context in which it was composed. Hughes's speaker acknowledges shared values—the speaker says that he, like most Americans, enjoys eating, sleeping, and being in love—but he leaves room for an expression of the crucial markers of difference that make "going home" to "write a page tonight" and making that page "come out of you" such a vexing proposition for the talented but quasi-homeless speaker.[5] By transforming his response to the teacher's

---

[4]In "Montage of a Simplicity Deferred: Langston Hughes's Art of Sophistication and Racial Intersubjectivity in *Montage of a Dream Deferred*," Daniel C. Turner explores how Hughes's "adaptation of techniques commonly associated with modernist poetics undercuts the popular notion of Hughes as merely a simple poet of the people" (2002, p. 22). Turner notes Hughes's "expert manipulation of colloquial or 'plain' language" as well as

[his] foregrounding of aesthetic frame and the artist's ironic distance from his subject ... a manipulation of other modernist artforms as framing devices, and a relativism of perspective. Hughes exploits this art of sophistication in order to countermand essentializing definitions of racial subjectivity.

(p. 23)

[5]In "Langston Hughes: Evolution of the Poetic Persona," Raymond Smith argues:

Hughes's efforts to create a poetry that truly evoked the spirit of Black America involved a resolution of conflicts centering around the problem of identity. For Hughes, like W.E.B. Du Bois, saw the black man's situation in America as a question of dual consciousness.

(2004, p. 37)

As Smith suggests, Hughes foregrounded the resistance of the desire "to pour racial individuality into the mold of American standardization," in his classic 1927 essay, "The Negro Artist and the Racial Mountain." In Smith's terms, "Theme" continues

assignment into a modernist lyric with dialogic features, and by challenging the basic assumptions behind the teacher's assignment (for example, that each student has a home to "go" to), Hughes's speaker ironically subverts the standard pedagogical hierarchy by instructing the teacher in the limits of his prompt. Especially since the speaker is young, black, and without a home, this inversion of teacher–student relations is certainly a major ironical element of Hughes's poem.

A childless bachelor who, Rampersad reports, was interested in asserting his "symbolic paternity" through his patronage of younger black authors in America and Africa after World War II, Hughes wrote "Theme for English B" as a representation of the middle-aged author's recollection of his self-creative moment (2005, p. 238).[6] By the poem's conclusion, the once disoriented, insecure self—"Me—who?"—asserts control over a discourse that begins in conversation with the instructor—"we two—you, me, talk on this page"—but concludes with a declaration of

---

in the tradition of the "Racial Mountain" essay "to integrate the two facets of double consciousness (the American and the Negro) into a single vision—that of the poet" (p. 38).

[6]By comparing and contrasting Hughes's memory of his year at Columbia in *The Big Sea* (1940) to "Theme," written almost a decade later, we notice how Hughes has revised his experience in the poem to illustrate themes of race and place. In "Theme," the Hughes persona is the only "colored" student in his class. In the "Columbia" chapter from *The Big Sea*, by contrast, Hughes focuses on his friendship with "Chun, a Chinese boy." Fellow outsiders, neither likes "the big university" (p. 83), and neither receives a fraternity invitation. In "Theme," Hughes's unique subject position goes unacknowledged by his teacher. In *The Big Sea*, white Columbia students ostracize Langston because of his race—as when the editor of *The Spectator* assigns him to "gather Frat house and society news, an assignment impossible for a colored boy to fill, as they knew" (p. 83). In *The Big Sea*, Hughes is detached from his classroom teachers at Columbia. Where the speaker in "Theme" challenges his white instructor, Langston in *The Big Sea* is not "interested" in any of his teachers with the exception of a "Mr. Watson, who read Mencken aloud all the time" (p. 84). Instead of attending classes, Hughes in *The Big Sea* explores New York City, going "to shows" and "attend[ing] lectures at the Rand School under Ludwig Lewisohn and Heywood Broun" (p. 85). The speaker in "Theme" importantly lives at the Harlem "Y." By contrast, Langston in *The Big Sea* lives at "Hartley Hall," a Columbia dormitory. He does not move "down into Harlem, where I began life on my own" at age "twenty" until "[A]fter the finals" when Langston broke ties with his father, who stopped sending him tuition money (p. 85).

independent ownership of the theme. The final line of the lyric reframes the student's response as the self-confident expression of a mature self who has achieved his linguistic "B-ing": "This is my page for English B," the predicted grade being an inaccurate representation of the cultured authenticity.

Quite likely Hughes's poetic narrator is the only student lacking a permanent address to call his own. Certainly, the teller is the lone African-American enrolled in a composition course at Columbia University presided over by a white instructor who commands his students, in strict iambic verse, to "go home and write a page tonight." The speaker foregrounds the struggle he experienced merely to arrive at the scene of composition. He devotes much of the first section of the poem to mapping the long trek down the steps from the hill of Morningside Heights needed to reach his boarding room at the Harlem "Y."[7] Arriving at his writing desk, he challenges on moral grounds the exclusionary nature of the universal ethos of the instructor's prompt:[8]

---

[7]In "Roots, Routes, and Langston Hughes's Hybrid Sense of Place," William Hogan focuses on the symbolically resonant imagery of rivers and mountains in Hughes's early poems and essays. "[I]n 'The Negro Speaks of Rivers' ... the river comes to stand for the common history and common experiences connecting people of color over distances of time and geography" (2004, p. 3). Hogan argues that:

> [O]ne of Hughes's cultural projects, particularly in his early years, was to try to build new and stronger types of African American community by reimagining the connections between African American culture and place. The landscapes Hughes imagines, whether they are nourishing rivers that connect and strengthen communities of color or mountaintops that black artists must ascend in order to be heard, work to unite the African American community.

(p. 3)

In "Theme," I would argue, Hughes continues to explore what Hogan calls a "hybrid sense of place." The difference is that Hughes is less focused on connecting African and African-American experiences across times and continents, as is the case in classic early poems such as "The Negro Speaks of Rivers," thus solidifying relations within the African-American experience, and is more interested in exploring interracial spaces as the Hughes persona pivots between spaces: Columbia, the Harlem Y, New York, and America, in which he negotiates shifting dynamics of self and other in a complex, multiethnic, and cosmopolitan environment.

[8]My thinking about "Theme for English B" as an expression of Hughes's moral critique of the communally shared ethos that informs the instructor's prompt even as it fails to account for the variability of subject positions is informed by Judith

I wonder if it's that simple?
I am twenty-two, colored, born in Winston-Salem.
I went to school there, then Durham, then here
to this college on the hill above Harlem.
I am the only colored student in my class.
The steps from the hill lead down into Harlem,
through a park, then I cross St. Nicholas,
Eighth Avenue, Seventh, and I come to the Y,
the Harlem Branch Y, where I take the elevator
up to my room, sit down, and write this page:[9]

Hughes spends approximately one-quarter of the poem (10 lines out of 41) not so much responding to the instructor's assignment to "let a page come out of you," but in demonstrating to the teacher that his assignment, in Judith Butler's terms, "postulates a false unity that attempts to suppress the difficulty and discontinuity existing within any contemporary ethos" (2005, p. 4).

Although left unexamined by the instructor, Hughes's speaker argues that three of the core beliefs informing the teacher's requirement must be debated and queried by the respondent who must recover to express himself as a linguistic "I."[10] The student's three critiques reveal how the assignment suppresses critical differences among a class of students that is by no means the monolithic lot that the instructor has, unthinkingly, supposed it to be. The student challenges the teacher's assumption that there is a transparent, one-size-fits-all, or universalist nature to the "you" to whom the teacher addresses his assignment. Further, he argues that the teacher's assumption that the written word is

---

Butler's reading of Adorno's *Problems of Moral Philosophy* (1963) in her *Giving an Account of Oneself* (2005).

[9]Of course, Hughes was born in Missouri, not North Carolina. The poet's willingness to blur the facts of his life experience speaks to how the creative author felt comfortable in taking liberties with the "truth" in order to serve the poem, in this case by allowing Hughes to align his personal narrative with that of the Great Migration from South to North.

[10]Ironically, the document that we now have as a record of that interrogation of the universalist moral ethos that informs the teacher's assignment is understood, by the mature Hughes, as the sum total of his response to an assignment that he is never able to complete on its own terms, but only in the deferred form of a belated lyrical interrogation of the nature of the lyric "I."

a direct, unmediated, and inherently truthful expression of the authorial self ("let the page come out of you and it will be true") is a morally flawed illustration of a romantic mythos. Why? What are the assumptions behind it? The assignment fails to account for the dialogic character of the self and the contingent nature of subject positions in a democratic, multicultural environment. Most crucially in the passage quoted above, the speaker questions the teacher's assumption that each student maintains a stable enough life that the instructor's command to "go home" to write will not itself be a source of uncertainty requiring serious inquiry and discursive confusion.

Where Descartes famously knew himself to exist through his ability to think, the speaker defines himself as in the Socratic tradition through his ability to "wonder," or, in other words, to speculate, to doubt, to be unsure, to be curious, as well as to experience the sensations of amazement and surprise at his own uncanny relation to self, to teacher, to the "white page" upon which he is implored to inscribe himself as an "I." Figuratively speaking, the African-American script points instead to the ever-expanding "home" sites of Harlem, New York City, and America in general.[11] It is evidence of Hughes's late radical bent that the comfortable home owner, but struggling artist, who was weathering the somewhat spurious charges by politicos and aesthetes for lacking the nerve to speak truth to power, can recover in "Theme" with fidelity the playful tone of the child. By questioning the assignment, ironically, this imaginary self can take the assignment more seriously, and respond to it more deeply, than the instructor could have thought.[12]

In the process of questioning the questioner, the speaker takes advantage of the assignment to unravel the nature of his own self only to reassemble it *as* a wandering figure. In Butler's terms, the young speaker's "subject forms itself in relation to a set of codes,

---

[11] It is significant in this regard that Hughes chose for the second volume of his autobiography the title *I Wonder as I Wander*.

[12] Unlike the speaker, who is sensitive to his audience and who sets his "page" up as one half of a dialogue with his interlocutor, the instructor's assignment, represented in parodic form as a piece of iambic verse, seems uninterested in the specific subject positions and unique life worlds of his students, and especially of the one "colored" student in the class.

prescriptions or norms and does so in ways that not only (a) reveal self-continuation to be a kind of *poiesis* but (b) establish self-making as part of the broader operation of critique" (2005, p. 17). Situated at the juncture of passage from adolescence to civic personhood, or self-conscious adulthood—the speaker challenges an understanding of self as being transparently stable. Instead, he interprets the self as something that does not exist in isolation from other selves. Rather, the self becomes visible in the linguistic process of sharing dialogue and in the context of various environments ranging from the Columbia classroom, to the neighborhoods of the upper-crust blacks who lived in St. Nicholas, to the Ur-site of the young man's space of questioning, the transient residence of the Harlem "Y" (or Harlem Why):[13]

> It's not easy to know what is true for you or me
> at twenty-two, my age. But I guess I'm what
> I feel and see and hear, Harlem, I hear you.
> hear you, hear me—we two—you, me, talk on this page.
> (I hear New York, too.) Me—who?

The instructor's iambics signify an unselfconsciously harmonious relationship between European literary tradition and modern American self-expression as well as a regularization of speech rhythms into the prosodic formation that is meant, as in Shakespearean verse drama, to approximate, but also to privilege as aristocratic, the quality of the spoken word. By contrast, Hughes represents the speaker's response in what critics have called a "stream of consciousness." While displaying puns, internal rhymes, assonance, and a rhythmic tempo, the speaker's lyric response transcends the iambic beat that would contain it.[14] Instead of

---

[13] In "There's No Way Not to Lose": Langston Hughes and Intraracial Class Antagonism," Ian Peddle discusses Hughes's complex awareness of the intersections of race and class conflict, including conflicts among blacks based in social and economic differences (2004). The speaker's trek through the various socio-economic strata within Harlem on his way to the "Y" speaks to Hughes's sensitivity to "intraracial" distinctions in a poem primarily focused on interracial themes.

[14] In this sense, the speaker is certainly correct to challenge the degree of "freedom" possessed by his white teacher since on a prosodic level his assignment reveals an atavistic attachment to tradition, not to liberationist change.

constricting his "black" voice into the "white" regulated line lengths of accentual stress, the speaker creates a free form comparable to what the radical stylist Charles Olson called a "field of action." As in Olson's "Maximus" poems, Hughes's line traces the movements of a mind in the process of its wondering about its relationships to audience. Indeed, the instructor's "you" (which the instructor rhymed with "true" in his assignment) becomes rhymed in the last word of the stanza quoted above with the question "who?" Hughes challenges the foundation of the asymmetrical power relationship between the white instructor and the black student by deconstructing the basic tenets of the former's command, which appears in the student's paper in parodic form as a vestige of the very kind of lyricism that Hughes and other modernists had, in the words of Ezra Pound, "broken the back of" in the 1920s. Is America really a "home" for this young black man? Is all of New York City as safe a zone as "home," the place that Robert Frost reminded us, where they have to take you in? Is the Harlem Y (like the B/Be of the title another pun suggesting questioning Y/Why) a stable place to write?

By the late 1940s most readers of Hughes's poetry considered him to be a long way from the author who wrote "Put one more 'S' in the USA," but "Theme for English B" recovers his once dormant but now festering radicalism. The radical nature of "Theme" is especially evident if we understand the white instructor to be a synecdoche representing in condensed form a version of the many privileged white figures in the private and public spheres of the poet's life. I am thinking of how Hughes, for the quite legitimate reasons of putting bread on the table, a roof over his head, paying for secretaries to help him prepare his manuscripts, and securing publication from distinguished white-owned commercial presses— wrote in part with an eye towards securing the approval of patrons such as Carl Van Vechten, "Godmother" R. O. Mason, and Noel Sullivan, and publishers such as Blanche and Alfred A. Knopf.[15]

---

[15] In "Refined Racism: White Patronage in the Harlem Renaissance," Bruce Kellner elaborates on the ambivalent contribution white patrons made to the development of the Harlem Renaissance:

Despite their good intentions, white intellectuals and philanthropists bestowed mixed blessings in support of black artists and writers during the Harlem

Later, in the first few years of the 1950s, Hughes toiled under the suspicious gaze of the censors for NBC, CBS, and, finally, members of the McCarthy House Un-American Activities Committee such as Roy Cohn and David Schine. I am not trying to make a direct, one-to-one comparison between the instructor from "Theme" and the many white authority figures in the poet's life. I do think it is fair, however, to perceive "Theme" as a vicarious challenge to white power, a mature poet's lyrical sublimation of his artistic resistance to the American state power in the period in which he wrote the poem. By imagining a young black speaker who turns the tables on his instructor, he was able to explore the complex and subversive negotiations with the McCarthy era during the Cold War. He expressed himself with a constant eye looking outward to the way his self-representation would play to various publics, including the censors, publishers, politicos, and patrons who authorized his voice.

Fearing that identifying with the Left would compromise his livelihood as a homeowner in Harlem, Hughes recalls in "Theme" an early moment when he risked alienating a white authority. In the process, he produced a poem that questioned the degree of the white man's freedom—the teacher is only "somewhat" more free than the speaker—and that signals the black speaker's own independent desire—he expresses suspiciousness in "being a part of" the white man's world:

> You are white—
> yet a part of me, as I am a part of you.
> That's American.
> Sometimes perhaps you don't want to be a part of me.
> Nor do I often want to be a part of you.
> But we are, that's true!
> As I learn from you,
> I guess you learn from me—

Renaissance. Their involvement contributed indirectly to the Black Arts Movement of the 1960s, yet the cost to the 1920s is undeniable. The black writer both thrived and suffered, torn between well-meant encouragement from the white race to preserve his racial identity (usually described as "primitivism") and a misguided encouragement from his own race to emulate the white one.

(2004, p. 53)

although you're older—and white—
and somewhat more free.

Now the student's "you" has reprised the moral authority of the teacher's original command that the paper "come out of you." Indeed the roles of both the instructor and the pupil are completely reversed. The student destabilizes the power relationship between the two interlocutors to the point where each learns from the other. I think anyone reading this "page for English B" would have to conclude that, in fact, the student becomes the teacher and the teacher the student.

The period after the conclusion of World War II and into the onset of the Cold War was not the best of times for Hughes's reputation as a major figure in African-American letters. Not as radical politically as a Paul Robeson or a W. E. B. Dubois in a period of Red Baiting, Hughes lost face among the Far Left for repudiating his most controversially radical poems from the 1930s such as "Goodbye Christ" and "Put one more 'S' in the USA." Viewed by many as a figure of compromise and conciliation, he tried to maintain his income and mainstream visibility through lectureships and commercial publications as America entered the period of McCarthyism. At the same time, many leading literary critics viewed Hughes as insufficiently radical in his literary forms. With the rise of the once New Criticism, which privileged the allusion and self-reflection of High Modernism, appealing to traditionalists because of its association with conservative writers such as T. S. Eliot and its critique of Social Realist narratives by authors such as John Steinbeck, influential scholars, such as the white Southern "fugitives" assembled at Vanderbilt downgraded such populist idiom and racial themes while elevating the esoteric poetics of the later Melvin Tolson.[16] Ironically, Hughes re-imagined

---

[16] As literary historian Vincent Leitch writes, the New Criticism was in fact a heterogeneous practice. But, as Leitch indicates in his cultural history of the movement, one can easily understand why Hughes's poetics ran counter to the basic tenets of the more doctrinaire forms of New Criticism in the 1940s and 1950s. In its purified forms, the New Criticism's stated values by and large certainly would not have been especially sympathetic to Hughes's poetry. Where in "Theme" Hughes linked poetry with social and biographical concerns in a dialogic form that emphasized different subject positions in an urban setting, doctrinaire New Criticism emphasized formal

the Cold War climate as an atmosphere to critique America in unexpected forms and genres.

Discussing Hughes during the Cold War, Jonathan Scott argues:

> For creative artists like Hughes, the anticommunist movement's narrowing of themes and subjects, as well as genres and forms by which they could be expressed, to only those which affirmed God, family, and country helped to create the conditions for a systematic negative critique ... in his writing for young people.
>
> (2006, p. 33)

Scott focuses on the radical compositional principles set forth in *First Book of Rhythms* (1954), which "came directly out of Hughes's teaching experiences at the Laboratory School in Chicago, where in 1949 he led interdisciplinary writing workshops for eighth graders" (2006, p. 42).

Instead of such grammatical skills as subject–verb agreement, Scott shows that Hughes framed assignments that illustrated rhythm patterns, a collage aesthetics, and that worked towards the axiom, "No one writes like anyone else" via the exposure to and practice of collective writing activities (p. 44).[17] Hughes's

---

unities, and an agrarian critique of modernist cosmopolitanism. As Leitch writes, Cleanth Brooks characterized New Criticism as a formalism that "separates literary criticism from the study of sources, social backgrounds, history of ideas, politics, and social effects, seeking both to purify poetic criticism from such 'extrinsic' concerns and focus attention squarely on the 'literary object'" (1988, p. 26). Where the New Criticism famously discounted reader response by suggesting their approach assumed an "ideal reader," Hughes's "Theme" pays attention to how his speaker's background influences how he reads and responds to his teacher's assignment. For a complex analysis of how a more relaxed form of New Criticism that takes into account "the need for historical perspectives in evaluating humane letters" may be applied to African-American authors such as Richard Wright and Ralph Ellison, see Chester J. Fontenot, Jr.'s "Angelic Dance or Tug of War?: The Humanistic Implications of Cultural Formalism" (1981).

[17] Scott writes:

> Hughes's method is an ingenious way of getting students thinking in terms of the rhythm patterns of prose and poetry writing, of lyrical flow, of word sentences, transitions, cadences, and caesuras. Already there is the room to start and stop as suits the writer, but in a disciplined, rhythmized way. In other words, many of the frustrations of the college writing instructor—run-on sentences, comma

concern with pedagogy, experimental responses to compositional
assignments, and the relationship between writing instructions
and a progressive social democratic agenda, so evident in *First
Book of Rhythms*, are equally evident in "Theme for English
B." Scott's analysis of Hughesian method of composition in *First
Book of Rhythms* resonates with how Hughes responds to his
teacher's assignment in "Theme for English B." Hughes's semi-
autobiographical student writer emphasizes knowledge of the self
in relation to the other, including the other within the self. Further,
Hughes's self-portrait emphasizes the "condition of movement"
rather than stasis. "Theme for English B" recovers the poet's origins
as simultaneously a political radical *and* a formally innovative
poet, thus answering in a single text the politically radical critics on
the Left and the aesthetically avant-garde, but socially conservative
New Critics on the Right. Hughes upsets the border between prose
discourse and complex lyric expression. By so doing, he destabilizes
the relation between radical politics and avant-garde poetics, which
in "Theme for English B" amounts to the same thing.

---

splices, improper use of punctuation, etc.—are answered in this exercise: how to
give life to the rhythms of the natural world ... on paper.

(2006, p. 46)

3

The Erotics of Close Reading: Williams, Demuth, and "The Crimson Cyclamen"

Distinguished William Carlos Williams scholars who have focused on his relationship to the visual arts have tended towards formalistic analysis. Here are three examples:

1. When Williams—particularly in the 1920s—or [Charles] Demuth dealt with subjects they admired, such as flowers, their reaction was to take them entirely out of life where they could decay and disappoint. Both Demuth's flower paintings and Williams's flower poems present their subjects as timeless, richly abstract, beautiful designs (Guimond, 1968, pp. 48–9).

2. The tension created by such a syntactic ambiguity can be directly related to the Cubist technique of including the ambiguous or contradictory overlapping of planes, or of fusing, or metonymically displacing, the material qualities of objects, so that a pipe becomes transparent while a glass or a carafe is opaque (Halter, 1994, p. 88).

3. [Demuth's] commentary on the American scene emerges from the formal means that [he] has exercised. His Cubist-Realism, as some critics have designated his style, exploits the geometry inherent in the building, thereby creating its own pictorial

structure ... [T]he clarity of lines (even in the passages that characterize the lower street in the closest approximation of Cubism), the rays that unite sky and building, the brightness of the colors, and the elegant twists of smoke all combine to create an aesthetic experience in marked tension with the drab architectural realities of such towns (Tashjian, 1978, p. 67).

In these examples, the language of formalism obscures other interesting aspects of Williams's fascination with painters and painting. For one, the idea that blurring the boundaries of art forms (poetry and painting) was an expression of a transgressive poetics as it went against such modernist pieties (think Greenberg, think Kandinsky) as the separation of arts and the purity of form. For another, and perhaps most intriguing, the fact that many of the artists he came into contact with lived lives that I would characterize as dissident, or nonheteronormative, or queer.

The relationship with Charles Demuth is an excellent case in point. As noted, scholars center discussions of their relationship on the mutual interest in defining a new type of American art that accepted the realities of urbanism and industrialism as appropriate subject matter, but that was, stylistically, influenced by European Modernism's attention to experimental forms and sleek designs. Critics emphasize the Futurist influence—the possibly ironic celebration of machine-age culture in the smoke stacks, grain elevators, skyscrapers, and auto plants that constituted what Demuth called "My Egypt." There is discussion of how Williams wanted to be a painter when young, and Demuth, then studying art at Drexel, a writer, and of how they knew each other in Philadelphia. A note about their first meeting in 1903 over a bowl of prunes at Mrs. Chain's boardinghouse on Locust Street is *de rigueur*. Williams is quoted as not realizing Demuth was gay, and Demuth himself not realizing it.

The closest commentators come to suggesting the queer dimensions of Demuth's work is when they acknowledge, as do Peter Schmidt and Tashjian, that his flowers and industrial landscapes possess a veiled or displaced "erotic" dimension, even as the art works lack a specific sexual content. Of course, much of Demuth's work, especially his watercolors, is overtly, even scandalously, bawdy and homoerotic, but these works are not discussed in the context of Williams's interest in his art. Williams himself felt that the content of much of Demuth's work barred it from public appreciation. In Demuth's "Three Sailors on the Beach," a water-color from 1930, the artist depicts one of his most overt scenes of public homoeroticism through the image of men about to engage in fellatio. Demuth implicated himself in the scene by placing his own initials inside a heart-shaped tattoo upon the arm of one of the sailors.[1] As Tashjian does helpfully point out, "Distinguished Air" (1930) depicts sailors admiring a giant phallus (based on a Brancusi) at an art gallery—a scene that Demuth drew from an episode deleted from a 1925 story by Robert McAlmon. These works are unambiguous examples of what David Jarraway in *Going the Distance* calls "dissident subjectivity" (2003) through a transgressive sexuality that flew in the face of bourgeois norms. Of course, from Williams's point of view, transgressive subject matter was itself a badge of honor. He linked eccentricity to an experimental poetics associated with newness, with American Modernism, with a kind of ugly beauty and democratically nonex-clusive poetics. Demuth's anthropomorphized flowers and phallic machines were of a kind with Duchamp's urinals, O'Keefe's flowers, and Marin's mountains, which Williams owned, and referred to as breasts. Demuth did a work of an industrial nature with gangly tubes in honor of Williams and both men understood the work as erotic. Williams was not pleased.

"The Crimson Cyclamen (To the Memory of Charles Demuth)" [1936] is an example of a poem that benefits from a close reading informed by a "queer" approach, that is to say, to use Jarraway's sense of the term, a reading that challenges essentialist ideas about a person's identity as a sexual being with a fixed gender. The poem itself anticipates the critical reception that I have been describing. The poem pivots between a florid, overflowing description of the eroticism (and homoerotics) of flowering as a figure for human sexual relationships, and the language of formalism that signifies intellectual reserve and aesthetic restraint. Consciously or not, the language of formalism suggests Williams's discomfort with

---

[1]The practice of suggesting homosexual love through the initials of the artist's name is also apparent in Marsden Hartley's *Portrait of a German Officer*, in which, as Jonathan Weinberg notes, "An epaulet twists into the letter E, which stands for Hartley's given name, Edmund," as part of the memorial to Karl von Freyburg, "who died in the early stages of World War I" (1995, p. 3).

his imaginative entry into the life of the flower through intense seeing. The formal tones work to distance, remove, conceal, or cool down, the heated and Romantic description of flowering. The speaker's way of seeing the flower (microscopically, cubistically, imaginatively) becomes a form of active engagement with the visual object to the point where the differences between seeing—as a figure for reading and writing—and actively creating, between witnessing and cocreating, mark Williams's efforts as a trans-gressive or "queer" poetic act. The poet both courts and rejects his imaginative entrance into the visual space through the language of formal restraint.

An example of the play between formalism (as veil) and eroticism (as covert subject matter) comes from the end of stanza 2 and the beginning of stanza 3 of the poem. First, the erotic imagery of stanza 2:

> ... In
> September when the first
> pink pointed bud still
> bowed below, all the leaves
> heart-shaped
> were already spread—
> quirked and green
> and stenciled with a paler
> green
> irregularly
> across and round the edge—

> (Williams, 1991, *Collected Poems* (CP), vol. 1, line 420)

And now, from this sexual drama with the not-yet-aroused phallic "pink pointed bud" and the "heart-shaped" leaves "already spread," we move to the formalistic, to the microscopic close reading of the leaves in terms of design, pattern, logic, and shape:

> Upon each leaf it is
> a pattern more
> of logic than a purpose
> links each part to the rest,
> an abstraction

playfully following
centripetal
devices, as of pure thought—
the edge tying by
convergent, crazy rays
with the center—
where the dips
cupping down to the
upright stem—the source
that has splayed out
fanwise and returns
upon itself in the design
thus decoratively—

(CP, vol. 1, line 420)

Williams himself imagines close reading as an uncomfortably "queer" act in "The Crimson Cyclamen." It is a transgressive activity that he enters into with passionate intensity, but then pulls away from (and back into the language of formalism), as if disturbed with the loss of boundary between self and other, object and seer, writer and artist, witness and cocreator.

Another passage shows how mere seeing turns into eroticized projection:

The young leaves
coming among the rest
are more crisp
and deeply cupped
the edges rising first
impatient of the slower
stem—the older
level, the oldest
with the edge already
fallen a little backward—
the stem alone
holding the form
stiffly a while longer—
Under the leaf, the same
though the smooth green

is gone. Now the ribbed
design—if not
the purpose, is explained.

(CP, vol. 1, line 421)

This is extraordinary seeing, seeing as active engagement, as cocreation, and seeing as creative writing, really. I wonder, how does the speaker see "under" the leaf? This is (to use the formalist idiom) cubist seeing, seeing from different angles, different distances, from the present and the past tense (the setting shifts from winter to September), seeing not just old and young leaves, but the older and oldest leaves (how can he tell?), seeing leaves in various stages of the life cycle, emerging, withering, seeing as a mixture of understanding, explaining, probing.

Williams deciphers the "design" of the "ribbed" leaf so that the leaf itself seems to be inscribed. The seer marks the "pink" flower as if he were writing upon it:

The stem's pink flanges,
strongly marked,
stand to the frail edge,
dividing, thinning
through the pink and downy
mesh—as the round stem
is pink also—cranking
to penciled lines
angularly deft
through all, to link together
the unnicked argument
to the last crinkled edge—

(CP, vol. 1, line 421)

Seeing is thus represented as a literal and figurative act. The verbal act creates the meaning of the silent visual object through the narration and description.

It is in the speaker's act of close reading the flower that much of the sexual drama of the poem unfolds. Williams's act of seeing the flower becomes an expenditure of creative energy that is likened in the poem to the work that the sun does in preparing the flower to blossom. The sun in the poem is from the start a figure for the male imagination, and is associated with sky, thought, and writing, as in the following passage from stanza 1 in which the sun is a phallic symbol that "pierces" the flower's petals, creating a variety of colors, including the crimson:

And though the light
that enfolds and pierces
them discovers blues
and yellows there also—
and crimson's a dull word
beside such play—

(CP, vol. 1, line 419)

The poem, however, suggests that this masculine principle, this way of seeing associated with sun, thought, and logic, is insufficient to create the aesthetic bliss that Williams describes in sexual terms of passion and lust.

The flower is a stereotypical figure for the female: silent, passive, receptive, and earthy. If the first stanza suggests a heterosexual union of male and female, of sun and petal, of generation through difference, then stanza 2 suggests a homosexual model of creative productivity, of generation through mirroring, of generation through like with like:

It is miraculous
that flower should rise
by flower alike in loveliness—
as though mirrors
of some perfection
could never be
too often shown—

(CP, vol. 1, line 419)

As in the biblical Genesis, there are two creation stories, only in this creation narrative the first version involves Adam and Eve, and the second one two Eves. The male principle of creativity through logic, thought, and via the language of formalism only takes the speaker part of the way towards a full appreciation of the flower and its potential for blossom:

But half hidden under them
such as they are
it begins that must
put thought to rest—

wakes in tinted beaks
still raising the head
and passion
is loosed—

its small lusts
addressed still to
the knees and to sleep—
abandoning argument

lifts
through the leaves
day by day
and one day opens!

The petals!
the petals undone
loosen all five and
swing up

The flower
flows to release—

(CP, vol. 1, line 422)

These stanzas mark a major shift in the poem away from the prior effort of the speaker to make the flower blossom through intellectual labor and the beginning of the poem's evocation of pleasure via a sexualized relationship to the object that is described in the bodily terms of passion and lust.

Rather programmatically, Williams proposes in "The Crimson Cyclamen" that masculine and feminine principles must coalesce so that it is the combination of masculine—thought, sky, light, logic, sun—and feminine—moon, dark, underground, odorous—that produces the blossoming. But the queer thing is that the Crimson

Cyclamen (associated in the title with the memory of Demuth) is ambiguously gendered, if we follow the masculine/feminine paradigm I outlined above.

> Such are the leaves
> freakish, of the air
> as thought is, of roots
> dark, complex from
> subterranean revolutions
> and rank odors
> waiting for the moon—

                                        (CP, vol. 1, lines 420–1)

The "freakish" leaves are both masculine ("of the air") and feminine ("of roots"). In fact, as the poem progresses from the expression of pure mind to the full blossoming that is described in orgasmic terms, the flower begins to defy gender categorization, for it is both erect and receptive:

> The petals!
> the petals undone
> loosen all five and
> swing up
>
> The flower
> flows to release—
>
> Fast within a ring
> where the compact
> agencies
> of conception
>
> lie mathematically
> ranged
> round the
> hair-like sting—
>
> From such a pit
> the color flows

over
a purple rim

upward to
the light! the light!
all around—
Five petals

as one
to flare, inverted
a full flower
each petal tortured

eccentrically
the while, warped edge
jostling
half-turned edge

side by side
until compact, tense
evenly stained
to the last fine edge

an ecstasy
from the empurpled ring
climbs up (though
firm there still)

each petal
by excess of tensions
in its own flesh
all rose—

rose red
standing until it
bends backward
upon the rest, above,

answering
ecstasy with excess

all together
acrobatically

not as if bound
(though still bound)
but upright
as if they hung

from above
to the streams
with which
they are veined and glow—

the frail fruit
by its frailty supreme
opening in the tense moment
to no bean

no completion
no root
no leaf and no stem
but color only and a form—

(CP, vol. 1, lines 422–4)

This is the moment of merger, a spillage that confuses terms, defies logic, and conjoins categories. The design is the color. The five petals (a nod to Demuth's "I Saw the Figure 5") are one, signifying the erasure of difference. The petals are at once "not as if bound" and yet "still bound," they are masculine and feminine in one. They are moving, climbing up, and yet "firm there still." They are both erect and receptive.

Williams links the consummation of sexual passion and the appearance of colorful beauty with states of illness, violence, and deformity, as well as with the gender confusion or fusion I have spoken of above. The petals are "tortured/eccentrically," the fruit is "frail," but "by its frailty supreme," and the petals are "inverted." Was not an "invert" the name for a homosexual in this period? Is not the flower in bloom—frail, sexually ambiguous, ill, and yet the producer of aesthetic pleasure—a figure for Demuth

in Williams's imagination, a figure that Williams is both attracted
to and repulsed by? Is not the fruition of this coupling of earth
and sky a work of art that, as Auden says, does nothing, produces
nothing ("no bean/no completion/no root ... but color only and a
form")?; the generation, not of another life, but of a work of art.

In "I Saw the Figure 5" (1928), Demuth's emphasis on the
color red, his figuring of the number 5 as an image that Williams
considered to be a portrait of the poet, his representation of his
own initials as well as several versions of Williams's throughout
the picture plane, and his inclusion of light bulbs resembling the
marquee of a movie theater might be read as part of an encoded
language that suggests the homoerotic nature of the homage to
Williams.[2] Williams's poem "The Great Figure" itself occurred in
the context of his interest in art produced by gay men. He recalls in
his autobiography that he jotted down the notes to the poem at the
doorway of Marsden Hartley's studio on Fifteenth Street after he
had "dropped in ... for a talk, a little drink maybe and to see what
he was doing" (A 172). Williams goes on to remember that, "As I
approached his number I heard a great clatter of bells and the roar
of a fire engine passing the end of the street down Ninth Avenue.
I turned just in time to see a golden figure 5 on a red background
flash by" (p. 172). It is impossible to know precisely why the sound
of bells would have made such an impression on the poet as he
was about to enter Hartley's studio, but perhaps something of the
clandestine nature of the visit (a drink in the middle of the day with
a gay experimental painter), might have seemed enough of an act of
social dissidence that Williams became especially aware of a sound
associated with the policing of homosexual life.

Demuth and Williams were of course lifelong friends. They were
involved in a kind of interarts dialogue throughout their lives.
Williams, for example, who displayed a Demuth flower painting
in his home at 9 Ridge Road, had published "The Pot of Flowers"
in *Spring and All* (a book he dedicated to Demuth). In 1936, he
published the long elegy that appeared in *Adam and Eve in the
City*, "The Crimson Cyclamen," with Demuth's watercolors of

---

[2]Weinberg points out that the "red tie" became a gay symbol and George Chauncey
has shown in *Gay New York* (1994) that the movie theater became a primary space
for same-sex trysts.

flowers, his lifelong subject, on his mind as a metaphor for the
growth and decline of the artist who died in 1935, possibly of
an overdose or underdose of insulin (A pp. 184–5). According to
the "Charles Demuth" chapter of the *Autobiography* (Williams,
1951), Williams served as a kind of unofficial doctor or therapist
to Demuth, a diabetic who only had insulin available to him near
the end of his life. Williams recalls incidents in which he inspected
Demuth's badly scratched back for infection at his Washington
Square Studio (apparently the outcome of a particularly wild
love affair, not a serious illness), and also visiting Demuth in
a Morristown, Pennsylvania, sanitarium with Marianne Moore
where "we had great talks" (p. 152). Although Williams's concern
for Demuth was often represented as clinical, an extension of
his medical practice, his imaginative fascination with Demuth's
"dissident" lifestyle is also a part of the relationship, both personal
and artistic, and I have tried to explore these aspects in my own
close reading of "The Crimson Cyclamen."

As I will note in my essay on Michael S. Harper's "Dear John"
letter to John Coltrane, W. J. T. Mitchell in *Picture Theory* defines
"ekphrastic fear" as:

> the moment of resistance or counterdesire that occurs when we
> sense that the difference between the verbal and visual repre-
> sentation might collapse and the figurative, imaginary desire
> of ekphrasis might be realized literally and actually. It is the
> moment in aesthetics when the difference between verbal and
> visual mediation becomes a moral, aesthetic imperative rather
> than ... a natural fact that can be relied on. (154–5)

Spectators experience "ekphrastic fear," Mitchell asserts, when
they perceive the confusion of genres in terms of an unrestrained
intersubjective encounter – what Mitchell calls a "dangerous
promiscuity" – in a nonart context.

Williams's creative encounter with Demuth's watercolor, I argue,
evidences what Mitchell terms "resistance or counterdesire" to
the poet's libidinal investment in his queer colleague's work. In
his poem, Williams mediates ekphrastic fear through the language
of formalism. Commenting on Demuth's abstract design features,
Williams seeks to restrain the vertiginous blurring of self and other,
viewer and artist, that, ironically, he manifests through a reading

of the watercolor that exceeds an account of its formal contours. Williams's lyric encounter with Demuth and his watercolor thus exposes the mess of unruly desire as well as the poet's failure to contain it through the language of detached, clinical observation. Unlike the critical accounts of Williams's relationship to visual culture that I glossed at the start of the chapter, I have tried to trace a lyric encounter between Williams and Demuth that mirrors my own experience of reading texts in ways that slip in and out of formal concerns and thus must reflect fears, desires, and fears about desire.

4

Queering Time:
Allen Ginsberg, "America,"
and the Cold War

I

By linking Allen Ginsberg's mid-century poetics with its counter-cultural critique of Cold War paranoia, conformism, and what Theodore Adorno termed "the Culture Industry," as I will go about doing in this essay, I am not offering a groundbreaking approach to the legendary Beat author who died in 1997. In seminal poems such as "America," the main lyric I will treat in what follows, as well as in "Howl," "A Supermarket in California," "Sunflower Sutra," and "The Green Automobile," Ginsberg desublimated mainstream America's fear of eccentricity. He crossed racial and sexual boundaries at once by expressing "deviant" behavior, including intercourse between white and black men. "Howl" displayed Ginsberg's fascination with what Norman Mailer called "white negroism," or the problematic—because it was risking the reduction of blacks to latter-day minstrel figures—association many Beats held between African-American culture, sexual liberation, and spiritual release from Alan Nadel's "containment culture" through music and dance.[1] "Howl" lauds those "best

---

[1]Interrogating how binary thinking and its inevitable slippages and paranoia informed American society in the 1950s, Alan Nadel in *Containment Culture:*

minds of my generation" who "purgatoried their torsos night after
night/with dreams, with drugs, with waking nightmares, alcohol
and cock and endless balls." And it was, after all, Ginsberg's 1956
long poem that led to a watershed First Amendment obscenity case
in San Francisco in 1957. As biographer Barry Miles reports:

> On May 21, 1957, acting on orders from Captain William
> Hanrahan of the San Francisco Police, Juvenile Division, two
> police officers went to City Lights Bookshop and bought a copy
> of Howl. The officers then obtained a warrant for the arrest of
> Lawrence Ferlinghetti as the book's publisher and as owner of
> the bookstore ...The Howl trial was under way.
>
> (1989, p. 227)

As Miles, American Studies scholar Walter Moore, and the poet
Ed Sanders in his narrative poem *The Poetry and Life of Allen
Ginsberg*, point out, the publicity and controversy surrounding the
profanity case, ironically, brought Ginsberg, "Howl," and the San
Francisco Beat culture to the forefront of the mainstream American
imaginary. "I suppose the publicity will be good," wrote Ginsberg,
while vacationing in Tangiers in March 1957, to publisher Lawrence
Ferlinghetti (Morgan, 2006, p. 236). Conservative publisher Henry
Luce's *Life* magazine devoted a spread to the poem, poet, and
controversy. This was only the start. In his narrative poem *The
Poetry and Life of Allen Ginsberg*, Ed Sanders writes of how the

---

American Narratives, Postmodernism, and the Atomic Age notices how Cold War
texts—political documents, films, and literary works—"reconcile the cult of domesticity with the demand for domestic security" (1995, p. xi). Containing the Red
Menace, Nadel asserts, was mirrored in how the archetypal woman of the 1950s
was cast as the domestic figure who must symbolically contain the unruly male
libido. Films such as *Pillow Talk* (1959), Nadel claims, participate in "the social,
political, and theological agenda that attempted to contain sexual activity in the
same manner that it attempted to contain communism" (p. 128):

> If containment ... names a foreign and domestic policy, it also names the
> rhetorical strategy that functioned to foreclose dissent, preempt dialogue, and
> preclude contradiction. The United States, empowered by the binding energy of
> the universe, was to become the universal container.
>
> (p. 14)

trial, and Ginsberg's victory, "catapulted him into a worldwide fame" (2000, p. 37).

I join other scholars and poets in situating Ginsberg's mid-century lyrics in the context of the Manichean ethics of a Cold War imaginary.[2] My reading of "America" differs, however, in that I argue Ginsberg's conformist bent, which exists within his nonconformist persona (and actions), ironically, authorizes a "queer" form of lyric dialogue that extends to Ginsberg's conversation with an Ur-site of what Adorno and Horkheimer termed "the Culture Industry," *Time* magazine. By "queer" lyric dialogue, I am thinking of the definition of "queer" set forth by E. Patrick Johnson and Mae G. Henderson in *Black Queer Studies*, as disrupting "dominant and hegemonic discourses by consistently destabilizing fixed notions of identity by deconstructing binaries such as heterosexual/homosexual, gay/lesbian, and masculine/feminine as well as the concept of heteronormativity in general" (2005, p. 5). Indeed, Ginsberg's semiosis deconstructs Cold War discourse (conservative mainstream/radical progressive) on a deep structural level. His expression of conformist impulses, including his self-described "obsession" with *Time* magazine, upsets the Cold War's dualistic mindset.[3] Implicated in and critical of "America," Ginsberg addresses the nation as if it were an imaginary state outside the self. At other times "America" represents the apostrophic "you" as a desublimated projection of the status quo. Turning the monologic lyric genre into a zany dialogue, Ginsberg occupies multiple positions including conformist citizen, nation, and inexplicable other within the state. The persona is public and private, oppositional to and informed by mainstream ideological rhetoric found in *Time* and on television.

---

[2] Anne Hartman, Mark Doty, Paul Breslin, Craig Svonkin, and Steven Gould Axelrod.

[3] In "Coteries, Landscape and the Sublime in Allen Ginsberg," Justin Quinn focuses on how the poet queers the "sublime" genre that is "traditionally viewed as a moment that jettisons personality and history in favor of vision of a reality that remains obscure in everyday life" (2003, p. 1) by "socializ[ing] and 'familiariz[ing]' the sublime": friends, family, and even the larger patterns of national fate are no longer abandoned by the rhapsode, but are imbricated within the very texture of his transcendental experience. Quinn's analysis of how Ginsberg queers (or blurs binary distinctions) between two dominant modes of American literature—the sublime and the quotidian—is resonant with my argument that Ginsberg in "America" challenges the Manichean ethics of the Cold War imaginary.

The speaker is antagonistic towards Eisenhower's "military industrial complex" and yet his rhetoric is informed by its belligerent
agendas. Ginsberg's character as excluded oddball in "America" is
simply too volatile to serve the Cold War binary.

As I will explain, Ginsberg's queer poetics in "America" include
his ambiguous relation to mainstream media and especially to
Luce's *Time*. Through a close reading of Ginsberg's comments
in "America" about *Time,* as well as his association of writing
with commerce, alongside an analysis of essays and reviews about
Ginsberg that appeared in *Time* and its sister publication *Life*, I
show how Ginsberg destabilizes Nadel's Cold War "containment
culture." Exploring Ginsberg's conversation with *Time* also allows
me to examine questions about the relation between literature and
popular culture. Expressing ambivalence towards *Time*, Ginsberg
engages with what linguist George Lakoff calls "bi-conceptualism."
By contrast, *Time* and *Life*, in their ripostes to his texts, attempt
to reduce Ginsberg to the mono-conceptual frame. He is cast in
Time as deviant in a contemporaneous book review concerning
the Beats, and treated in *Life* as an ironically pro-American Cold
Warrior via his advocacy for free speech and individualism. In
the 1980s, when Ginsberg had signed a six-figure contract with
Harper & Row, *Time* regards his commercial success as a sign that
the "Culture Industry" had thoroughly absorbed one of its most
notorious critics.

II

Certainly, we may read "America" as the poet's archival rehearsal
of Alternative Histories of Progressive Movements in the U.S.
"America" references Leon Trotsky, William Burroughs, the
"Wobblies" (Industrial Workers of the World), Marx, Tom
Mooney, the Spanish Loyalists, Sacco and Vanzetti, the Scottsboro
Boys, Scott Nearing, and Ella Bloor. As poet Kenneth Rexroth
has stated, Ginsberg's work is "an almost perfect fulfillment of
the long, Whitman, Populist, social revolutionary tradition in
American poetry" (p. 2, "Allen Ginsberg": The Poetry Foundation
website). Early in "America," Ginsberg's lyric voice *is* that of
a conventional counter-culturist. At first a specter of Whitman

returning to observe the outcome of his handiwork a century after *Leaves of Grass*, Ginsberg confronts a progressivist's nightmare. He enters what the poet Robert Lowell referred to as "the tranquilized fifties" and into the belly of what President Eisenhower, in his farewell address, termed "the military industrial complex." In Whitman fashion, Ginsberg in "America" establishes a public dialogue with a nation understood as a textual manifestation of the corporate body.[4]

In the early strophes, Ginsberg voices countercultural critique. He accuses "America" of a litany of right-wing sins in an interrogatory manner that, one could argue, mimics the grilling of witnesses at the Army-McCarthy "Witch Hunt" hearings. Unlike the Red Scare trials, however, "America's" inequities range from being sexually repressed— "When will you take off your clothes?"— to political repression of radical movements. Personae non gratae in the U.S. imaginary occupy a distinguished, if unacknowledged, place in the American polity: "When will you be worthy of your million Trotskyites?" Following a title that riffs on "America the Beautiful," Ginsberg accuses the land of "amber waves of grain" of hoarding commodities and insensitivity to the sufferings of another formerly colonized country: "America, when will you send your eggs to India?"

Later in the poem, however, Ginsberg occupies an "I" in a series of declarations that express Cold War paranoia from the perspective of a threatened corporate body ("Asia is rising against me."). He takes agency for oppressive politics, and repressive social and sexual mores ("I have abolished the whorehouses of France. Tangiers is the next to go") associated with the "you" of "America" earlier in the poem. In this later stage, even when Ginsberg authorizes his "I" to express attitudes more typically associated with a Beat sensibility, the poet frames this countercultural "I" via economic and industrial discourses. We notice how Ginsberg's "I" floats between different perspectives, at times making it difficult

---

[4]The poetic space is the appropriate discursive space for Ginsberg's psychoanalytically driven desublimation of the self in dialogue with its own otherness because, as Whitman acknowledged in his acceptance of contradictions ("Do I contradict myself?/Very well then ... I contradict myself; I am large ... I contain multitudes"), poetic logic privileges ambivalence and ambiguity in ways that are inadmissible in rationalistic forms of discourse. In poetic discourse, the slippery, unstable nature of language is not only admissible, but privileged.

to establish if the pronoun's referent is "America" or "Ginsberg."
In the following segment, Ginsberg's tone is indebted to entrepreneurial hucksterism and his poetics resemble an assembly-line form
of productivity that Marx famously linked to alienated labor. Late
in the poem, the speaker's oppositional stance is informed, however
parodically asserted, by an industrialist's mindset:

> My national resources consist of two joints of marijuana
>   millions of genitals an unpublishable private literature that
>   jetplanes 1400 miles an hour and twentyfive-thousand
>   mental institutions.
> I say nothing about my prisons nor the millions of
>   underprivileged who live in my flowerpots under the lights
>   of five hundred suns. [...]
> I will continue like Henry Ford my strophes are as individual
>   as his automobiles more so they're all different sexes.
> America I will sell you strophes $2500 apiece $500 down on
>   your old strophe.

Ginsberg wrote these lines in the context of the National Security
State, as well as the ramping up of desire for products through
television, advertising, and the development of a consumer society
in a heated-up post-war economy.[5]

Ginsberg links writing with Detroit's assembly lines and the
selling of "strophes" through the installment plan. Less than a
decade earlier, Frankfurt School theorists Theodor Adorno and
Max Horkheimer in their (1947) *Dialectic of Enlightenment* had
argued that the critical space of High Art had become coopted
into a capitalist nexus that they termed "The Culture Industry."
German-Jewish exiles living in the midst of Hollywood's studio
system, Adorno and Horkheimer argued:

> The cultural commodities of the industry are governed ... by
> the principle of their realization as value, and not by their own
> specific content and harmonious formation. The entire practice

---

[5] A classic dramatic representation of the post-war shift to a consumer society occurs
in Arthur Miller's *All My Sons* (1947) when Joe Keller refits a factory that once
made war munitions to produce washing machines and refrigerators.

of the culture industry transfers the profit motive naked onto cultural forms. Ever since these cultural forms first began to earn a living for their creators as commodities in the market-place they had already possessed something of this quality. But then they sought after profit only indirectly, over and above their autonomous essence. New on the part of the culture industry is the direct and undisguised primacy of a precisely and thoroughly calculated efficacy in its most typical products.

(Adorno, 1975, p. 13)

In line one of "America," Ginsberg implicitly announces his alternative masculinity: "America I've given you all and now I'm nothing." He was someone who, now "nothing," has "given"— rather than someone who "takes"—(consumes) "his all." Self-worth cannot be defined by productivity, rationality, militarism, social status, and especially not by bank account, which in his case amounts to a grand total of "two dollars and twenty-seven cents." In the passage quoted above concerning "national resources," we notice a shift in thinking. Instead of "nothing," the speaker enjoys a surplus of eccentric commodities that exceed a rational assessment of his value.[6]

---

[6]The subtitle of Nadel's study on the Containment Culture refers to "the Atomic Age." The threat of Soviet nuclear power led American planners to view the Red Menace as requiring containment, but Nadel shows the proliferation of atomic power disabled the desire for containment. Noting Undersecretary of State Dean Acheson's "committee to investigate the problem of atomic energy," Nadel writes:

Repeatedly these recommendations attempt to stabilize exactly the distinctions that atomic power destabilizes: the distinction between national interests and international, between dangerous and nondangerous activities, and, most important, between the legitimate and illegitimate authorities for making these distinctions.

(1995, p. 21)

We may interpret Ginsberg's remarks about the extraordinary speed of the poet's "unpublishable private literature" ("1400 miles an hour") as well as his "national resource" of "millions of genitals," which, in Stanley Kubrick's Dr. Strangelove or: How I Learned to Stop Worrying and Love the Bomb (1964) are associated with nuclear missiles and the comment about "the lights of five hundred suns" as referencing, however obliquely, elements of a culture of atomic power that, as Nadel suggests, could not be contained by the Cold War binary.

Ginsberg chides American consumerism, mainstream media and
religion, industrialism, militarism, anti-Sovietism, and suppression
of an alternative history of American progressivism, anarchism,
and anti-racism. And yet he participates in this culture as well:

> I'm addressing you.
> Are you going to let your emotional life be run by Time
>   Magazine?
> I'm obsessed by Time Magazine.
> I read it every week.
> Its cover stares at me every time I slink past the corner
>   candystore.
> I read it in the basement of the Berkeley Public Library.
> It's always telling me about responsibility. Businessmen are
>   serious.
> Movie producers are serious. Everybody's serious but me.
> It occurs to me that I am America.
> I am talking to myself again.

Founded in 1923 as America's first weekly newsmagazine, *Time*,
reports the magazine's website, was a "newsmagazine which
summarized and organized the news so that 'busy men' could
stay informed." In no way were "busy men" encouraged to think
of *Time* magazine alongside "Howl" and *On the Road* (1957)
as part of a cultural continuum rather than of the latter two as
distinct and adversarial discursive systems. And yet in "America"
the speaker declares himself one of the "busy men" who wants
his news contained—that is, "summarized and organized" in
a tidy package. Indeed, the faces *Time* celebrated on its covers
each week take on an interpellative function in "America."
A textual manifestation of a surveillance culture designed, as
Nadel argues, to contain behavior deemed a threat to a family-
centered, heteronormative system of work and status through
consumption, the *Time* covers, for Ginsberg's speaker, serve a
punitive function. The covers signify his inadequacies. They also
convey his tonal failure to imagine the serious and responsible
faces of world leaders on the covers of *Time* as a mirror reflecting
his (ostensible) lack of seriousness and responsibility. (Ginsberg
speaks in the poem of the difficulty of writing poetry in his "silly"
mood.) The *Time* cover becomes a personal cover, or means of

concealment. Ginsberg interprets *Time* as a "how to" manual that simultaneously seduces and repels.

The *Time* cover is a source of shame for Ginsberg in "America." There also is an ironic suggestion of its role in how he manifests deviant behavior. His reading of *Time* in the basement (presumably where the bathrooms are located) of the Berkeley Public Library may signify a literal and figurative "cover" for clandestine meetings in the less easily surveyed subterranean space of a public building. "Its cover stares at me every time I slink past the corner candystore./I read it in the basement of the Berkeley Public Library./It's always telling me about responsibility." The speaker is acutely "responsible" to *Time*. He responds to its construction of an American psyche, even as he finds himself unable to conform to its strict expectations for a flat line emotional affect.[7]

III

In a *Time* 9 June 1958 review of *The Beat Generation and the Angry Young Man*, edited by Gene Feldman and Max Gartenberg, the anonymous critic rebukes the "central Beat character" as "a model psychopath" (Hyde, p. 54). The reviewer's sarcastic voice and dismissive tone indicate he or she intends to produce less an analytical critique of Feldman and Gartenberg than an ideologically-driven screed aimed at stirring up the *Time* audience's revulsion at Beat identity. The reviewer terms Ginsberg the "discount-house Whitman of the Beat Generation" (p. 54). Citing "New York Times's critic J. Donald Adams" the reviewer adds that "Howl" "should be retitled 'Bleat'" (p. 54). *Time* reads the Beats as "sheep": effeminate pacifists who don't think for themselves.

---

[7]Writing in the semiotic mode of a poetics that exceeds the demand for semantic stability in conventionally transparent journalistic prose such as *Time*'s or scientific discourse, Ginsberg in "America" explores how the two apparently oppositional but actually compositionally coordinated elements of his performance merge to the point where the Other is the Self and the Self is the Other. We are meant to puzzle over Ginsberg's fascination with Henry Luce's conservative, anti-Soviet periodical, but we are also encouraged to regard the term "Time" in relationship to other places in "America" in which Ginsberg ponders metaphysical and ontological questions of being in time.

They have buckled under the pressure of Cold War nuclear brinks-
manship and spit on the organizational man's gray flannel suit:

> He is a rebel without a cause who shirks responsibility on the
> ground that he has the H-bomb jitters. His disengagement from
> society is so complete that he treats self as the only reality and
> cultivates sensation as the only goal. But the self-revolving life is
> a bore, a kind of life-in-death that requires ever intenser stimu-
> lants to create even the illusion of feeling.

(p. 55)

The end game for such "disengagement from society" is a quick
death: "The future of the Beat Generation can be read in its past—
the James Deans and Dylan Thomases and Charlie 'Yardbird'
Parkers" (p. 55). Never mind that Dylan Thomas was a Welsh
poet not associated with Beat poetry. The review continues, "The
Angry Young Man is a rebel with a cause, a disorganization man
in transition who will eventually make his peace with a society in
which he means to make good" (p. 55).

The *Time* reviewer's invective against Beat culture is especially
irresponsible because of its willful misreading of Ginsberg's poetry
as formed by "a disengagement from society [that] is so complete
that he treats self as the only reality" (p. 54). In fact, the self in
isolation from society is precisely what Ginsberg's signature poems
from the 1950s—"Howl," "America," "Sunflower Sutra," and
"A Supermarket in California"—set out to remedy through the
creation of a different society via homosocial friendship. As poet
Mark Doty correctly observes, "'Howl,' considered in 2005, seems,
more than anything else, a poem of visionary friendship, of the
longing to be part of a questing (albeit erratic) company" (p. 2).
In part through its ambivalent reckoning with *Time*, Ginsberg's
"America" disables the magazine's desire to contain his social
influence by dismissing the poet as a suicidal psychopath.

IV

In "America," Ginsberg uses silly humor for a shrewd rhetorical
purpose. The irreverent tone enables him to occupy a discursive

and emotional space different from, and yet contingent upon, the realm of seriousness and responsibility that he associates with *Time* and corporations such as the Ford Motor Company. In a line of Jewish comics from Groucho Marx to Lenny Bruce, Ginsberg absorbs, ventriloquizes, and parodies contemporary discourse. He mimics the Cold War binary in a queer style that is so excessive in its Black Face performativity and its Red Scare paranoia that these restrictive aspects of the American social text become destabilized to the point of absurdity.

> America it's them bad Russians.
> Them Russians them Russians and them Chinamen. And them
>   Russians.
> The Russia wants to eat us alive. The Russia's power mad. She
>   wants to take our cars from our garages. [...]
> Her wants our auto plants in Siberia. Him big bureaucracy
>   running our filling-stations.
> That no good. Ugh. Him make Indians learn read. Him need
>   big black niggers. Hah. Her make us all work sixteen hours
>   a day.
> Help.
> America this is quite serious.
> America this is the impression I get from looking in the
>   television set.

In terms of rhythm, grammar, and diction Ginsberg relies on Borscht Belt comedy and Dadaism. He also mimics the "broken" English associated with African Americans and Native Americans. It's an intriguing trope, putting anti-Communist discourse into the mouths of the most alienated and marginalized in America— thereby undermining the critique of the Cold War rhetoric and the racist discourse that Ginsberg sees going along with it. At the same time in phrases such as "them Russians and them Russians and them Chinamen. And them Russians" Ginsberg's repetition of the terms dissociates sign and signifier. The "meaning" of national signifiers—Russian, China—becomes unstable. Listeners are enchanted by the jazzy syncopation. Ginsberg offers a *da da dum* (anapestic) rhythm —"and them Russians" (unstressed, unstressed, stressed, unstressed) metrics that reaches an end stop only to turn into a surprising caesural pause as Ginsberg offers one more "And them Russians" after the period. This literally off-beat prosodics that combines Dadaism, jazz, and a schmaltzy Yiddish theater one-liner rhythm replicates, and through discursive excess, dislodges, words from their ideological moorings. It becomes, to use Ginsberg's term, "silly" to imagine Russians taking over American filling stations. My reading of "America" as a queering of the Cold War binary helps connect Ginsberg's ambivalent biographical relation to 1950s America to his poetry. My reading problematizes representations of him as a counter-cultural pariah. Even such a distinguished historian as Morris Dickstein has described Ginsberg as occupying the counter-cultural position: "the Beats tended to mythologize each other and aimed to provoke middle-class outrage. Their antinomianism could lead them to idealize the addict, the criminal, and the madman as 'angelheaded hipsters' or doomed victims of society" (1991).

By contrast to Dickstein, and as Bill Morgan's (2006) biography of the poet *I Celebrate Myself* indicates, Ginsberg, at the time of "America's" composition, was by no means certain about where he stood in relation to heteronormative, consumerist America. Unlike Kerouac, who quit college after a knee injury caused him to lose his football scholarship, Ginsberg made it his business to complete his degree at Columbia in spite of nervous break-downs and his suspension after writing anti-Semitic graffiti on the window of a Columbia dormitory. At Berkeley, he worked towards a Master's Degree with the hope of following his father Louis's example as a language arts instructor. He accepted jobs in marketing research in New York and San Francisco, and pursued straight relationships even as he explored gay sex with otherwise straight or bisexual men such as Kerouac, Neal Cassady, and Peter Orlovsky. Far from lamenting the fact, as he does in "America," that "Burroughs is in Tangiers I don't think he'll come back it's sinister," Morgan reports that at precisely this time Ginsberg hoped Burroughs would make himself scarce. Ginsberg wanted to develop his romance with Sheila Williams, "a pretty twenty-two-year-old woman from Salt Lake City" (2006, p. 182) with whom he lived in her "homey apartment on the side of Nob Hill, promising to split her seventy-five-dollar-a-month rent" (p. 183). As Morgan reports, "He knew that William [Burroughs] would make impossible, possessive demands on him that he wouldn't have the strength to escape ... Allen's only hope was to stall

Burroughs's visit to San Francisco, so he wrote immediately to ask him to wait awhile" (p. 183).

It is certainly true that Ginsberg challenges the 1950s codes of masculinity in "America" through his then-illegal participation in gay sex. In an ironically veiled moment of outing in "America," the speaker declares, "I sit in my house for days on end and stare at the roses in the closet." The comment reminds us of Gertrude Stein's "a rose is a rose is a rose," which slips semiotically into the phrase "eros is eros is eros," and to Marcel Duchamp's cross-dressing image of himself in Man Ray's photograph of 1921 "Rrose Sélavy" (translation: eros, that is life). And of course there is the famous last line of the poem in which Ginsberg tells America that he is "putting [his] queer shoulder to the wheel." But his behavior during his San Francisco period, and especially his travels in Mexico just prior to it, suggest his exploration of what Paul Breines would call the "tough Jew" image meant to contradict the feminized Yeshiva Jew image that Daniel Boyarin has recently recovered from denigration. Besides his Melvillian quests with the Merchant Marines, Ginsberg, as Morgan reports, performed the role of imperial-colonial archeologist explorer. He led an expedition into a virtually impenetrable forest to observe recently excavated Mayan ruins.[8]

Ginsberg chides America, and therefore the national imaginary he internalized, for letting "your emotional life be run by Time magazine." Simultaneously, Ginsberg, as biographer Bill Morgan has noted, compared his heterosexual relationships to those found in *House Beautiful* magazine. He sought journalism positions in San Francisco and in New Jersey. As Walter Moore has noted,

---

[8]In a perceptive 1977 review of "Howl" and "Kaddish," James Breslin outlines Ginsberg's ambiguous relationship to mainstream codes:

> It is certainly mistaken to imagine a recreated Ginsberg floating into San Francisco on a magic carpet, dressed in robes, with flowing hair, hand cymbals and a "San Francisco Poetry Renaissance" banner. The Ginsberg that emerged in "Howl"—Ginsberg the rancorous and somewhat gloomy mystic seer—must in some sense have been there, but he was apparently hidden at first beneath a deferential and conventional exterior. In fact, it would be more accurate to imagine him arriving in a three-button suit, striped tie, and an attaché case.
>
> (Breslin, 1985, p. 405)

Ginsberg wished to benefit from publicity surrounding the "Howl" obscenity trial in *Time*'s sister publication, *Life*:

> In letters right before and during the trial, Ginsberg wrote to numerous journalists and critics, explaining the context and significance of *Howl*. In an April 1957 letter to Ferlinghetti, after the book's seizure but before the trial, Ginsberg wrote: "I suppose the publicity will be good ... Be sure let the *Life* people in SF know about situation, they might include it in story... Send story to *Village Voice*, they've been digging the scene. ..." Further, "I guess the best way publicity wise is prepare some sort of outraged and idiotic but dignified statement, quoting the Customs man, and Eberhart's article and Williams, and *Nation* review, mimeograph it up and send it out as a sort of manifesto publishable by magazines and/or news release."
>
> (Moore, 2011, unpaginated)

"Howl" faced censorship because of its anti-establishment rhetoric and celebration of homosexuality. Moore, however, shows that "through his letters, Ginsberg displays a close awareness of and involvement with the media as a player in what cultural theorist Theodor Adorno calls the 'Industry'." Whether Allen Ginsberg completely lost creativity and freedom as a result of his involvement with the media is up for debate, but regardless, his savvy sense of publicity must be noted.

V

One may read "Mainstreaming Allen Ginsberg," a *Time* article by R. Z. Sheppard published in February, 1985, one month after Harper & Row brought out *Collected Poems 1947–1980*, as the magazine's belated riposte to the poet's tongue-in-cheek statements about his obsession with *Time* in "America" three decades earlier. The title signals *Time*'s boast that is not merely reporting on the author's "mainstreaming" through his shift of publication venue from Ferlinghetti's City Lights to Harper & Row. Sheppard enacts the poet's absorption into what Adorno and Horkheimer described as the "entire practice of the culture industry [that] transfers the profit motive naked onto cultural forms" (Adorno, 1975, p. 13).

Ginsberg self-mockingly commodified his poetry—"America I will sell you strophes $2,500 apiece $500 down on your old strophe." By contrast, Sheppard informs readers that *Collected Poems* will fetch the tidy sum of $27.50 per copy, a price, one assumes, Harper & Row's finance department calculated to recoup the $160,000 advance the publisher had paid the poet to sign a six-book deal. If "America" represents Ginsberg's deliciously undecidable relation to *Time*, an Ur-text in Adorno's coopting Culture Industry, Sheppard's article reads like a Reagan-era attempt to contain a repressed subject of the Cold War's heyday at the cusp of its dissolution.

With the subtitle "Pushing 60, the poet has a six-figure contract," Sheppard pronounces the rebel as thoroughly rehabilitated. That is to say, the late middle age author has cried Uncle to commercialism. For better or worse, Ginsberg still influences contemporary America. Sheppard casts the poet as precursor to a media that transforms alternative private lives into titillating morning talk show fodder for housewives. Words and ideas from the "bearded rebel from Paterson N. J." who "flaunted the subjects of drug use and homosexuality with an explicitness that would have unnerved Walt Whitman" have been reconfigured as banal TV freak fodder: "[M]illions of housewives casually tune in to hopheads and gays on The Phil Donahue Show."

Stylistically, Ginsberg and Donahue were light years apart. One was a queer bearded leftist Jewish intellectual from Northern New Jersey, the other a big white-haired Catholic Notre Dame grad with a Midwestern twang, three-piece gray suit, and gee whiz persona. Where Ginsberg's partner was Peter Orlovsky, Donahue married "That Girl," Marlo Thomas. Where Ginsberg wrote his signature poems in Berkeley, Donahue got his start as a TV reporter in Dayton, Ohio, before moving his talk show to Chicago. And yet Sheppard grants that Ginsberg's irreverent life and experimental verse have served to bridge Whitman, America's seminal queer 19th-Century bard, and today's no holds barred reality TV culture. Privacy is publicized, as it was in Whitman and Ginsberg, but now self-exposure is a for profit enterprise in a scopophilic society. Ginsberg represented artistic culture while *Donahue* is mass culture devoid of artistic value. That said, the poet opened the door for sensationalistic talk shows when he took poetry from the page to the stage through events such as the legendary reading of "Howl" at the Six Gallery Reading on Fillmore Street in San Francisco in 1955. *Donahue* seems to be pure voyeurism, while "Howl" carries a message of freedom and self-expression. Nonetheless, Ginsberg helped usher in the distribution of poetry as a type of mass media through the appearance of *Howl*, *Kaddish*, and *Planet News* in the Pocket Book series of Lawrence Ferlinghetti's City Lights. Even High Culture favorite Robert Lowell stated in a *Partisan Review* interview with Frederick Seidel that his ground-breaking confessional style and the relaxed diction in *Life Studies* were indebted to his hearing Ginsberg read on the West Coast. Donahue extended his long thin microphone with a straight arm into the audience and with his head turned away from the speaker. The microphone seemed less a phallus than a listening device that measured a safe distance between himself and the "hopheads and gays" who performed their freakishness before a studio audience of other astonished normals. In Sheppard's article, *Donahue* may thus be read as a program designed to desublimate, by projecting onto a national television audience and—by making it into a freak show — contain the unruly dialogue between Ginsberg's subject position as one of abjection and belonging in "America."

Is Ginsberg's "mainstreaming" through the contract with Harper & Row a sign that he has fulfilled the promise of Whitman, who at the conclusion to his "Preface" to the 1855 first edition of *Leaves of Grass* wrote, "The proof of a poet is that his country absorbs him as affectionately as he has absorbed it"? Perhaps. Sheppard stresses that *Collected Poems* is "only the first step in drawing Ginsberg to mainstream publishing and ratifying his presence between hard covers." Presumably the "hard covers" are meant to contrast with the "soft sheets" under which the queer poet once enacted his sexual proclivities with angelic boys. The *Time* essay illustrates how a radical American character may be absorbed into Adorno's Culture Industry and the capitalist nexus that it underwrites. Even in Sheppard's treatment, however, Ginsberg defies easy categorization, as he is "[a]pproaching his autumnal years." Sheppard notes that the figure who threw a "poetic tantrum ... at an academic system that rejected his rude unconventionality" is now a National Book Award-winning author (ironically for *The Fall of America*) and "member of the National Institute of Arts and Letters." Ginsberg is literally and figuratively contained in time (the magazine, his "autumnal years," and a media that absorbs alternative cultures by displaying deviance as voyeuristic pleasure via shows such as *Donahue*).

Sheppard celebrates the shift from Ferlinghetti's City Lights to Harper & Row, but Ginsberg defies containment. No longer cast in dashikis, but "sports jackets, slacks, shirts and ties," Ginsberg differs from a man in a gray flannel suit or *Donahue* double-breasted wannabe. Sheppard acknowledges that Ginsberg remains antagonistic to the consumer society that *Time* displays because he bought the threads "secondhand at the Salvation Army." Similarly, Ginsberg's dwelling is antagonistic to real estate as economic asset. The article mentions that lower Manhattan is in the midst of gentrification and yet Ginsberg occupies a "$260-a month apartment in Manhattan's run-down East Village." It resembles, in a queer sort of way, the Beat Generation's latter-day communal home. Peter Orlovsky, identified as "a former lover and longtime companion," lives "across the hall," and the "Ginsberg apartment is a popular rest stop for old companions passing through New York." The bard has become something of a persnickety house mother for surviving Beats whom he refers to, quite ambivalently, as "hideous human angels." Ginsberg laments his trouble keeping "the place clean" because of frequent travels to destinations such as Colorado's Naropa Institute. "Clean" here means sans mud, not sans grass. He has taken to putting a sign on his bedroom door "that asks guests to remove their shoes," not, as one might have assumed in the past, to facilitate the lotus position or the nuzzling of toes, but rather to avoid tracking in dirt.

The apartment resembles a cock-eyed version of middle-class conformism. It signifies a queer parody of a mainstream homeowner's sensibility. A renovation has been attempted, but gone awry. There is a "kitchen sink in the living room." Lacking a "working front bell," a "visitor must call up from the sidewalk and wait for the poet to throw down a key rolled up in a sock." Charming, but how impractical! Ginsberg may have grudgingly become a financial winner with the publishing deal with Harper & Row, but Sheppard acknowledges that poets, even those as notorious as Ginsberg, must still sing for their supper: "At 58, Ginsberg is confronting one of life's simple truths: one cannot step into the same cash flow twice." This statement seems overtly mean-spirited. Sheppard mocks Ginsberg's anti-establishment bent through the riff on Heraclitus's quip about how life's flux is like a river flow. "I don't know if I can keep it up any longer. I'm getting too old to run around," Ginsberg laments. The passage suggests his sexual escapades may be over in the days before Viagra, as well as his inability to support underground literary allies and political movements. A weary Cold Warrior, Ginsberg is classified as ending up on the wrong side of history. He is a relic with "papers and projects that relentlessly pile up around him." The fact that Stanford would pay him a million dollars for his personal archives in 1994 only supports Sheppard's thesis. Even the detritus of a rebellious mind can be catalogued and sold to the highest bidder. A split figure, Sheppard concludes his piece by suggesting he can gaze into the best mind of a prior generation: "one [eye is] wide and innocent, gazing at eternity; the other narrowed and scrutinizing, looking for his market share." Sheppard defines Ginsberg's association with mysticism as "innocent," and so the other eye must be trained on "experience." The Culture Industry, often associated with a postmodern realm of fantasy and simulation, is in Sheppard's essay defined as what is real, because it is associated with finances, not, like poetry (unless it can be sold) imagined.

VI

Sheppard takes a victory lap for the Culture Industry during the Reagan era at the nadir of the Cold War. By contrast, a full-length feature story from May 1966 by Barry Farrell in *Time*'s sister publication *Life*, takes a different tack in its public dialogue with the poet. "The Guru Comes to Kansas: Allen Ginsberg, Wild-Haired Wild Man of the Beat Poets" covers his visit to the University of Kansas in Lawrence on a Guggenheim grant. A quick glance at Wikipedia's annual report for 1966 reveals a year of extreme destabilization in the United States and Cold War turmoil throughout the world. Amidst reports of massacres and U.S. airplane bombings of Hanoi and Haiphong, Vietnam is regularly in the news. U.S. troops in Vietnam now number 250,000 and tens of thousands of anti-war demonstrators picket the White House and the Washington Monument. The Cold War is heating up with the

House Un-American Activities Committee investigating Americans who have aided the Viet Cong, Mao Zedong officially declaring a Cultural Revolution in China, and Fidel Castro ordering martial law in Cuba in the wake of fears of a U.S. attack. While Martin Luther King Jr. has begun to speak out against the Vietnam War, Bobby Seale and Huey P. Newton found the Black Panther Movement. U.S. youth culture is moving into the acid rock era with new releases from The Doors and The Jefferson Airplane and The Beatles in the studio to record *Sgt. Pepper's Lonely Hearts Club Band*. LSD is made illegal in the United States. John Lennon declares The Beatles are "more popular than Jesus now."

Rather than the exhausted relic of bygone days of social radicalism that Sheppard argues he had become by 1985, Ginsberg is at the height of his influence among young people worldwide in 1966. A visiting dignitary described as having the aura of a "monk," he strolls through the University of Kansas Student Union, settling in to danish and tea while "imploring faces shine with want of Allen's talk" (Farrell, 1966, p. 79). A figure who cannot be taken lightly as an irrelevant, if irreverent, queer kook, Ginsberg now has adoring acolytes flourishing in the heartland between Berkeley and the Bowery. In Kansas "even home-economics majors now seem able to hear all he has to say with wonderful, terrifying sophistication" (p. 80). After he reads to thousands of fawning Jayhawk undergraduates, "[t]he students are deeply excited—less so, it seems, by the buckets of sexual revelation than by the larger spectacle of a man so completely able to tell the whole truth about himself, however difficult it is to bear" (p. 89).

Ginsberg is a Warholian superstar, but not only for fifteen minutes. One year earlier, on 1 May 1965, over 100,000 "students of Prague elected him King of the May" (p. 80). Sheppard cannot deny Ginsberg's position as "a major literary figure known around the world and looked up to by the young" (p. 79), and yet he stubbornly resists the consumer nexus—no million dollar deals on the horizon for his manuscripts from Stanford or six-figure deals with Harper & Row. At the end of the article, Ginsberg is depicted in a photograph as a shirtless, skinny, and praying ascetic in India "where he spent months living in a $2-a-month tenement in the holy city of Benares" (p. 90). Even his famous poems hardly make a buck: "Howl has sold through 16 printings, [but] Allen continues to live under an old vow of 'relative penury' — $3,000 a year or so, and the rest for whoever needs it" [p. 90]). Farrell is thus assigned a complex task. He must acknowledge Ginsberg's undeniable sway over Midwestern young while explaining to worried parents why this "guru" is actually benign, and even sensible.

The trick for *Life*'s readers is not to panic about Ginsberg's effect on youth culture. To stay calm, Farrell suggests readers overlook the wild locks, accept that he is pro-grass, anti-war, and is known to shed his clothes at poetry readings, as well as endure his recitation of what comedian George Carlin in 1972 called "The Seven Words You Can Never Say on Television." Far from advocating for a political revolution, however, Farrell casts Ginsberg less as a mendacious and mean-spirited phony such as *Leave it to Beaver*'s Eddie Haskell and more in the mold of Beaver Cleaver or Dennis the Menace. As a kid, Ginsberg, in Farrell's portrayal, was basically decent, if neurotic and maladjusted. He was gullible enough in his Columbia days in the mid-1940s to get in with some really bad seeds around Times Square. Ginsberg recalls his father Louis's reaction to his arrest for fencing goods Herbert Huncke had stored at his Columbia apartment ("Huncke was far too sympathetic a creature for Allen to throw out") (Farrell, 1966, p. 84): "What a mess! Like was my father ever upset—it really brought him back. He—a nice middle-class teacher, a poet, there in Paterson—the idea of anybody going to jail was horrifying to him" (p. 85). After pep talks from a non-judgmental therapist, he "began to shift perilously toward respectability and steady employment—book reviewer, market research consultant. He traveled some, wrote poems, relished his friends" (p. 85). Sounds promising, but Farrell writes that Allen only came into his own once he accepted himself as a basically harmless misfit. So he happened to like guys named Peter more than gals named Paula, didn't feel right in a suit and tie, and got a kick out of writing out his inner feelings in long flowing lines. Maybe not bring home to meet mom material, but revolutionary? No worries. Farrell's piece is part of the domestication of Ginsberg that enabled him to become part of (or coopted by) mass culture.

In fact, Farrell casts Ginsberg as a moderating influence on hot-headed Kansas undergrads. They, not he, are bent on personal ruin and political destruction. For example, at his danish and tea meeting at the campus café with Kansas students, Ginsberg, described as wearing a "great Hasidic beard" (p. 79), is asked about the symbolism of his "wild beard and sunburst hair" (p. 79).

Refusing to interpret his hair style as a symbol of freedom and rebellion à la the Broadway musical ("Oh say can you see/My eyes if you can/Then my hair's too short"), Ginsberg takes the tack of Zen master, not social revolutionary: "It's not a flag or anything. It's just there" (p. 79). Another student recalls "talking about blowing up railroad stations" only to be told by the Thoreauvian guru that it was "better to sit in front of the draft board" (p. 79). Near the end of the feature, Allen is joined at—where else?—a Chinese restaurant by a young poet who has carved an "X" into his cheek with a piece of broken glass as a "one letter suicide note." To the *poète maudit* or nihilistic Jim Morrison—"I'm nothing ... and death is nothing" (p. 90)—Ginsberg plays practical Jewish mother: "Now you just eat your soup" (p. 90).

Framing Ginsberg as a Yiddishe Mama in drag, Farrell contains Ginsberg's literary radicalism by reading his poetry as an expression of Romantic individualism and Wildean aestheticism. Agitprop à la Clifford Odets is not Ginsberg's bag: "Art is something discovered from your own real nature," he is quoted as saying. A poem that celebrates the "best minds" "who burned cigarette holes in their arms protesting the narcotic tobacco haze of Capitalism" (*Collected Poems*, 1995, p. 135), Ginsberg is quoted as treating "Howl" as interior self-expression that exists "outside social communication":

> I started it with the idea of writing what I really felt, summing up my life for the soul's own ear, tapping the sources of what was really inside me and expressing these things directly— outside literature, of course, outside the possibilities of social communication.

> (1966, p. 84)

Regardless of subject matter or its relation to the poet's life or political and social commitments, Farrell assures *Life* readers that the bottom line for Ginsberg is the work: "Allen keeps the best of himself for his writing. In the end he is, as he says, 'always careful to keep myself together and pursue Poesy & have a forwarding address'" (p. 88).

It turns out Ginsberg needs the "forwarding address" for reasons other than receiving edited manuscripts from publishers. In 1965, Communist governments in Czechoslovakia and Cuba banned him from extended visits in these two thorns in America's side. These expulsions represent a key subtext to *Life*'s benign treatment of Ginsberg in 1966:

> Whatever early hopes Allen might have cherished for people's regimes were dashed last year when he was expelled from both Cuba and Czechoslovakia in the space of the same springtime. In Cuba he was asked to leave "for violating the laws."//"I asked them which laws they meant, of course," Allen says, "and this Brown Shirt answered. 'You'll have to ask yourself.' A pure Kafka bureaucracy shot!"

(p. 89)

Casting Ginsberg in a Cold War milieu, his appearance as a celebrity with an extremely loud voice in favor of sexual liberation is underwritten by the fact that, according to Farrell, the Fascistic treatment in Leftist lands "struck him mute." Since Ginsberg is tongue-tied—if implicitly taking a stand on — the fundamental political issue of the day in a Cold War environment, *Life* may display him as an unthreatening symbol of American freedoms of speech and the press: "Allen raised no fuss about these ungentlemanly departures; the appalling irony of becoming a cold war hero struck him mute" (p. 89). Needless to say, Farrell's characterization of Ginsberg as timid is unfair. Activist as well as poet, he showed courage in fighting on behalf of First Amendment issues in the "Howl" trial and he was on the front lines of the gay rights movement, and against the Vietnam War, nuclear power, and political oppression in places ranging from Chicago to Prague.[9]

---

[9]As the "Allen Ginsberg Project" website reports:

> The "Howl" obscenity trial served as a catalyst in fomenting Ginsberg's lifelong obsession with First Amendment issues in particular, and political activism in general. Using his fame as an international podium, Ginsberg spoke out on such controversial issues as the Vietnam War, gay rights (he listed his lifelong companion, Peter Orlovsky, as his spouse in his Who's Who entry), and drugs (he was an early participant in Timothy Leary's psilocybin and LSD experiments). At times, his opinions landed him in trouble: he was expelled from Cuba and Czechoslovakia in 1965 and, like many outspoken artists and activists, became the subject of a voluminous FBI dossier. His opinions and knowledge, however controversial, were highly solicited. He testified before Senate subcommittee hearings on drugs and his political essays were in constant demand. Accredited

VII

In the dialogue I am establishing between Ginsberg, *Time*, and *Life*, I want to give the poet the last words by discussing a poem that overtly associates poetry with its cooptation in a financially-driven Culture Industry, the issue Ginsberg queered in "America." In November of 1974, Ginsberg in "Mugging" engaged Whitmanic long lines and William Carlos Williams-like objectivist detailing of urban life to record his experience of being mugged. The poet was accosted after leaving the "red door" of his apartment on East Tenth Street, his decade-long neighborhood in the Lower East Side of Manhattan. In "Mugging," Ginsberg is no longer cast, as was the case in "A Supermarket in California" (1955), as a lunatic wandering at night "down the sidestreets under the trees with a headache self-conscious looking at the full moon" before heading into a surreal depiction of the epicenter of consumerism—the "neon fruit supermarket" to go "shopping for images" (*Collected Poems*, 1995, p. 144). In "Mugging," Ginsberg heads out by himself at night, but "young fellows" (p. 633) deploy common objects as weapons to hold him in custody. The thugs eventually trip him down to the pavement. They drag him, not into the super-market where he had, in the earlier poem, encountered the specter of prior queer masters Whitman and Garcia Lorca, but "onto the fire-soiled floor of an abandoned store, laundry candy counter 1929" (p. 634).

As was the case in "America," Ginsberg upsets binary thinking about his identity. During the assault, he represents himself as puzzled about what is going on and why. At the same time, he calmly reflects on his possessions, and keeps his cool in the face of danger. He meditates about, of all things, the various credit cards and identification cards in his "old broken wallet," checks in with his Buddhist sensibility by repeatedly chanting "Om Ah Hum," and "slowly reclined on the pavement" (p. 633). Once inside the old store where the crooks search his body for watch, wallet, and hidden money, he tells them to "take it easy." In a Whitman-like

---

with coining the term "Flower Power", Ginsberg became a figurehead of the global youth movement in the late 1960s.

(http://www.allenginsberg.org/index.php?page=bio)

gesture of homosocial affection, he tries to calm the boys with tenderness (and perhaps attempts to turn the crime into a tryst) by putting his "palm on the neck of an 18 year old fingering my back pocket" for money while chanting "Om Ah Hum there isn't any."

Part one of "Mugging" (the second part of the poem, written in December of 1974, recounts the event's aftermath) concludes in serio-comic fashion. While one boy roughly removes the poet's "Seiko Hong Kong" from his wrist, another tells the victim, who has continued to chant his mantra, "Shut up and we'll get out of here" (p. 634). The writer asserts that his irritating incantation "didn't stop em enough," but the boys abandon him, it seems, to escape all that chanting. A further irony, and this one relevant to my analysis of Ginsberg's relation to the consumer nexus that he allegedly disavowed in "America": the boys foolishly assume their victim is quite literally made of money as they search his body for big bills and jewelry he doesn't possess (I presume "Seiko Hong Kong" signifies a brand name knock off). But the boys leave intact the one object of real financial value: "my shoulder bag with 10,000 dollars full of poetry left on the broken floor" (p. 634).

As in "America," Ginsberg in "Mugging" destabilizes his relation to the national imaginary, not by characterizing his persona as embracing the counter-culture, but by noting his queer encounters with society in general. In "Mugging," Ginsberg signifies in complex ways to the street kids. He passes as a comfortable member of the mainstream who is worth accosting for his cash, but it is unclear whether he "passes" as straight or if they are targeting a gay man. The boys are mistaken to assume his mainstream status because his "snakeskin wallet" is "actually plastic" and because it contains, not untold riches, but a measly "70 dollars my bank money for a week" (p. 634). They misjudge his middle-of-the-road status because they can't read his mind. As he walks down East Tenth Street at dusk he is not anticipating visiting Bloomingdale's or getting a slice of pizza at Ray's, but rather is musing about Timothy Leary, the Weathermen, and "F.B.I. plots" (p. 634). Ginsberg's is a counter-cultural mind. But at the same time, the boys are correct to associate him with consumerism. His wallet holds cards signifying membership in the ACLU and Naropa, but along with these signs of apartness, there is also, oddly enough, his draft card, and credit cards from American Express, Manufacturer's Hanover's Trust, Mobil and Shell.

The mugging itself is a highly ambiguous affair. Is it his queerness that marks him as a target in the first place? Is there an association of his Jewishness with money? Certainly Ginsberg takes a surprisingly long time to figure out why he is being touched. When a "boy stepped up, put his arm around my neck," Ginsberg is expecting affection: "tenderly I thought for a moment" (p. 633). Ginsberg regards his experience as a strange admixture of terror, pleasure, and comic performance art even after the "umbrella handle" presses "against my skull" (p. 633). He starts chanting while observing the bystanders who watch him fall victim without raising a finger to help. The tone is detached objectivism, but at the same time comically confused about how to interpret an act of malevolence against himself: "as I went down shouting Om Ah Hum to gangs of lovers on the stoop watching/slowly appreciating, why this is a raid, these strangers mean strange business with what—my pockets, bald head, broken-healed-bone leg, my softshoes, my heart—" (p. 633).

In *Ego Confessions*, the volume in which it first appeared, "Mugging" follows the poem "Ego Confession" in which Ginsberg wants "to be known as the most brilliant man in America" and takes credit for overthrowing "the CIA with a silent thought" and had "many young lovers with astonishing faces and iron breasts" (p. 631). Perhaps because of egotism, Ginsberg in "Mugging" cannot decide whether the boys want his money (pockets), his metaphorical family jewels (pockets), his intellect (bald head), his rhythmic panache (softshoes), or deep romance (his heart). He doesn't know if he is Whitman admiring the roughs and the brawny workers on a stroll "out of my home ten years" where there are "gangs of lovers on the stoop" or if he is a stranger among "strangers [who] mean strange business" (p. 633). It is even unclear whether this event goes on "out" in the actual world or "in" a surreal environment signified by the account of the poet being "dragged slowly onto the fire-soiled floor" (p. 634). Given that Ginsberg was born in 1926, there is a suggestion that he is being returned to an aboriginal moment of re-birthing. If so, Ginsberg emerged into an America that has become a lawless environment populated by dangerous gangs who now threaten the safety of the aging bard. Carrying credit cards and poetry worth thousands of dollars, his body becomes a bricolage. He now embodies the Culture Industry, or at least, from the point of view of the boys doing the mugging, its materialistic fruits. But the fact that he can turn the event into poetry means that he also embodies the poetic muse and the power of self-expression that the poet fought to preserve throughout his long career. Like Whitman, Ginsberg is in the end ambiguous and contradictory. He embodies self-commodification as he'll sell the poem of the event.

5

Active and Passive Citizenship in Emma Lazarus's "The New Colossus" and Judith Ortiz Cofer's "The Latin Deli: An Ars Poetica"

In *The New American Exceptionalism*, Donald E. Pease relies on sociologist Ghassan Hage's description of "two utterly different ways" of "national belonging" that he calls active and passive (2009b, p. 28). The active citizen, Hage notes, includes "[t]he nationalist who believes him or herself to 'belong to the nation,' in the sense of being part of it, [which] means that he or she expects the right to benefit from the nation's resources, to 'fit into it,' or 'feel at home within' it" (quoted in Pease, 2009b, p. 28). Inhabiting what Pease calls the "national will to manage the spatial field," the maternal speaker in Emma Lazarus's "The New Colossus" (1883) enacts an "active" mode of what Hage calls "national belonging." Lazarus's speaker, in other words, experiences a sense of agency, entitlement, and a feeling of being at home. She aligns her will with the fantasy of America as what Pease calls a "State of Exception," following Italian philosopher Giorgio Agamben's *State of Exception*.[1] By

---

[1] See Agamben (2005).

contrast to how Lazarus represents her lyric speaker as a citizen who feels at home within the nation, the immigrants, described as "poor wretched refuse," remain silent throughout the poem, and thus "passive" in terms of governmental belonging. In "The New Colossus," America is represented as a "State of Exception" in that the new empire is imagined as a benign ("mild-"eyed)—rather than martial—and maternal—rather than male—figure that offers a "world-wide welcome" to displaced exiles from discredited Old World empires.[2]

In "The Latin Deli" (1993), the Puerto Rican-born poet Judith Ortiz Cofer (b. 1952) self-consciously reimagines the passive status and silent posture of the immigrants of Lazarus's poem. Writing in a different climate in which a diasporic, bifurcated, and multi-cultural poetics was widely accepted by this time, Ortiz Cofer's revision of Lady Liberty into a patroness at a Latin deli suggests that the language of "The New Colossus" and the figure welcoming immigrants to America were ripe for revision. Ortiz Cofer replaces the "active/passive" model Lazarus sets up between her speaking subject and the silent immigrants about whom she speaks in her address to another nation (give me *your* tired ...) with a multi-lingual and dialogic conversation. Ortiz Cofer's poem represents the linguistic disposition of two sets of speakers: the Mother of Exiles, recast as an immigrant shopkeeper, and her unruly, unassim-ilated, and often dissatisfied customers. Both sets of speakers are ambiguously situated within the active/passive model. Ortiz Cofer represents an individuated set of immigrants as they assess, in realistic, rather than idealistic, terms, the difference between what Pease would call the "exceptional" promise of the national realm beyond "the golden door," described at the end of the Lazarus poem, and the lived experience of displacement, loss, and exile in a new country in which they do not quite "feel at home."

An expression of a mythic American monoculture in tension with an emerging multiculture, "The New Colossus" offers an

---

[2]Ironically, although Lazarus repudiates Greek culture's martial and masculine elements in "The New Colossus," she does in poems and essays promote what Ranen Omer-Sherman calls "a new robust body" of the Jew, "rehabilitated" through work on the "broad prairie" of the American plains. Further, in her poems in support of Zionism such as "The Banner of the Jew," Lazarus praises the "ancient strength" and "martial fire" represented in "traditional Jewish literature."

ambivalent message to the arriving immigrants. Although the immigrants are welcomed, the form, tone, diction, and style in which the welcome is framed signify that the new cultural realm will exclude their difference from the Lazarus's speaker's linguistic disposition. Ranen Omer-Sherman notes the contrast between the speaker's sentiment (welcome) and the form and tone in which that sentiment is expressed (reservation): "[A]t the same time that her lyrics sympathize with the immigrant's plight, Lazarus positions herself at a great distance from the masses." It is Lazarus's voice, not theirs, that is the authorized vocal expression of the nation as a unified corporate body. The immigrants' linguistic disposition will not be validated as an admissible element of their entrance into the United States.[3] Unless a linguistic transformation occurs, the poem's classical frame strongly implies, the immigrants will remain passive citizens, uncanny figures for the National Other within the context of the National Same. David Bleich speaks of the poem's "generous" spirit as well as characterizing it as a "charitable gesture" (2000, p. 180), and it is true that, as Max Cavitch reports, "Lazarus helped greet and care for some of the earliest arrivals [of Eastern European Jews], including the young Abraham Cahan, at Ward's Island in 1882" (2006, p. 9). But I am focusing on the significant form of the sonnet as Lazarus's establishment of a border between her situation as a native American-Jewish subject in the position to offer charity and the immigrants to whom her poem refers to as belonging to another realm, the "*your* tired, *your* poor,/*Your* huddled" that is aligned with the "Keep, ancient lands, *your* storied pomp."[4]

My discussion of "The New Colossus" focuses on the ethical implications and cultural contexts of the most significant—but

---

[3] Max Cavitch notes:

> [T]he beginnings of modern nationalist consolidation came with the creation in Jewish languages of a culture parallel to the national and cosmopolitan cultures of Europe and America. The voices – particularly the Yiddish and Hebrew voices – of the parallel culture, however, quickly came to be a focus of contempt, not only among non-Jewish commentators, such as Lazarus's friend Henry James, but also among assimilated Western Jews.
>
> (2006, p. 17)

[4] Intriguingly, Lazarus did employ a Whitman-style long line in her Zionist prose poem of the same period: "By the Waters of Babylon: Little Poems in Prose."

rarely commented upon—aspect of her most famous poem, the decision to frame her public welcome to the exiles we associate with the Ellis Island experience in the Ur-form of the High European lyrical (that is, individuated) tradition: an Italian sonnet. The form, ornate diction (I am thinking of archaic-sounding phrases such as "tempest-tost, air-bridged harbor" and "storied pomp"), detached perspective, and classical allusiveness ("the brazen giant of Greek fame") signal the poet's ambivalence towards associating her own identity as an established American citizen ("Here at *our* sea-washed, sunset gates") and assimilated American Jew with that of the newly arriving immigrants, including the many Eastern European Jews who made up a substantial part of the Ellis Island experience.

"Born in New York City to a well-established family of mixed Sephardic (Spanish Jewish) and Ashkenazi (German Jewish) ancestry," Lazarus, write Jonathan Barron and Eric Selinger, "gained early fame for a poetry that was as thoroughly assimilated and uninterested in things Jewish as she was" (2000, p. 6). In form and style, Lazarus is announcing her affiliation with and mastery of a class of poems associated with representing the experience of the European elite who, ironically, are accused of discharging the very immigrants Lazarus is called to welcome ("The wretched refuse of *your* teeming shore"). Writing as if her speech act is seamlessly aligned with the political will of the newly empowered American nation ("Give *me*"), she is establishing her status as an American citizen through her assertion of national difference from the newly arriving immigrants: "The wretched refuse of *your* teeming shore./ Send these, the homeless, tempest-tost to *me*." As Allen Grossman has explained, the ten-position line is "stained" with its aristocratic association because its most renowned practitioner, Shakespeare, chose that line to represent the social discourse of nobility in his dramas. "Blank Verse ... is the order speech takes when it gives the picture of the well-formed social person – as in Shakespearean talk, where only 'gentle' persons speak Blank Verse and only gentle persons are well-formed" (1989, p. 282). Grossman goes on to argue that the line of ten, associated with the lyric speaker, could be contrasted with what he calls the line of the folk, the ballad measure that, I am suggesting, would have been the more familiar generic mode of welcome to the immigrant communities addressed in "The New Colossus." Lazarus begins her poem by dissociating the disposition of Frederic Auguste Bartholdi's "Liberté éclarent le monde" statue that would reside in New York harbor—Lazarus's sonnet was "placed in the statue's pedestal in 1903" (Cavitch, 2006, p. 2)—from the Colossus at Rhodes ("Not like the brazen giant of Greek fame"). But even here her act of dissociation ironically calls to mind the ancient template of martial and imperial power.

In Americanizing herself, Lazarus thus takes on many of the vocal traits of high European culture. As Max Cavitch reports in "Emma Lazarus and the Golem of History": "When Lazarus wrote 'The New Colossus' in 1883 she was, as a Jew, a presumptive member of a traditional extraterritorial caste in the process of imagining and inaugurating its own national future" (2006, p. 6). This contrasts strikingly with the newer wave of immigrants, who nevertheless might remind established Jewish Americans of their problematic status. Contextualizing the vexed relation between long-established Jewish American citizens such as Lazarus and the Eastern Europeans who were immigrating to the United States to escape the Czarist Pogroms of 1882, Ranen Omer-Sherman reports:

> Strikingly less assimilated and "modern" than their American counterparts—indeed perhaps "beyond salvation"—the new exiles aroused cultural anxieties across the spectrum of the established Jewish community. Nineteenth-century Jewish Americans were vexed by the new/old risks of becoming visible to the surrounding culture.
>
> (2002, p. 172)

In form, genre choice, diction, and the detached tone of voice that enacts the will of the state, Lazarus expresses the "cultural anxieties" spoken of by Omer-Sherman. She indirectly addresses the immigrants through the established American speaker's ventriloquizing of a silent object —"'Keep, ancient lands, your storied pomp!' cries she/With silent lips"— that at once rejects and repeats the discourse of empire that will only admit the immigrants to its shores with reservations. Ironically, the immigrants themselves remain silent, undifferentiated objects of the speaker's address to another nation: "Give me [America] your [Old World] poor."

If Lazarus writes from the perspective of active belonging, Ortiz Cofer gives the voices of her poem over to the Immigrant Others—including Lady Liberty herself—who now reside uneasily within the national border of the United States as a kind of Other Within. This Other-Within-the-Nation in Ortiz Cofer represents the inassimilable remnants of a contemporary immigrant experience that Lazarus understood as only available to the state of becoming American by excising visible signs of difference. Where Lazarus enforces a national fantasy of exceptional treatment of displaced persons by representing the immigrants as they anticipate what lies behind the "golden door," Ortiz Cofer represents the immigrants who already reside, however uneasily, within the United States as they look backward and try to account for the unrecoverable losses and displacements from their past lives. They are what Hage calls "passive" American subjects whose language and interior fantasy space (in which they dream, remember, and imagine) place them in a kind of limbo between two worlds, neither of which feels like a home of genuine belonging. The customers in the Latin Deli thus bear witness to the limits to Lazarus's representation of an imaginary future that at once erases the new American subjects' histories and simultaneously predicts (through silencing) the erasure of the continuity between their prior selves and the passive American subjects they are becoming.

Revisioning us/them relations in "The Latin Deli: An Ars Poetica"

The terms "Latin" and "Ars Poetica" in Ortiz Cofer's title recall the kind of Horatian classicism evident in the formalistic elements and allusions in Lazarus's poem. Ortiz Cofer, however, converts these terms away from their European connotations and towards the specific elements of contemporary Hispanic (Latin in terms of Latin American) immigrant experience in a deli that caters to the dietary preferences and, more important, linguistic yearnings and affective desires, of immigrants displaced from their Spanish-speaking lands of origin. The customers described in "The Latin Deli" hail from Puerto Rico—Ortiz Cofer was herself born in Hormigueros, a rural village in Puerto Rico in 1952—Cuba, and

Mexico. The poem's title echoes Horace, and also alludes, ironically, to Archibald MacLeish's notorious statement of a modernist dissociation of poetry from discursive reflections on society and politics—"A poem must not mean but be" (2007, p. 280). In Ortiz Cofer, however, the economic situation and cultural space of the Latin Deli, with its shelves stocked and bins filled with Spanish language versions of food and drink items, become aligned with the space of poetry. The goods in the shop are likened to words in a nostalgic poem as they recall a lost world of unrecoverable memories. Occurring through the "comfort/of Spoken Spanish," the interaction between proprietor and patron underlines the multicultural situation and bilingual context in which Ortiz Cofer revises the immigrant poetics of Lazarus's signature poem. By describing the shopkeeper as "the Patroness of Exiles," Ortiz Cofer directly echoes Lazarus's description of Lady Liberty. In so doing, Ortiz Cofer asserts that her poem will be a literary revision. The word "poetry" occurs only once in the poem, but Ortiz Cofer wants readers to understand the deli, with its patrons and proprietor, as embodying the poetic and dialogic space. The shop owner is placed in an ambivalent position as both American entrepreneur and empathetic immigrant exile. Her "art of poetry" occurs in how she interacts with her shop patrons.

A crucial difference between "The New Colossus" and "The Latin Deli" is apparent in how the two authors situate the female figure of Liberty in relationship to the exiles. In Lazarus, the Liberty speaker constructs a binary, or "Me/Them," relationship between her perspective and the immigrants. She speaks as a member of the already established community of American citizens that will offer its ambivalent welcome to the "poor wretched refuse" of the Old World. "The New Colossus" invokes the Ekphrastic tradition to ventriloquize the statuesque object—Lady Liberty—that represents a turn of the twentieth-century version of U.S. exceptionalism. Writing on the cusp of "The American Century," on the heels of imperial forays into the Philippines and Cuba during the Spanish American War, and on the front end of the Ellis Island Experience, Lazarus represents America in idealistic terms as a benign, maternal, welcoming version of a classical empire emerging onto the world stage as a major power.

A Sephardic/Portuguese/German-American Jew from a well-established and prosperous family that could trace its roots in America back to the Civil War period, Lazarus expresses a harmonious symmetry between her lyric voice and the statue. The statue, in turn, stands as a physical manifestation of the nation, a gargantuan representation of America's exceptional and yet imperial status in relation to discredited Old World Powers, that opens its borders to Europe's "wretched refuse." In the process of making the silent object speak about a silent subject, Lazarus performs her own situation as what Hage calls an "active" citizen-subject. In a doubling of the persona of lyric speaker as the gatekeeper at America's shoreline, the speaker's (Lazarus, lyric speaker, Lady Liberty as national personification) will is amplified, publicized, and transformed into the vocal equivalent of a physical monument that surveys the border of the nation: "Her mild eyes command/The air-bridged harbor that twin cities frame." Through the process of *noblesse oblige* that ironically mimics the aristocratic system associated with the Old World, the speaker of "The New Colossus" literally represents America as she adjudicates the outcome of the "wretched refuse's" sea voyage from the Old World to the New.

In Ortiz Cofer, the Latina storekeeper disrupts the Lazarus us/them scenario even as it maintains distinctions between the subject positions of the storeowner and the various immigrants who shop in her store. On the one hand, the patroness in Ortiz Cofer is associated with an archetypal American entrepreneurial enterprise, the small business. Discussing the patroness with a tone that mixes admiration for her efforts to supply goods and a linguistic context to assuage the homesickness of her customers, Ortiz Cofer is well aware that she is, to a degree, capitalizing on the desperate (and unfulfillable) longing for the recovery of smells, tastes, and sounds of a native culture. This scene will, in Homi Bhabha's terms, mimic but "never quite" match up to the real thing back home: Ortiz Cofer writes that the patroness "spends her days selling canned memories/while listening to the Puerto Ricans complain/that it would be cheaper to fly to San Juan/than to buy a pound of Bustelo coffee here."

In the final stanza, Ortiz Cofer adds that her wares, if bought at the A&P "would not satisfy/the hunger of the fragile old man lost in the folds/of his winter coat." The patroness quite literally capitalizes on her clients' loss, displacement, and uncanny desire for a taste of home away from home. The ham and cheese she sells are generic. What, then, is the value-added to the "plain" good that the patroness can offer to the "fragile old man" who is willing to pay extra to purchase from her? What the patroness adds is also what separates her from the Lazarus Liberty figure: the dialogic, interactive, and linguistic unassimilability of her relationship to the exiles. It challenges the "them-ing" of the exiles, and provides an inadequate but nonetheless desirable locus of empathetic caring (rather than sympathetic *noblesse oblige*).

Although she sells "canned" (that is, prepackaged, kitschy, or artificially staged) memories, she does important healing work by "listening to the Puerto Ricans complain," even if this is directed toward her own high prices on coffee. She provides "the comfort of spoken Spanish" and the silent care of "her look of maternal interest." She represents the mother tongue and the motherland—"she smiles understanding." The patroness sells products that fail to deliver the promise of a fulfilling return to the original space in which comparable (but never quite the same) products were first experienced in a situation of comparative atonement with the national surroundings. The patroness, however, offers an affective compensation for the failure of the product itself to provide pleasure to the purchaser. She accomplishes this task through spoken, gestural, and unspoken languages ('her look of maternal interest," "her listening the Puerto Ricans complain," how she "smiles understanding").

The patroness, in other words, provides through the transmission of products that fail to deliver the promise of a fulfilling return to the original space in which comparable (but never quite the same) products were first experienced in a situation of comparative atonement with the national surroundings, an affective compensation for the failure of the product itself to provide pleasure to the purchaser via the spoken, gestural, and unspoken languages. She provides a space in which "the comfort of Spoken Spanish" can take place—a shared position of being simultaneously inside the cultural nexus of American capitalism in which branded goods become the medium of interpersonal exchange, and also of a shared "Themness" or uncanny outsideness in terms of identification as a full-fledged American citizen.

Where Lazarus flattens linguistic difference at the American border through imitation of an English aristocratic form, Ortiz Cofer desublimates the linguistic signifier of inassimilable difference among the Cuban, Mexican, and Puerto Rican exiles through the inclusion of elements of the Spanish language. These exist uneasily, italicized—*dolares, Suspiros, Merengues, jamón y queso*—in relation to the primarily English lexicon. In the poem, however, these terms become signs of absence, displacement and loss, rather than of a recuperation of the lost home space via the full admission of the language of the other world in the new one. The expression of these Spanish terms as the patrons "walk down the aisles of her store" (the store aisles signifying the lines of the poem) signifies the emptiness of the linguistic gestures in relation to the persons and places they are meant to compensate for. The Spanish names of products are spoken "as if/they were the names of lost lovers" or, conversely, represent "the stale candy of everyone's childhood."

Ortiz Cofer represents the relationship between shopkeeper and customer as comparable to the one between a poet and a reader. We might think of the shop itself, with its "narrow aisles" and linguistically bilingual products, as the poetic space, and the products as the terms of the exchange, or mediation, between poet and reader. By revisioning the commercial as a poetic space, Ortiz Cofer attempts to transform the alienating site of consumer exchange into an intimate space of human solidarity among the immigrant communities. But in terms of power relations between patron and exile, owner and guest, it is one of the exiled customers—the "fragile old man lost in the folds/of his winter coat"—who is in the active position with his ordinary discourse. It is the "fragile old man's" list of grocery items—an example of ordinary language that a poet such as William Carlos Williams in "This is Just to Say" transformed into a found poem—that becomes transformed through his rehearsal of it to the patroness into an extraordinary, that is to say, lyric, expression. He "brings her lists of items/that he read to her like poetry." This moment in the final stanza is the only point in a poem called "An Ars Poetica" in which the consumerist exchange is directly described in terms of poetry. The moment is especially complex because, although Ortiz Cofer writes that it is the fragile old man who recites his list "like poetry," the poet also suggests that the recitation becomes lyrical because he is saying the list aloud (probably in Spanish) to the patroness. In other words, it is only in the linguistic and cultural space—the never quite adequately consoling home away from home that is the Latin Deli, as this space is presided over by the patroness who, in stanza one, encourages customers to do their "talking lyrically"—that the list becomes charged with lyric meaning. The fragile old customer's list becomes a poem through an act of co-creation between writer (shopper) and reader/interpreter (patroness). However much the patroness encourages lyric expression, there is no question that lyric power is shared between immigrants in a way that cannot be said to take place in Lazarus. In "The New Colossus," Lady Liberty speaks on behalf of American Power in relation to the arriving immigrants.

Ortiz Cofer relates poetry to the low tradition of found artifacts by associating the grocery list with spoken word poetry, but also throughout the poem associates the role of the patroness and the products she sells with the elevated, even sublime, discourse of religious mystery. As much as I have described the store as a poetic space and the products as the terms of the linguistic play of affection between patroness and customer, it is also a church or shamanistic setting in which the mercantile exchange is transformed into a scene of soul work. The patroness performs the task of insight into the spiritual needs of her clients. From the start of the poem, the patroness is associated with the Virgin Mother of Catholicism. Ortiz Cofer's description of a "plastic Mother and Child magnetized/to the top of an ancient register" at once parodies and invokes an association between the "presiding" female shopkeeper and the figure of Mary. The term "ancient register" can be read literally as a description of the aging storage area for cash (no electronic computer eye to scan prices via bar codes here).

On a figurative level, the poet is encouraging readers to associate the moment of trade in this Latin Deli with an "ancient register" of the buying and selling of goods. Her privileging of human-to-human exchange (as found today, for example, in the resurgence of local farmers' markets) between buyer and seller in a specialty shop harks back to the feel of the Latin Delis of South American culture that this store is meant to replicate. The products— "dried codfish" and "green plantains"—are described as "votive offerings," an adjective meaning "showing or symbolizing a wish or desire" or "given, done, or offered in fulfillment of an oath or vow." Ortiz Cofer is suggesting the products are showcased to deliver on a "hunger" that does not merely satisfy the bodily need for sustenance, but rather is meant to appeal to something deeper, more ephemeral; a kind of "soul food" is at stake here. It is precisely the patroness's attempt to speak to her clients' "dreams and their disillusions" through the products she displays and the attention to their emotional/affective needs that are missing, erased, ignored, or sublimated in Lazarus.

As Ortiz Cofer's poem starts by linking the patron to Mother Mary as a figure of spiritual care, it ends with her in the position of mystic healer or soul caregiver. The patron works with "the others,/whose needs she must divine, conjuring up products/from places that now exist only in their hearts—/closed ports she must trade with." Finally, the patroness is in the shamanic position of doing work for the heart and the mind rather than the stomach. "She must divine" their needs, implying that communication with her patrons occurs on the level of deep unspoken intuition. Her "products" are not to be found in any international commodity market because the "ports she must trade with" are "closed." Ortiz Cofer registers a radical dissociation between present and past for the exiles, and yet the patroness understands that the "things" these exiles require from her have been utterly internalized into an interior space of affect. Rather than ventriloquizing the voice of the state, Ortiz Cofer desublimates the missing curiosity about the soul needs of the "them" that had remained "them" in "us" in Lazarus.

I have been critical of Lazarus's expression of an "active" relationship to governmental belonging that is contingent upon her detachment from the newly arriving immigrants at Ellis Island. But in closing I would like to complicate my own binary interpretation of "active" versus "passive" belonging in Lazarus by acknowledging her role in the fostering of the kind of diasporic poetics represented by Ortiz Cofer. As Omer-Sherman reminds us:

> Though no immigrant herself, Lazarus's is one of the first attempts to grapple – albeit reluctantly at times – with the possibilities of extending America's proud notion of "newness" to those who truly were new Americans. In this sense, she must be credited with founding a new textual dynasty of ethnic voices who will seek to assert their cultural heritage against the dominant culture.

> (2002, p. 187)

Further, I want to make a note of the poignancy of Lazarus's desire to express her personal voice via a silent monument that she associates with Greek Classicism. This ekphrastic move in effect registers Lazarus's own diasporic relationship to both the American voice that she wishes to ventriloquize as well as the displaced European culture endowment to which her sonnet's formalism aspires.[5] By noticing the limits of Lazarus's empowerment as the "active" voice of a national citizenry, as well as the ways in which "The New Colossus" expresses the speaker's compassion, if not empathy, with the newly arrived immigrants, we may follow Steven Rubin in reading the sonnet as "an eloquent statement of Lazarus's final affirmation of America and her recognition of the role it was to play in welcoming oppressed people" (Rubin, 2000, p. 203). We may also interpret Lazarus as an ambivalent precursor in dialogue with Ortiz Cofer's diasporic poetics.

---

[5] I want to express my gratitude to Donald Pease, who, in a response to an earlier draft of this essay, pointed me in the direction of this line of thought about Lazarus's own relationship to a diasporic poetics.

6

Queer Desire as Mediated through the Horn and the Pen: Elegy as Love Letter or Love Letter as Elegy in Michael S. Harper's "Dear John, Dear Coltrane"

Michael S. Harper (b. 1938) is a leading poet known for his homages to critical figures associated with the African-American experience, including such notable authors as Robert Hayden, Alice Walker, Zora Neale Hurston, and jazzmen such as Charlie Parker, Elvin Jones, Dexter Gordon, and most especially John Coltrane. "Dear John, Dear Coltrane" (1970) is Harper's much-anthologized, jazz-influenced homage to the legendary saxophonist who died of liver cancer at age 40, possibly exacerbated by heroin addiction, in 1967. Critics regard it as a seminal illustration of the poet's strategy of simultaneously historicizing and making mythic the life and times of key figures associated with the African-American experience and its self-representation.

Lisa Dunick (2004) reads Coltrane as Harper's metonymic figuration of African-American history and aesthetics:

The pain of slavery, which led to slaves attempting to escape through the swamps of the south, is the same pain from which the blues stems. Thus, ["Dear John, Dear Coltrane"] links the blues, with all of its ties to slavery and a specific African American aesthetic, directly to the pain of the jazzman's dying body and represents this personal and communal pain as productive. The historical and personal pain represented in the dying body of the jazz musician repeats and intensifies throughout the poem.

Harper himself has stated that he learned from African-American blues and jazz musicians to conjoin the personal and the social: "Black musicians have always melded the private and the historical into the aesthetics of human speech and music, the blues and jazz" (Harper, quoted in Byrne, 2008).

Harper is already something of an establishment figure, even as the establishment has grudgingly made room for experimental stylists such as Harper's Brown University younger colleagues, C. D. Wright and Forrest Gander. His work regularly appears in mainstream anthologies, he holds a chair in English at Brown, and he has served as the Poet Laureate of the state of Rhode Island. I will approach his work taking the premise of *Reading the Difficulties*, a recent collection of essays focusing on contemporary Language poetry, which encourages readers' interaction with poetry that "deletes accustomed cues of comprehension" to restage our comfortable assumptions that Harper's poems are already framed—and tamed—as mainstream expressions of African-American uplift.

My reading of "Dear John, Dear Coltrane" engages with an eclectic set of approaches ranging from queer studies, W. J. T. Mitchell's work on ekphrasis, Eliotic mythopoesis, and biographical and historical material on Coltrane's life and times. I lean towards what Eliot, in "'Ulysses,' Order and Myth" (1923), regarded as Joyce's "mythical method," by associating Harper's work with elegy via the poet's own commentary on the Orpheus legend. I put myth criticism in conversation with the poem's historicity, however, by showing how the author engages with the "Dear John" letter trope from World War II. Because the first half of the poem's title—"Dear John"—alludes to a private love letter, albeit a break-up one, I address the homoerotic subtext of the speaker's elegiac address to Coltrane. My purpose in bringing such an unruly assortment of reading strategies to bear on Harper's text is to remove it from the category of poems already understood and easily known by readers. Emphasizing the poem's multiple aspects, I want to move readings of "Dear John" away from an exclusive focus on how "Coltrane becomes a link for Harper to connect the historical with his own personal family history," as the poem's theme is described on the Poetry Foundation website.[1] I want to place "Dear John" in the direction of texts such as A (1978) by Jewish-American experimental modernist Louis Zukofsky. I argue that Harper in "Dear John" foregrounds indeterminacy, reader response, and what Charles Altieri, writing on Zukofsky, called the "mobility of mind" that I see also characterizing Harper's fluid, multivalent, and sonically driven lyric (Fink and Halden-Sullivan, 2013, n.p.).

A poet who has stated, "I've enjoyed the play of putting things together that don't belong together" (Rowell, 1990, p. 786), Harper collapses paradoxically contrary elements such as space and time, history and myth, love lyric and elegy, an improvisatory jazz aesthetic and the fragmentary collage stylings and mythologizing impulses of Eliotic High Modernism, and the contradictory positioning of the Orphic dynamic in which the singer simultaneously looks backward and forward (Belasco and Johnson, 2008, p. 1428). He does so, I argue, to reveal and conceal the problematic of queer desire among black males that Hazel Carby has explored in *Race Men* (1998). My invocation of the concept of "queerness" in this essay speaks to a quality of unstable categories of sexuality. Homosocial and socially disruptive aspects of "queerness" conjoin in "Dear John, Dear Coltrane."

In "Playin' the Changes," Carby discusses the homosocial dimension of the male jazz ensemble in the context of Miles Davis's legendary quartets and quintets from the 1950s, which at times included Coltrane on sax. Carby also addresses the misogynistic, homophobic, and anti-maternal dimensions of Davis's development as a jazzman. She shows that Davis viewed musical collaboration as a homosocial encounter, if not also displaced homoerotic expression, that represented for Davis a "freedom" from what he viewed as the inhibiting aspects of domesticity. Davis interpreted

---

[1] See http://www.poetryfoundation.org/bio/michael-s-harper.

parenting and family life in general as distractions from his desire
to express himself in the all-male space of the jazz group. Perhaps
the reaction of a frustrated patriarch who felt cut off from greater
social power, Davis was known to inflict violence upon the women
in his life, such as his wife, the noted actress, Cicely Tyson.

By no means do I wish to conflate the very different person-
alities of Davis and Coltrane. My point is that Harper reads the
self-inflicted—through drug injection and alcohol—and racially
inflected violence against the black male body, in the case of
Coltrane, as the modes through which the musician becomes
transformed, via a process of desexualization and reengendering,
into a mythic figure, which enables Harper to express his desire
for Coltrane in the highly ambiguous form of an elegiac love
letter to a man who is still alive at the time of the composition.
A subject of several Harper poems written before and after the
musician's death, Coltrane is represented most memorably in
"Dear John, Dear Coltrane," a liminal poem composed *before* its
titular subject's death, but published as the title poem of Harper's
first book *three years after* Coltrane's death. Because of the poem's
collage-like surface, radical tonal, temporal, and stylistic shifts,
idiosyncratic wording, extreme imagistic compression, and associative logic, one is challenged to read "Dear John, Dear Coltrane"
as an elegiac love letter between the "I" and the "you," each a
talented black male artist, although Coltrane enjoyed the kind of
status to which Harper could only aspire. This chapter, however,
views the difficult modernist surface as subterfuge, as I read "Dear
John, Dear Coltrane" in terms of a black queer desire that is cast
as an ephebe's (or young poet's) homage to Coltrane's horn.

Harper's gender reversal of the Orphic tale in his representation
of Coltrane as Orpheus *and* Eurydice speaks to the larger issue
of queer desire that I am exploring in a poem that is a personal
love letter by a male speaker to a male beloved, set in the City of
Brotherly Love. In a 1972 interview, Harper noted that, "I loved
John Coltrane and I loved his music. I loved the kind of intensity
he brought to his playing and I loved his commitment" (Lenz,
1984, p. 294). Harper's queer desire is, however, sublimated under
the formal guise of the poem's mythic and historicized surface
that is consistent with critical approaches to Harper's poetics.
Schooled in the difficult aesthetics of Post Bop, Cool, and Free Jazz,
Harper brought avant-garde jazz elements such as Miles Davis's

conception of "modal" jazz to contemporary poetics.[2] But Harper
was also immersed in the High Modernist aesthetics of T.S.
Eliot, whose mythic image—by way of Sir James Frazer's *Golden Bough*
(1922) and Jessie Weston's *From Ritual to Romance* (1920)—of
the Fisher King as a sacrificial figure, whose wounding inaugurates a barren land and whose burial and symbolic restoration
restore cultural fertility in *The Waste Land*, is referenced through
the image of Coltrane's body as simultaneously culturally regenerative and personally devastated.[3] Imagining his task as poet to
be alchemical in its ability to transform junk into treasure, if of a
spiritual sort, Harper reads Coltrane's impending physical death
and spiritual rebirth as an implantation of seed that will regenerate
a land in crisis that reflects the discredited American history of
racial discrimination.

In a parallel way, Coltrane turned his heroin addiction into a
search for musical innovation and perfection. Upon his return to
Philadelphia after leaving Miles Davis's band in the mid-1950s,
Eric Nisenson reports, Coltrane began the process of purification
from alcohol and heroin addiction that led to his belief that "he

---

[2]Harper referenced "modal" jazz in his own commentary on the poem:

> The antiphonal, call-response/retort stanza simulates the black church, and
> gives the answer of renewal to any question raised—"cause I am." It is Coltrane
> himself who chants, in life, "a love supreme"; jazz and the blues, as open-ended
> forms, cannot be programmatic or abstract, but modal ... Coltrane's music is the
> recognition and embodiment of life-force; his music is testament in modal forms
> of expression that unfold in their many modal aspects. His music testifies to life;
> one is witness to the spirit and power of life; and one is rejuvenated and renewed
> in a living experience, the music that provides images strong enough to give back
> that power that renews.

> (Quoted by Byrne, 2008)

[3]In her study of *The Waste Land*, Nancy K. Gish writes:

> In the Grail stories, as Weston describes them, there is always a land that has
> been laid waste, made barren and sterile, by the illness or wounding of a king
> called the Fisher King ... There is also a knight in quest of the Holy Grail ... If he
> fulfills his quest and either asks or answers certain questions correctly, the king
> will be restored and the land renewed by the coming of rain. The Grail stories
> share with the ancient rituals the restoration of a waste land to life and fertility.

> (1988, p. 43)

might find the mind of God" by playing "every possible harmonic permutation" (2001, p. 82). During his horrendous withdrawal,

> he experienced the spiritual epiphany that changed his life. In the middle of this ordeal, he felt touched by God. He made a bargain with God: if God would get him through the pain of withdrawal, he would devote his life and work to a spiritual quest.
>
> (p. 80)

Harper, we could say, was himself beginning such a quest, but with a mythologized version of Coltrane as his icon.

An elegy paradoxically written prior to the disappearance of its subject, the poem thus proleptically enacts the transformation of "Dear John," the flawed human embodiment of an inspired horn man with a voracious appetite, into the iconic "Dear Coltrane," the disembodied symbolic figure, and martyred saint, of Black Power resistance to white hegemony during the Civil Rights era and unrest, in what Sly Stone called America's "Chocolate Cities." In an interview, Harper referred to Coltrane as "a banner for an attitude, a stance against the world" (Rowell, 1990, p. 791). Harper also praised Coltrane's "energy and passion" as perhaps akin to the nature of oppression generally and the kind of energy it takes to break oppressive conditions, oppressive musical structures, and oppressive societal structures" (Brown, 1986, p. 211).

Stephen Fredman has recently noted that a shamanistic tradition of transformational poetics influenced experimental U.S. authors in the 1960s and 1970s, such as Robert Duncan, Allen Ginsberg, and Jerome Rothenberg. Junk (in this case garbage, not heroin), as Fredman argues, is converted from an abject object of disaffection into a significant aesthetic frame in the salvage work of West Coast collage artists such as Duncan's lover, Jess. May we not consider Harper's revisionary treatment of Coltrane as a junkie whose addiction facilitates his transformation into a figure of spiritual power? Enacting the process that Fredman, referring to Duncan, calls "a spiritual desire to convert abject experiences into meaningful ones" (2010, p. 157), Harper transforms Coltrane into a metaphoric vehicle (or signifier) who literally and figuratively performs as the tenor (both sax *and* signified) for the contemporary legacy of the healing tradition of soulful singing—DuBoisian sorrow songs—once located primarily in the Southern black church.[4] By so doing, Harper encourages readers to associate sacred music with a long heritage of resistance to the dehumanizing institutions of slavery and Jim Crow. As Joseph A. Brown reports:

> The world in which Michael Harper lives is not significantly different from the world of Paul Laurence Dunbar or John Coltrane. That world is the real and legendary America, a world where the souls of black folk are continually threatened with dreams which turn into nightmares.
>
> (1986, p. 211)

The legacy of resistance through artistic and sacred music and art plays out in the diasporic post-war context of Coltrane's post-conversionary free jazz compositions performed in what Harper calls the "Electric City." Harper is referring to sites in the urban North such as Philadelphia, where Coltrane recovered from heroin addiction in large part through the care of his first wife, Juanita Naima Grubbs. Philadelphia in 1957 was also where and when Coltrane altered the direction of his music towards what the musician, in a text entitled "Dear Listener" (1964), described as "a humble offering to Him. An attempt to say 'THANK YOU GOD' through my work, even as we do with our hearts and our tongues."

Coltrane imagined himself in the last decade of his life as a purified vehicle through which to announce God's majesty, but Harper represents Coltrane as a "diseased" figure in the "Dear John" poem (Harper, 2005, p. 236). Hooked on opiates and alcohol, sexually impotent, and suffering from major organ failure, he is, ironically, too "sick" to "play *Naima*," a statement that alludes to the classic 1959 composition that first appeared on *Giant Steps,* named for Coltrane's first wife, Juanita Naima Coltrane (née Grubbs), the woman who contributed to his recovery. In the poem,

---

[4] "Coltrane's grandfather, who lived in the family home, was minister of St. Stephens AME Zion Church in Hamlet" (Nelson, 2000, p. 1048). Coltrane scholar Lewis Porter considers "Psalm," the last part of "A Love Supreme" to be a "wordless recitation" of the devotional poem Coltrane wrote and published as a liner note in the album (Porter, 1999, p. 244).

Harper also hints that Coltrane was no longer able to perform sexually with his wife, signifying the traumatic violation of the black male body via the common tropes of emasculation and castration. Harper's thesis is that Coltrane's heroin addiction—an epidemic that ravaged jazz musicians of his generation including Bill Evans, Sonny Rollins, and Miles Davis—at once disabled and inspired, polluted and eventually cleansed, the musician as he reinterpreted his music as a sacred discourse. Coltrane's new understanding of his art as salvific, however, occurs, at least in Harper's rendering, simultaneously with a symbolic death of the sax man's desiring and desirable black male body.

The very title of the poem signals Harper's stammering intent to pay homage to the romanticized public image of Coltrane as junk-sick genius whose music became the vehicle for the expression of his (and his culture's) pain. The title also suggests the poem will be in part a love lyric via the romantic associations of the "Dear John" letter that became especially prominent during World War II, when many newly empowered Rosie the Riveters back in the States refused to wait for their "Dear Johns" to return from the war. In drafting an elegy to Coltrane prior to the musician's death, it is as if Harper is saying goodbye to the man he loves before that man can say goodbye to him. Harper, who often heard Coltrane perform live, demonstrates that he can only express the depth of what in a prose statement he calls his "tenderness" for "Dear John" via the mediation of an elegiac meditation. He projects affection via Coltrane's "tenor," a ventriloquization of Coltrane's affective life through an instrument associated with the emission of African-American suffering. He represents Coltrane as a black Hamlet figure, a disabled and tortured artist, via Harper's reference in the poem to Coltrane's birthplace of Hamlet, North Carolina (Coltrane grew up in High Point, North Carolina).

Reflecting Harper's strategy of, in his terms, "blend[ing] historical information, myth, and voice" (Rowell, 1990, p. 788) so that historical figures are converted into archetypal personifications of the relation between death, absence, witness, and the testimony of suffering, Harper states, "I guess Coltrane was my Orpheus" (p. 791). For Harper, Coltrane quite literally embodies history in the context of a denigrated, diasporic, addicted, and yet creative black male self that, at least for Charlie Parker, ventriloquizes pain ("If you don't live it, it won't come out of your horn"). Coltrane's body in Harper's proto-elegy is rendered as archive, documenting historical trauma, but if Coltrane is Harper's Orpheus, the "image for a standard of manliness in the arts" according to Harper (2005, p. 791), then we must ask the question: Is Harper Eurydice, or is he Orpheus's double?

In the Greek myth, of course, Orpheus, the bereaved male singer with his mournful lyre, descends into the underworld in order to recover his deceased beloved, felled by a viper on her wedding day. A classical analog to the biblical narrative of Lot's wife, Orpheus loses Eurydice forever to Hades and Persephone when he cannot abide by their instruction to refrain from looking back at her while the couple make their precarious return, on unfamiliar, steep terrain, to the land of the living. The archetypal lyricist whose music is contingent upon the experiential loss of the female beloved, Orpheus is the male prototype of the poet as traumatic victim of irreparable loss, the emotionally wounded survivor. (As Allen Grossman has argued in his classic essay on the "founding stories of poetic production," Philomel, transformed into a nightingale after a violent rape by King Tereus, is the traumatic image of the originary female poet.)[5] By contrast to the version found in classical examples of the tale, such as Ovid's, in Harper's account Orpheus/Coltrane, *the male singer*, is left behind in a psychic underworld of drug addiction, organ failure, geographical dislocation, and sexual dismemberment. (Orpheus, we recall, was torn apart, according to antique legend, by a frenzied group of Bacchic women, protesting the musician's refusal to love other women after the death of Eurydice.) In "Dear John, Dear Coltrane," it is Orpheus's dismemberment that inaugurates Harper's position as the belated survivor, jilted and jilting lover, and queerly imagined elegist. It is Harper/Eurydice, as surviving poet, who looks back to Coltrane/Orpheus as inspirational metonym for African-American

---

[5]Susan Stewart writes in *Poetry and the Fate of the Senses*:

> Bereft of Eurydice from the moment of his fatally forbidden turn, when he dooms her to be his inspiration, "he must attempt to fill her absence with compensatory song" (256). So Eurydice stands in for Orpheus, punished for his transgression, and he her, making art out of her fate. Across the gulf of time and the river Styx, she prompts him, as he keeps looking back to her.

(2002)

historical suffering and possible redemption through music and a ritualistic transubstantiation of the disabled black male body into martyred saint.[6] The Orpheus story has appealed to poets because it is a narrative of the crisis, on personal terms, of looking backward (against a command by a non-human authority not to do so). Because of the inconsolable losses the story identifies with looking backward, the poet must gather the courage to go forward into a future without a beloved at his side, but with a sorrow song to lift up to the world as a compensation of last resort.

On a formal level, "Dear John, Dear Coltrane" is Orphic in its overall structure. At the poem's opening, Harper *looks back* to invoke the mutilated and commodified black male body in the post-Reconstruction era through an image that the poet has noted refers to "Sam Hose, who was lynched and dismembered in the Atlanta riot of 1906"—"sex fingers toes in the marketplace" (Harper, 2005, p. 235). He then *looks forward* to project the demise of Coltrane. It is here that Harper re-members the narrative of the slave trade and degradation of the black male body in the Jim Crow South by reimagining it in the contemporary setting of the late 20th-Century urban jazz context. Coltrane's body becomes a sacrificial reenactment of the entire history of Harper's looking backward. Coltrane relinquishes control of his body through the injection of opiates that musicians of his generation believed inspired their performances, but Harper is there to quite literally integrate Coltrane's body organs—his enlarged heart, for example—as if through transfusion, into the sonic dimensions and narrative modalities of his own elegy to the Orpheus who has become his Eurydice. Harper's gender reversal of the Orphic tale in his representation of Coltrane as Orpheus *and* Eurydice speaks to the larger issue of queer desire that I am exploring in the poem that is a personal love letter by a male speaker to a male beloved.

In this proto-elegy that manifests the problem of representing black masculinity and queer desire, I read Harper on Coltrane in the context of what Dwight A. McBride, in an essay on James Baldwin,

---

[6]The impact of *A Love Supreme* has been extensive enough to encourage the founding of a church. Ashley Kahn reports, "Every Sunday, San Francisco's St. John Coltrane African Orthodox Church draws an unusually mixed congregation, local regulars and young, T-shirted visitors, to praise God, behold Coltrane as a saint, and play and sing along to the music of *A Love Supreme*" (2002, p. 11).

the first openly gay black male writer, has described as a "hetero-sexist strain" in "African Americanist discourse" (2005, p. 68). Harper's expression of affection for Coltrane is an implicit critique of what Cornel West sees in *Race Matters* as the "machismo" stylizing of the black male body that, West argues, has become the strategy

> of acquiring power in the patriarchal structures of white America and black communities. For most young black men, power is acquired by stylizing their bodies over space and time in such a way that their bodies reflect their uniqueness and provoke fear in others.
>
> (quoted in Carby, 1998, p. 32)

Harper's willingness to honor the desexualized body of Coltrane, and then to write a "love letter" to the physically disabled musical hero, works against West's image of the "machismo" style of contemporary young black men, which "solicits primarily sexual encounters with women and violent encounters with other black men" (West, quoted in Carby, 1998, p. 32). I am working under the confines of what McBride calls "the politics of black respectability" that, he argues, led to "the necessary disavowal of black queers in dominant representations of the African-American community" (2005, p. 71) and, in general, encouraged an embrace of a "race-centered identity bias" at "the expense of other critical forms of difference" (p. 72). I argue that John Coltrane, the embodied figure, must become martyred saint, dismembered Orpheus, and a figure of violent emasculation, before Harper can write his paradoxically predictive elegy and belated break-up love letter to him.

"Dear John, Dear Coltrane" is in its way a traditional elegy and a loss-based love lyric. An "I" expresses affection for a beloved, a "you," who is absent, but whom the speaker wishes to call to mind in the transhistorical, but never adequate, linguistic form of consolation for irreversible loss. But the instability and ambiguity of the "you" referents to pronouns and other apparently specific but actually indeterminate referents to identity markers—"these minds," "this life,"—speak to an open secret about the queerly unstable relation between the male "I" persona of the poet and the "you" to whom Harper addresses this homage. Keith Leonard (1977) writes, "In the volume, John Coltrane, who Harper knew, is both the man and his jazz, the talented and tragic musician, and his holistic worldview and redemptive music." Following Leonard, we notice Harper's difficulty with locating a stable position through which to address the uncertain nature of the referent to the speaker's address. Is Harper's poem a personal lyric to a former lover? The first part of the title is addressed, as in a letter, to a specific "Dear John." But the poem is also addressed to "Dear Coltrane," and thus is cast as an impersonal public address lamenting the physical, psychic, and creative deterioration of a major artist. From this second perspective the poem is not a personal lyric. Instead, like other poems paying homage to iconic artists who cannot be separated from their art, it is concerned with what folk singer Don McLean in "American Pie" (1971), referring to the death in a plane crash of early rocker Buddy Holly in 1959, called "the day the music died," from Milton's poem about Shakespeare to Auden's elegy for Yeats, to Frank O'Hara's for Billie Holiday. The poem enacts Harper's trouble finding the appropriate stance to address his feelings of loss, love, and care for the departed "you," John, as well as for his lament that Coltrane's famous sax, through which, Harper writes, the musician would, "blow/into the freezing night/*a love supreme, a love supreme* —," will be silenced (Harper, 2005, p. 236). But the poem's difficulty may itself be understood as a dodge. Did not Eliot, through ploys such as the dramatic monologue in "The Love Song of J. Alfred Prufrock" (1915) and via his theory of impersonality in "Tradition and the Individual Talent," and Gertrude Stein through her opaquely referenced object poems in *Tender Buttons* (1914), famously conceal queer desire through varieties of difficult idioms, broken forms, and, in Eliot's case in *The Waste Land* (1922), a mythic manner? In Harper, the collage style of the poem shifts dramatically from sampling passages found in Coltrane's vocal refrain in "A Love Supreme" (1964) to enacting the mutilative violence, subjugation, eroticization, commodification, and enslavement of the black male body in the post-Reconstructionist Jim Crow South into which the musician Coltrane was born in North Carolina in 1926 ("Sex finger toes/in the marketplace") metonymically. The poem then alludes to an Eliotic mythography of Coltrane as a Fisher King. His Christ-like death signals a possible rejuvenation of a land in the purification of its sins: "genitals gone or going/seed burned out,/you tuck the roots in the earth/turn back, and move" (Harper, 2005,

p. 235). There follows a narrative passage in which Coltrane's biographical journey from North Carolina to Philadelphia becomes a synecdoche for the Great Northern Migration of rural blacks to the industrial cities of the North and Midwest after World War II. It melds into the consequent transformation of rural folk blues, developed by Mississippi Delta figures such as Robert Johnson, and unselfconscious New Orleans jazz as steamboat entertainment into urban, electric, and self-consciously avant-gardist movements. The poem then swings into a long italicized passage performed in a funky call and response style reminiscent of the incantations of the black church spiritual. Finally, it returns to a series of biographically and autobiographically evocative, if opaque, passages.

By the poem's concluding passages, Coltrane's biographical history of addiction, recovery, spiritual epiphany, and illness during the 1950s and 1960s are thoroughly recast in mythic terms. Harper interprets the musician's health and vitality as sacrificed to produce not a musical performance—for Coltrane is described as "So sick/you couldn't play *Naima* ..." (Harper, 2005, p. 236)—but a transformational instrument of cultural regeneration and homosocial affection. Harper reads Coltrane's afflictions—addiction, disease, sexual impotence—as a symptom of a history of oppression, dispersal, castration, and spatial dispossession upon the black male body that gave itself up to make a healing sound: "your diseased liver gave/out its purity,/the inflated heart/pumps out, the tenor kiss,/tenor love:/*a love supreme, a love supreme—/a love supreme, a love supreme—*" (pp. 236–7). Coltrane's diseased body becomes, ironically, a figure of purification for its audience, a filter that is simultaneously in the process of exhaustion and that discharges ("gave/out") a substance that the poet reads in terms of affective dissemination: sex (tenor kiss) and love (tenor love).

In poetry, the "tenor" is the "subject" or "signified" dimension of a metaphor and the "vehicle" is the "signifier" that conveys the metaphorical connotative or figurative meanings onto the "tenor." In offering the phrases "tenor kiss" and "tenor love," Harper, a sophisticated analyst of his genre who received his MFA at the University of Iowa in 1963, was invoking the deep tonal register of Coltrane's horn, but also playing with the classical terminology analysts of poetry use to discuss the relationship of signifier ("vehicle") and signified ("tenor") in metaphorical constructs. We are left to puzzle out the signifiers, or "vehicles," that carry

the "tenor" terms of "kiss" and "love" in the following passage:
"your diseased liver gave/out its purity,/the inflated heart/pumps
out, the tenor kiss,/tenor love:/*a love supreme, a love supreme —/a
love supreme, a love supreme—*" (pp. 236–7). Is it possible that
Coltrane's diseased body itself becomes the signifying "vehicle"
that signifies the "tenor" terms of "kiss" and "love"? In order
for Coltrane to express his affection for an audience that includes
Harper, and in order for Harper to transmit that affection in
terms of poetic discourse, a displacement must occur in which the
embodied figure of the musician—the signifier or "vehicle"—is
exchanged for what he signifies as a linguistic marker of emotive
value, as a "tenor" signifying "kiss" and "love." We end up with
two "tenors," but the vehicles are erased, made absent.

Harper reads Coltrane's self-inflicted injuries through drug use
as part of a shamanistic ritual. Coltrane's production of spiritually
uplifting music is contingent upon, literally feeds upon, the deterioration of the musician's body—"you cook up the thick sin 'tween/
impotence and death, fuel/the tenor sax cannibal/heart, genitals,
and sweat/that makes you clean" (p. 236). The extreme condensation of these lines, the elision of verbs that would facilitate the
assignment of agency, the eccentric phrasing that pulls together
abstract concepts such as "sin" with the vernacular of addictive
behavior ("cook up"), the strange personification of the sax as a
"cannibal" that, apparently, feeds on the musician's vitality, and
the associative logic of the narrative, make any paraphrase of the
passage an act of folly. But it is fair to say that Harper is suggesting
the emasculation of Coltrane's identity as a virile black male figure
is, through the injection of opiates, recast as a paradoxical process
of cleansing and baptism. "John" reemerges as "Coltrane," a sacrificial figure of sacred desire whose phallic self is sublimated into a
figure of emasculated healing.

Harper has spoken of the influence of Coltrane's "sheets of
sound" on his own poetics.[7]

---

[7]Eric Nisenson reports that it was during a mid-1950s

stand with Monk at the Five Spot, [that] Coltrane developed a style that Ira
Gitler has very aptly described as "sheets of sound." This is a technique in which
Coltrane plays long series of arpeggiated chords, almost as if he were deter-
mined to find every possible chord permutation within a single solo ... Melody

Coltrane functions as an analogy to a theory of sonics ... [S]ome of the notions of phrasing, tropes, metaphor, and stanza relationships, have much to do with my way of hearing music, and stanza relationships, have much to do with my way of hearing music, and how language works for me in the process of composition.

(Rowell, 1990, p. 791)

Approximating in lyric form the sonic qualities, repetitive phrasings, and call and response elements ("Why you so black?/ cause I am") of Coltrane's "A Love Supreme," Harper rotates the axis of Coltrane's vertically-oriented expression of affection for God (or Allah). (Indeed, many listeners have heard the phrase "Allah Supreme," not "A Love Supreme," when listening to Coltrane's tenor incantations.[8]) Coltrane's statement of a man's love for God's mercy following his recovery from addiction via his tenor instrument is converted, through linguistic remediation and psychological projection, into an ambivalent, partially veiled, horizontally-oriented, and decidedly queer expression of Coltrane's love for Harper through the mediation of Coltrane's horn: "the inflated heart/pumps out, the tenor kiss,/tenor love:/*a love supreme*"(Harper, 2005, p. 237).

Harper enables Coltrane's High Cult composition to become disseminated in and through the poem. Given the inchoate, collage-like style of the poem, Harper relinquishes the signs that would differentiate where Harper's contribution begins and Coltrane's musical legacy ends. In the "blues" poetry of a prior generation of High Cult African-American poets such as Langston Hughes,

---

is sometimes virtually ignored; the pure sound of those roiling arpeggios is the substance of these solos.

(2001. p. 80)

[8]One reviewer on the Amazon.com website page for *A Love Supreme* writes:

The opening bass line is one of the most recognizable in any music to date. "Acknowledgement" is an ode to (the Christian) God, but many claim that "Allah Supreme" is chanted as a look back to a previous time when he came into contact with Islam.

(http://www.amazon.com/A-Love-Supreme-John-Coltrane/product-reviews/
B0000A118M)

and in the fictional journey by a classical composer to the Deep South to collect black spirituals for his composition in James Weldon Johnson's *The Autobiography of an Ex-Coloured Man* (1912), anonymous folk music is treated as a starting place for fine art literary expression. By contrast, Harper does not contain the flow of Coltrane's embodied expressivity. Instead, Harper queers the traditional ekphrastic encounter. He destabilizes notions of authorship by imagining his poem as an act of unruly collaborative co-creation between two men who specialized in different media forms. It is important to note that *A Love Supreme* is itself based on a Coltrane poem entitled "A Love Supreme." If a voice could be said to be lyrically reproduced in Harper's poem, it is the specter of Coltrane's. Although the phrase "A Love Supreme" is literally sung in Coltrane's actual composition, Harper has noted, "it is Coltrane, himself, who is singing" the final couplet in "Dear John, Dear Coltrane" (Belasco and Johnson, 2008, p. 1431). Harper's poem performs masculinity and authority differently because its author works dialogically. He collaborates with Coltrane in a work that slips between music and poetry.

In closing, I want to situate Harper's admission of Coltrane's sonics into his poetics by making an analogy between the queer subtext of "Dear John, Dear Coltrane" and the formalist aspect of its interdisciplinary aesthetic. In *Picture Theory* (1994), W. J. T. Mitchell argues that the traditional desire among painters and poets to distinguish between the arts by paying attention to their unique formal features (in other words, the formalist aesthetics associated with the High Modernist poetics of a critic such as Clement Greenberg) speaks to a resistance to the kind of dialogic co-creationism and sonic indebtedness to Coltrane evident in Harper's poem. Mitchell describes:

the moment of resistance or counterdesire that occurs when we sense that the difference between the verbal and visual representation might collapse and the figurative, imaginary desire of ekphrasis might be realized literally and actually ... It is the moment in aesthetics when the difference between verbal and visual mediation becomes a moral, aesthetic imperative rather than ... a natural fact that can be relied on.

(1984, pp. 154–5)

As I noted in chapter three, spectators experience "ekphrastic fear," Mitchell asserts, when they perceive the confusion of genres in terms of an unrestrained intersubjective encounter—what Mitchell calls a "dangerous promiscuity"—in a non-art context. In Mitchell's analysis, the observer's translation of one art form into another replicates the merger of self and other in a system of social relations based on the establishment of difference between persons. From the perspective of "ekphrastic fear," narration compromises the integrity of art. By so doing, it is analogous to the erasure of distinctions between "me" and "not me" in the sphere of social relations. By directly admitting elements of modal compositional techniques into his poem, Harper eschews "ekphrastic fear" by fusing an artistic homage to Coltrane with a worship of the (sick) body through which the art comes—especially since musicians physically embody and perform their art. At the same time, can we not suggest that Harper also expresses "ekphrastic fear" through his penchant for abstracting Coltrane's presence in the poem with what Eliot, in his essay on Joyce's *Ulysses*, called the "mythic method"?

7

Frank Bidart's Voice and the Erasure of Jewish Difference in "Ellen West"

Post-World War II American poets often adopted the persona of the imaginary Jew. This is especially true of those authors assigned the label of "confessionalism," Hilene Flanzbaum and Craig Svonkin have argued persuasively. By associating themselves with a symbol of the marginalized victim in the wake of the Holocaust, writers including Robert Lowell, Sylvia Plath, Randall Jarrell, John Berryman, and Elizabeth Bishop deflected attention from their (fully for Lowell and partially for the others) white, male, patrician subject positions. In the autobiographical prose section to *Life Studies* (1959), "91 Revere Street," Lowell emphasized the Jewish background of his great-great grandfather Mordecai Myers over and above more prominent Lowell ancestors. In Svonkin's reading, Lowell turned to a distant Jewish ancestor to "transgress the limits of an oppressive American society, and through that transgression gain much needed imaginative space" (2010, p. 110).

Like Lowell, his teacher, friend, and, I will argue, agonistic rival, Frank Bidart in 1977 chose a historically distant Jewish figure, Ellen West, a European woman who died in 1921, as alter ego for a signature long poem.[1] By contrast to Lowell, however, Bidart

---

[1]Published in *The Book of the Body* (1977), "Ellen West" is one of only five poems included in Bidart's second volume. It is also one of two long poems that bookend the volume (the "Arc," which concerns an amputee, is the other) spoken in a voice associated with a character other than the poet. In it, as Edmund White writes,

erases any trace of West's Jewishness from his lyric rendering of the source text—Ludwig Binswanger's *The Case of Ellen West* (1944–5; translated into English in 1958). Binswanger treated West's Jewish difference from an Aryan model of beauty, intelligence, creativity, and access to sublimity as a primary element of her identity. He interpreted West's Jewish difference as a source of body hatred, which led to her extreme anorexic behavior and, eventually, her suicide by poison three days after being discharged from Binswanger's Bellevue Sanatorium in Switzerland. A fair reading of Binswanger's case study, I will show, must place West's suicide in the context of a racialist ideology that, as Michael Mack has argued in *German Idealism and the Jew* (2003), associated the Jew with the unruly and abject body and the Aryan with a secular version of the Christian will to spiritual transcendence:

> [N]ationalist and racist discourse celebrates the Aryan body as healthy and strong. Taken at face value, this might strike one as essentially biologistic. This aggrandizement of the "Aryan" physique must not be confused with an espousal of materialism and "worldliness." On the contrary, what it glorifies is precisely the immanent overcoming of the body's immanence.
>
> In racist depictions, the Aryan physique is so intrinsically strong and healthy that it is without any imperfections. Here the body has overcome its bodilyness. We cannot find any signs of frailty and contingency ... The Jew's body, on the other hand, represents frailty, illness, and contingency.[2]

(p. 10)

"Bidart has reduced a book-length case of an anorexic woman into 15 pages of verse, the writhing, sleeping inner debates of a tormented soul" (2007, p. 110).

[2] As Mack argues: "Kant in fact saw in the Jews the opposite of reason's purity: they embodied the impurity of empirical reality, of 'matter'" (2003, p. 3). Mack continues:

> The Kantian and Hegelian body politic is one in which heaven takes the place of a contingent and imperfect earth. The Jews, however, represent this earthly remainder of incompleteness, of imperfection. The anti-Semitic stereotypes thus no longer fill the space of apocalypse. Instead, they now embody all that which hinders the construction of a perfect body politic in the here and now. They come to symbolize the worldly, which resists an immanent and imminent transformation into the other-worldly.

(pp. 4–5)

In part, Bidart offers a reading of Ellen West in line with Mack's thinking. He interprets his titular subject as someone who tried, but failed, to achieve a "fixed idea" of an identity that would, in her terms, "defeat nature," and so conform to German Idealism. Following Binswanger in this regard, Bidart represents West interrogating what her doctors call the "given" nature of her gendered identity. Through the deformation of her body to the point of disappearance (first through the abuse of laxatives, self-starvation, and eventually suicide through poison), Bidart represents West challenging her "given" subject position: "Why am I a girl?/I ask my doctors, and they tell me they/don't know, that it is just 'given.'/But it has such/implications–."

In "Ellen West," Bidart engages with an intertextual poetics by including "found" prose from the English translation of Binswanger's case history to lend historical veracity to lyric passages spoken by West. In his representation of Binswanger's text, however, Bidart omits key points that connect West's disgust with her "Jewish" body type to her internalization of an anti-Semitic discourse.[3] Bidart removes Binswanger's speculation that West privileged the blond, thin, "Aryan type" because she associated it with control that was assigned the value of transcendence over physical desires. Instead of focusing on the anti-Semitic discourse that animates West's body hatred, Bidart reads West's devaluation of the body and her wish for its erasure as in line with German Idealism and an aesthetic sublime. This chapter will explore the ethical implications of Bidart's invocation of Ellen West *as a historical figure*. To lend his poem a documentary ambience, he includes the following "note" at the end: "This poem is based on Ludwig Binswanger's "Der Fall Ellen West," translated by Werner M. Mendel and Joseph Lyons (*Existence*, Basic Books, 1958)." Invoking, as Helen Vendler has noted, a High Modernist aesthetic that conveys meanings through the juxtaposition of discursive fragments, Bidart interposes first person dramatic monologues and essayistic set pieces assigned to West's perspective with selections

---

[3] The Jewish attitude toward his or her body was, Sander Gilman writes, "so deeply impacted by anti-Semitic rhetoric that even when that body met the expectations for perfection in the community in which the Jew lived, the Jew experienced his or her body as flawed, diseased" (1991, p. 179).

from Binswanger. As in the source text, Bidart places dates on case history entries that chronicle the last period of her life as viewed by sanatorium clinicians who have access to her diaries, poems, and letters. Bidart describes his poem as based on a historical record of the final months of Ellen West's short life, but he distorts that historical record by significantly altering the dates on which Binswanger recorded his chronological observations of his patient, omitting essential information about West's historical situation as a Jewish woman who faced anti-Semitic attitudes towards conceptions of beauty in the Germanic cultural context of Europe in the 1920s, and changing West's relationship to her own poetry, her body, her testimony about what Bidart calls a "history of styles," and to nature. Bidart names his patient "Ellen West." Bidart does not treat the source text in a responsible manner. By that, I mean he does not handle Ellen West's narrative with a fidelity to what can be known, through the case study's textual traces, of historical circumstances. I would argue that Ellen West must be remembered as not only one of Bidart's obsessional character types, but rather as a person who exits in excess (or surplus) of what can be known in and through Bidart's reading of her as an aesthetician and idealist or of Binswanger's critique of her as failing to live an existentially authentic life because of her obsession with a fixed idea concerning the ideal body type.

Comparing how Lowell and other "confessionalists" adopted the mantle of the imaginary Jew in the 1950s and 1960s to access the aesthetically liberating position of the margin, and the far more ambivalent way Bidart at once evokes and erases the imaginary Jew in "Ellen West" in the 1970s, we should consider the different subject positions occupied by Lowell and Bidart. Flanzbaum rehearses Lowell's position:

When [Lowell] showcases his distant ancestor Mordecai Myers in the prose section of *Life Studies*, [he] does so because he understands that Jewish ethnicity provides an alternative to a repugnant and blameworthy national identity. In finding the exotic ancestor in a family steeped in blue-blood genealogy, Lowell redeems himself as a marginal figure and clarifies his position as poet.

(Flanzbaum, 1999, p. 32)

By contrast to Lowell's guilt-ridden association—addressed in poems such as "For the Union Dead"—with a "blameworthy national identity" during a period of nuclearism, militarism, Cold War paranoia, and the ongoing restrictions of civil rights, Bidart occupied a far more ambiguous position in mainstream American culture when he wrote "Ellen West." A queer son of a farmer from Bakersfield, California, Bidart (born 1939) wrote "Ellen West" as a displaced Bostonian. He held a decidedly non-elite (UC *Riverside*) college pedigree when he worked towards his uncompleted PhD on the poetry of Robert Lowell. Unlike the subject of his dissertation, Bidart did not require the vehicle of the alienated female Jew to occupy a marginal position. Following the Flanzbaum/Svonkin model in which privileged white, heteronormative poets adopted Jewish (or sometimes Black) personae to self-identify with what Svonkin calls "subaltern Others" (2010, p. 104), we are left to puzzle over Bidart's paradoxical decision to at once invoke a Jewish woman as alter ego in a major long poem, but then to erase signs of her Jewishness in his account of her short and unhappy life and her suicidal death.

Rather than casting West in her historical context as a victim of Germanic associations of the Jew with an abjected body in the 1920s, Bidart represents West as one of what Svonkin regards as his "Ahab" figures—in the tradition of classic New England literature from Melville to the early Lowell to the child murderer Herbert White from Bidart's first book of poems. To do so, I contend, Bidart must erase signs of West's embodied subjectivity, not to free the author's identity from what Svonkin calls "the limitations of his white, patrician persona" and thus to open the poet to the perspective of the colonized other (Svonkin, 2010, p. 105), but quite the opposite. To transform West into a poet who believes she must erase the body to "*defeat* nature" and to overcome a "*History of Styles*" that inhibit the transcendence that she interprets as a trope for poetic strength, Bidart must remove the Jewish difference of Ellen West's identity, which was the historically accurate motivation for her displeasure with her body (Bidart, 1990, pp. 112, 116). Bidart must do so, I argue, to facilitate the appearance of *his voice* on the page—in the displaced form of a maligned other—so as to assert himself as the logical heir to the Eliot–Pound–Bishop–Lowell tradition that he has synthesized through the paradoxically impersonal confessionalism evident in "Ellen West." He develops a hybridic post-confessional High Modernist poetics that seeks to transcend the body, history, nature, and ethnic difference in a quest for sublime meaning even as the vehicle for this transcendent narrative—the story of Ellen West—is animated by the issues Bidart wishes to transcend.

The degree to which Bidart dissociates, rather than identifies, with Ellen West leads me to read the poem as a statement of his desire for poetic majority. He reads Ellen's status as a failed, because "weak"—because feminized—poet. It is the marginalized double, Ellen, who dies in West's poem, I argue, so Bidart's characteristic "voice" can appear on paper in a form other than that of a belated version of Lowellian confessionalism. Dismayed by the limited vocal possibilities of the domestic monologic lyric, and yet still indebted to Lowell's exemplary treatment of psychic disturbance in poems set in McLean's Hospital such as "Waking in the Blue" from *Life Studies* (1959), Bidart simultaneously recovers his teacher as a dramatic, rather than merely lyric, poet, and also surpasses Lowell's "confessional" disclosures by representing West as a failed author of what she calls, in a diary entry recorded by Binswanger that Bidart includes in his poem, "hospital poems ... weak" (Bidart, 1990, p. 113).[4] By way of an Ur-figure of difference, ironically, Bidart reframes Lowellian confessionalism through a High Modernist formalism that is structured as a pastiche and made impersonal through dramatic monologue. He also *resists* a multicultural poetics based as it is on embodied difference, secularism, nature, mutability, and especially in the critique of the gendered roles of wife, mother, and sexual being. The predominant trope of contemporary American, identity-based, and body-centered poetics, "voice," is, in "Ellen West," deconstructed to the point that lyric embodiment is merely a belated textual trace. West's suicide note, for example, which Bidart places at the conclusion of

---

[4] According to the Poets.Org website:

> Lowell was admitted to McLean in 1958, though his infamous manic outbursts had already resulted in numerous stays at other mental institutions. Over eight years, he stayed there four times, corresponding frequently from his hospital address, and sending letters to Theodore Roethke, Ezra Pound, and even Jackie Kennedy. Written about his first stay at McLean, his poem "Waking in the Blue" ... was pasted on the wall of the nurse's station there for years.

his poem, is addressed to a female companion from the sanatorium, which West suspects the addressee will receive *after* she learns of West's death by poison.

In a celebrated portion of Bidart's poem, West's discussion of the later—from West's point of view, superior, because they are more nuanced and refined—Maria Callas's operatic performances benefit from the singer's disembodiment. According to West's reading of Callas in Bidart's poem, it is the physical deterioration of the once legendarily robust physique that produced what West refers to critically as "the usual soprano's/athleticism" (Bidart, 1990, p. 115) and that led to "crude effects, even vulgar" (p. 114). In a period (the 1970s) characterized by identity politics (although still marginalized in the academy), the body, and the intersection of persons with their natural environment and cultural setting, Bidart, through West's analysis of the dissociation of body from voice in the case of Callas, rejects all of these elements. Instead, by way of West's reading of Callas, he places his poetics in the context of High Modernism's desire for transcendence of the quotidian, ironically, through a poststructuralist viewpoint by animating what West refers to in the analysis of the late Maria Callas as "the *shreds* of a voice" (Bidart, 1990, p. 115). In Derridean fashion, the phrase "shreds of a voice" connects voice to text (paper shreds, physical voice does not). It also enables Bidart, an openly gay man born in a farm community in Bakersfield in 1939 and writing in the wake of Lowellian confessionalism in the Boston area in the late 1970s, to dissociate his own "voice" from the provincial subject position of his conventional identity. Further, Bidart associates his poetics with High Modernist heteroglossia (think *The Waste Land* and *The Cantos*) and High Modernist ventriloquization of other selves (think *Prufrock* and *Mauberly*) by extending the vocal range of the post-confessional lyric to include a Jewish Northern European woman known through a case history by Binswanger, the influential Swiss psychologist who attempted to meld existentialism, Heideggerian ontology, and Freudian therapy. Bidart resists postmodern identity oriented imaginings of selfhood by privileging as "NOT trivial" West's quest for transcendence from her body altogether (Bidart, 1990, p. 117). Echoing German Idealists such as Kant and Hegel, West's search is for a spiritual release that challenges what she calls the "'given' of my existence. This I is anterior/to name; gender; action;/

fashion;/MATTER ITSELF, –" (pp. 117–18). Through West, Bidart interrogates the lyric as a monologic vocalization of the embodied self. He challenges the dominant ethos of post-confessional lyricism that associates "voice" with embodied subjectivity. He implicitly critiques a difference-based multiculturalist imaginary.

Working in a mode comparable to High Modernist collage, Bidart greatly expands upon and complicates post-Romantic notions of lyric subjectivity. "Ellen West" is at least triply mediated and thus, in Bakhtinian terms, heteroglossic.[5] There is the author, Bidart, ventriloquizing Ellen West, herself a pseudonym for a female anorexic "non-Swiss" Jewish woman who committed suicide in 1921 after being released from Binswanger's care at the Bellevue Sanatorium. We also have excerpts from Binswanger's 1944–5 testimony concerning "The Case of Ellen West," which became known to Bidart through a 1958 translation into English from the German. Juxtaposed to his ventriloquization of West's "voice," the prose materials from Binswanger record fragments of clinical observations, dated and presented in chronological order, related to West's case, but written by male psychologists. In some diary entries the clinicians interpret fragments from other texts: poems, diary entries, and letters, authored by "Ellen West." Bidart's compositional structure is dialogic, but the poem itself is in dialogue with major movements in modern and post-modern 20th-Century poetics. While studying for his (uncompleted) PhD

---

[5]As David Mikics reports, the Russian theoretician Mikhail Bakhtin defined "dialogic" as "the productive conflict of distinct voices encountering one another [as] definitive of social life, especially as portrayed in novels. Bakhtin remarked, 'for the prose artist the world is full of the words of other people'" (2007, pp. 84–5). Bakhtin championed prose writers such as Rabelais and Dostoevsky, not lyric poets. It was in prose that authors could imagine the world as "polyphonic." Mikics adds:

> In Bakhtin's later work, *The Dialogic Imagination*, he develops his notion that the self is made up of a polyphony of voices: as individuals, we are the result of the endless hubbub of social life. Bakhtin argues that the novel is the genre in which this polyphony is most fully and energetically conveyed to the reader.
>
> (p. 85)

My chapter notes how the polyphonic and dialogic aspects of literature that Bakhtin located in prose can also be found in "Ellen West," an exemplary twentieth-century American poem.

in English at Harvard, Bidart was a confidante of Robert Lowell (Chiasson, 2007, p. 48). In form and subject matter, "Ellen West" represents Bidart's ambivalent response to a reductive version of Lowellian confessionalism.[6] Through his reproduction of Ellen West's story in tones, cadences, and grammatical markings easily identified with the poet's characteristic stylings of his voice on the page, Bidart demonstrates that he has developed a hybridic High Modern/post-confessional lyric. His work is deeply personal in its focus on same-sex desire and body image, and in its metaphysical and aesthetic concerns, and yet not merely based on autobiographical experience. In recording Ellen West's own analysis of her poems as "weak," as merely "hospital poems," it is as if Bidart were imagining a failed, and feminized, version of a post-Lowellian poet. He must transcend the embodied subjectivity of the author of "weak hospital poems" to dismiss his own provincial status as well as to displace his association with confessionalism—made

---

[6]I had the privilege of studying contemporary poetry with Bidart when I was a graduate student at Brandeis in the late 1980s and early 1990s. In seminar, we spent time close reading poems from Lowell's groundbreaking book, *Life Studies* (1959). Bidart encouraged seminarians to interpret Lowell's poetry as limited, rather than informed, by the "confessional" label attached to it by critic M. L. Rosenthal. To demonstrate Lowell's dialogic imagination, and to disprove the "confessionalist" moniker, Bidart paid special attention to the poem "To Speak of Woe that Is in Marriage." As the notes to the poem in the *Collected Poems*, edited by Bidart and David Gewanter, point out, "To Speak of Woe" is itself deeply in conversation with literary and philosophical traditions. The title of the sonnet is derived from Chaucer's "Wife of Bath"; the epigraph is taken from Schopenhauer's "The World as Will and Idea"; the poem itself "started as a translation of Catullus's *siqua recordanti benefacta*" (2002, p. 1045). Lowell placed the entire sonnet in quotation marks because the poem's speaker is not to be confused with a figure for Lowell's autobiographical persona. Rather, it is spoken from the perspective of the author's wife, the writer Elizabeth Hardwick. In conversation with other poems from Part Four of *Life Studies* such as "Man and Wife," "Home After Three Months Away," "Waking in the Blue," and "Skunk Hour," "To Speak of Woe that Is in Marriage" examines the themes of Lowell's well-publicized personal maladies, including his mental illness, addictions, manias, marital struggles, and infidelities. One could accuse Lowell of self-absorption because he restricts the lyric domain to the author's quotidian failings, and thus of abandoning poetry's association with historical, mythic, social, and political themes. But in seminar at Brandeis, Bidart stressed Lowell's extension of his poetic vision beyond the narrow horizon of the monologic self through poems such as "To Speak of Woe" that point to the novelistic, even heteroglossic qualities of Lowell's autobiographically-inflected lyrics.

manifest through his co-authorship of Lowell's last four books. Who more than Lowell would have been associated with "hospital poems" that, at least in a reductive reading, lacked the amplification of cultural significance beyond a recollection of the poet's own psychic disturbances and hospitalization at McLean's? M. L. Rosenthal (1991) performs one such reduction in a famous 1959 review of *Life Studies,* writing that "Lowell removes the mask. His speaker is unequivocally himself, and it is hard not to think of *Life Studies* as a series of personal confidences, rather shameful, that one is honor-bound not to reveal." West's comment that her poems only manage "to beat their wings softly" suggests a metaphorical figuring of the poem as itself lacking originality and sounding trite. Being, in Harold Bloom's terms, a "strong" poet does, for Bidart, signify a judgment of poetic quality, but also a symbol of masculinity in a poem. West views being "a girl" or "a wife," two of the gendered self-constructions against which she chafes throughout her testimony, as inhibiting memorable literary accomplishment.

We can read Ellen West's "weak hospital poems" as a critique of Lowellian confessionalism, but we may also read Ellen West as the "Elle in West" that is, the "she" (weak, provincial, marginal, queer) in the author identified by Lowell as the poet of the American *West.* In the 1970s, Bidart was best known for "California Plush" from the book, *Golden State.* In the University of Michigan Press's "Under Discussion" series volume devoted to his work, graduate student friends at Harvard in the early 1960s recall viewing Bidart as an exotic from the West. They recall Bidart's car ownership as a sign of his Western sensibility, as well as his interest in taking impromptu road trips to West Coast style diners such as the International House of Pancakes. In "Ellen West," the persona is both attracted to and repulsed by pancakes; "At twelve, pancakes/ became the most terrible thought there is ..." (Bidart, 1990, p. 112). Like West, whom Bidart represents as married, but deeply attracted to another woman at the sanatorium, Bidart is a queer person. His elegy in *Desire* (1998) for his long-time companion, the artist and poet Joe Brainard who died of AIDS, constitutes a major aspect of his later literary achievement. His descriptions of homoerotic attraction between West and "an elegant, very thin female patient" to whom West writes a suicide letter, as well as his description of West's queer fascination with a heterosexist relationship when she observes a man and a woman feeding each other in a restaurant—West describes the man as "so attractive" because "He was almost/a male version/of her, –/I had the sudden, mad notion that I/wanted to be his lover..."—enable Bidart to play a game of hide and seek as he simultaneously reveals and conceals his own queer identity (Bidart, 1990, p. 111).

In "Ellen West," Bidart follows Binswanger by representing West as an introspective, self-revisioning person. He shows West refining her perspective on key themes such as idealism, the body, and transcendence. Bidart, however, emphasizes West's interest in idealism in a way that at once universalizes, dehistoricizes, and inflects with his own psychosexual, agonic, metaphysical, and aesthetic issues her own testimony—again, at least what we can know of it through the remediation of her life story by her husband Karl and by Binswanger.[7] In the following lengthy passage, Bidart represents West engaged in self-revisioning. She meditates on her obsession with food, hunger, eating, and the association of her anorexic behavior with idealism and the desire to transcend her body:

—I *know* that I am intelligent; therefore

the inability not to fear food
day-and-night; this unending hunger
ten minutes after I have eaten ...
a childish
dread of eating; hunger which can have no cause,—

---

[7] Alan Williamson's celebration of Bidart's "Ellen West" picks up on Bidart's decision to universalize, rather than to historicize, West's affliction:

> It is Bidart's seriousness and triumph to make the reader feel that these extremes [in the behavior of Ellen West, but also Herbert White and Vaslav Nijinsky] are not curiosities but instances of universal moral and ontological problems – indeed, clarifications of the ways in which these problems may be beyond solution.
>
> (1984, p. 169)

Williamson does conclude that "At the same time, Bidart succeeds – largely through the brilliant poem-essay on Maria Callas and 'the History of Styles' that he puts into Ellen's mouth – in making the problem Ellen poses, the incompatibility of pure expression and material presence, seem in its own terms unresolvable" (p. 170).

half my mind says that all this
is *demeaning* ...

Bread
for days on end
drives all real thought from my brain ...

(Bidart, 1990, p. 117)

Engaged in a spirited internal debate about her eating disorder, West at first regards her obsession with bread as a "demeaning" and "childish" obfuscation of real thought. In the next part of the passage, however, Bidart represents West's deepest reflection on her malady in terms of philosophical idealism. She regards the eating disorder as a manifestation of her will to power over the desiring body. By refusing to succumb to her cravings for food, West, in Bidart's reading, expresses her wish to imagine a self liberated from the confinement of culturally imposed aspects of identity such as name and gender. In Bidart's analysis, her baseline desire not to have a body at all is an expression of her belief that identity is not limited to materiality:

– Then I think, No. The ideal of being thin

conceals the ideal
not to have a body—;
which is NOT trivial ...

(Bidart, 1990, p. 117)

In my reading of Binswanger's case study, West is far more critical of idealism. Her concern with body image is less a metaphysical issue than it is the manifestation of West's internalization of Jewish hatred in Northern Europe in the past of the twentieth-century.

In Binswanger's account, West's anorexic behaviors stem from a Jewish outsider's interpolation of disgust with the satiation of bodily pleasure through eating. In the case history, physical indulgence is associated with "Jewish bourgeois" identity. Further, in Binswanger, West is critical of her idealism. She writes to her husband of "the delusion which lies in my seeing this ideal as something worthwhile" (1958, p. 251) and adds, "I have made a mistake, this ideal is a fiction" (p. 250). She comes to "see the pleasure of eating as the real obsessive idea, it has pounced upon me like a wild beast" (p. 253). A fair reading of West's eating disorder places less emphasis on her desire not to have a body at all, which is Bidart's contention, than on her repudiation of her ethnically-encoded body in a period of racialist thinking that associated body type with levels of intelligence, spirit, will, and aesthetic prowess.

In "Feminism, Western Culture, and the Body," Susan Bordo discusses the case of Ellen West as well as that of other women who have suffered from severe eating disorders. Reading the body as a "medium of culture" ([1993] 2004, p. 165) in which "the [anorexic] subject at times becomes enmeshed in collusion with forces that sustain her own oppression" (p. 167), Bordo attempts to historicize normative images of the female body. She links varying ideals of female beauty to specific moments in U.S. history. Bidart hints at the historical underpinning of a specific moment in Northern European history when he alludes to West's concern with the ethnically encoded body through an intriguing but, in the poem, unexplored comment. He mentions that West detests the "fate" or "given" of her body type as "dark-complexioned" and "big-boned." Following Bordo, I want to historicize Binswanger's case study. By so doing, we can recover West's subject position in the context of the ethnic and racist typing that Binswanger's history strongly suggests contributed to her death, but that Bidart elides from his reading. Bordo writes, "I take the psychopathologies that develop within a culture, far from being anomalies or aberrations, to be characteristic expressions of that culture; to be, indeed, the crystallization of much that is wrong with it" ([1993] 2004, p. 141). Bordo's emphasis on reading the female body against a specific historical frame, and of reading the body symptomatically, is precisely what Bidart avoids doing through his erasure of Ellen West's Jewishness in his long poem. Arriving at a more ethical, because more historically accurate, picture of West, we see that her body trouble is not motivated by aesthetic dissatisfaction, as in Bidart, but by the anti-Semitic and racist coding of her time period—Europe in the 1920s—and, more acutely, the period of 1944–5 in which Binswanger first published in German his guilt-ridden, belated study of the patient he treated, but allowed to be released from his care, two decades earlier.

In light of his allusion to West's dislike of her being

"dark-complexioned" and "big-boned," Bidart's opening of the poem with her comment that "my true self/is thin, all profile/and effortless gestures, the sort of *blond*/elegant girl whose/body is the image of her soul" [italics mine], and her comment that "heaven would be three scoops of *vanilla* ice cream" [italics mine] does link "Ellen West" to a prominent code of racialist and anti-Semitic discourse (Bidart, 1990, p. 109). By contrast to Bidart's poem, however, Binswanger foregrounds West's Jewish heritage and the association of her Jewish background with an abjected body type and socio-economic position. Binswanger goes farther than Bidart by discussing—without, I should add, critiquing—West's case in terms of eugenic and phrenological assessments of body type and especially skull shape and size and a reading of facial features as depicting racially marked and hierarchically evaluated characteristics. In Binswanger, West's concern is not, as in Bidart, with having *a* body as an obstacle to the poetic sublime, but rather with detestation for *her* body. Jewishly encoded with its dark complexion and big bones, signifying a bourgeois type, and, as the case history suggests in ways that I will specify later in this chapter, implying a freakish excess of glandular activity leading towards a monstrous deformation of skull and body shape, West's body issues, once historicized, differ from the metaphysical and aesthetic issues of embodiment, style, and creativity that Bidart foregrounds in his reading of West.

In Bidart's poem, West is an aesthetician of pure forms. She is concerned with being trapped in the "history of styles" that she explores in the celebrated set piece on Maria Callas. By contrast, Binswanger reads West's eating disorder as an expression of her desire to conform to an Aryan body type that is marked not only as more beautiful than the big-boned, and dark-complexioned Jewish bourgeois type, but also as more inclined towards spirituality, creativity, and intelligence. As Binswanger writes, "She had feared that by becoming fat she would displease her previous fiancé (the student), and anyway, for her, being thin was equated with a higher intellectual type, and being fat with a bourgeois Jewish type" and "She had made it clear to herself that 'her obsessional idea' meant turning away from the paternal (Jewish) type" (1958, p. 260). Binswanger's emphasis on West's Jewish background and his narration of her obsession with blondness as a code for Aryan racial supremacy, German Idealism, and, as in Kant and Hegel, a secularized version of the Christian transcendence of the body in a metaphysics informed by Western dualism—Binswanger does use the term "Aryan" in a discussion of West's connection of blondness with purity and beauty—are not a minor part of his case study, but rather are foregrounded in the first paragraph of his "Case History" under the category of "Heredity":[8]

> Ellen West, a non-Swiss, is the only daughter of a Jewish father for whom her love and veneration know no bounds. She has a dark-haired brother four years older than she, who resembles his father, and a younger brother who is blond.

> (p. 257)

Binswanger's analysis of the three West men does not fit neatly into racial hierarchal categories that would regard the "blond" brother as well-adjusted, strong, and masculine, and the "dark-haired" older brother as the feminized neurotic Jewish male. In fact, Binswanger compares the "blond" younger brother—who marries a "blond," "thin," and "aesthetic" woman whom West envies—to West in terms of gender confusion and psychological disturbance. He is described as "'a bundle of nerves' and is a soft and womanish aesthete" (p. 237). Like West, he "was in a psychiatric clinic for some weeks on account of a mental ailment with suicidal ideas,

---

[8]Bordo rehearses the history of what she calls the "dualist axis" that she argues in part informs a privileging of the slender body in Western culture:

> the most general and attenuated axis of continuity, the one that begins with Plato, winds its way to its most lurid expression in Augustine, and finally becomes metaphysically solidified and scientized by Descartes. I am referring, of course, to our dualistic heritage: the view that human existence is bifurcated into two realms or substances: the bodily or material, on the one hand; the mental or spiritual, on the other... First, the body is experienced as *alien*, as the not-self, the not-me. It is "fastened and glued" to me, "nailed" and "riveted" to me, as Plato describes it in the *Phaedo* . . . All three – Plato, Augustine, and, most explicitly, Descartes – provide instructions, rules, or models of how to gain control over the body, with the ultimate aim – for this is what their regimen finally boils down to – of learning to live without it. By that is meant: to achieve intellectual independence from the lure of the body's illusions, to become impervious to its distractions, and, most important, to kill off its desires and hungers.

> ([1993] 2004, pp. 144–5)

and even after his recovery he remained easily excitable. He has married" (p. 237). At first glance, Binswanger appears to contest Aryan discourse—most prominently theorized in the anti-Semitic Jew Otto Weininger's *Sex and Culture* (1903)—by figuring the "blond" Jew as "soft" and mentally unstable. Because the section is entitled "Heredity," however, the point Binswanger is making, from a racialist perspective, is that the "blond" Aryan brother is merely a masked version of the Aryan type. His emotional, gendered, and psychological self has been corrupted by his father's Jewish identity. Like the blond son, who seems to be Aryan, but is in fact a neurotic and feminized Jewish type, the father appears on the surface to be an "externally very self-controlled, rather stiffly formal, very reserved, willful man of action" (1958, p. 237). But he is a sheep in wolf's clothes:

> [I]nternally, however, [he is] very soft and sensitive and suffering from nocturnal depressions and states of fear accompanied by self reproaches, "as if a wave of fear closed over his head." He sleeps poorly and is often under the pressure of fear when he gets up in the morning.

Writing in the midst of Nazi race rhetoric, Binswanger participates in a racialist and nationalist discourse. He suggests the Jew—recall that Binswanger begins his text by describing West through the strange formulation of being "a non-Swiss"—may appear to "pass" as Aryan to conform to gender roles and expectations. The Jewish father appears to be a "willful man of action," but in fact he is, like Joyce's Bloom, a womanly man who is "very soft and sensitive." West, like the effeminate brother, does marry, but throughout the case history she is described as expressing "the ardent desire to be a boy" (p. 239) and as lacking fully developed female genitals, making her unfit to bear children. The Jew in Binswanger may look Aryan—the brother is "blond"—but scratch the surface and the chameleonic, diseased Jew will be revealed. Given the racialist iconography of Germanic culture when West lived in Switzerland in the 1920s and then again when Binswanger re-membered her history during World War II, is it a surprise that West, throughout the case history, exhibits a detestation of the "given" of her body? Indeed, this is a form of Jewish self-hatred.

In the case history, Binswanger records two pivotal love affairs

West experienced in her twenties, one with "a [blond] student," another with "a cousin" (p. 247). Binswanger describes the period of the "love relationship" with the student, when West is 24, as "one of the happiest of her life" (p. 246). To illustrate his claims, Binswanger quotes from West's poem, "Spring Moods," in which she imagines herself, quite unsettlingly in my point of view, as a flying bird "[t]hat splits his throat in highest jubilation" (p. 246). During the affair with the "blond" student, West's obsession with her body image became destructive. Binswanger writes that she cannot "free herself of her 'fixed idea'" (p. 246), that she "avoids fattening foods, since she feels that she is nevertheless getting too fat, [and that] she undertakes a reducing diet" (p. 246). In this period, Binswanger reports, the "affair with the student turns into an engagement" (p. 246), apparently against the will of her parents, who "demand a temporary separation" (p. 246). West endures an "especially severe 'depression'," and "does everything to get just as a thin as possible" including the daily intake of "thirty-six to forty-eight thyroid tablets" (p. 246). "[C]ompletely emaciated," West "feels spiritually satisfied because she is thin … She has the feeling that she has found the key to her well-being. The engagement remains in effect" (p. 246).

In his poem, Bidart associates West's anorexic behavior with a "fixed idea" of spiritual transcendence that involves renunciation of embodied desire. By contrast, Binswanger does not associate the "fixed idea" or West's being "spiritually satisfied" with not having a body, but rather with achieving, through laxatives, extreme exercise on mountain hikes, and extreme dieting, the approximation of a body type that West associates with Aryan imagery of fashion and beauty, but also with a Germanic Idealism that associates the Aryan type with spiritual powers and aesthetic prowess. In the Fall, Binswanger reports, West travels, is diagnosed with a hyperthyroid condition, is prescribed bed rest and by "the following spring she weighs 165 pounds. Shortly afterward the engagement is broken off" (pp. 246–7). Binswanger does not elaborate on the cause and effect, but he implies that West's body image has contributed to the break-up. Bidart does not narrate the affair and separation from the blond student. Instead, he begins his quotations from Binswanger's case history after she decides to "marry her cousin," with whom she became engaged at the age of 26, and whom she marries, "after another meeting with the student [when] she breaks off with him for good" at age 28. Binswanger reads the disintegration of the love affair as an "open wound" (p. 247) that haunts West throughout the rest of her short life. For example, Binswanger considers a West lyric in which she describes herself as "unfruitful" and as a "discarded shell" and in which she begs a "Creator" (since West is elsewhere described as a non-believer, this clearly refers to the student) to "Take me back!/ Create me a second time/And create me better!" (p. 247). In her poem, West does not wish to disappear into a Platonic, Hegelian, or Christian version of Self, as in Bidart. Instead, she views herself as abject—"discarded," "unusable," a "Worthless husk"—and thus asks her "Creator" to reconstruct her self in a more pleasing manner (p. 247). Binswanger reads West's poem as "evidently aimed at her former fiancé, in which she asks herself if he ever loved her at all, if her body was 'not beautiful enough' to bear him sons" (p. 247). Feeling defective, West is eager to shape herself to please her blond paramour since he had the power to confirm or deny her status as a desirable and productive body.

In his set piece on Maria Callas, Bidart links aesthetics and a disembodied poetics. Imagining Callas listening with distaste to recordings of an earlier, more robust operatic style that she had since repudiated, West concludes that Callas allowed her body to deteriorate to symbolically detach herself from that prior fashioning of the self:

—Perhaps it says: *The only way*
to escape
the History of Styles

is not to have a body.

(Bidart, 1990, p. 116)

Binswanger suggests that West was indeed interested in the History of Styles, but her desire was not, as in Bidart on Callas, to escape from this history. Rather, West's goal was to conform to an Aryan model of fashion. As in Homi Bhaba's reading of mimicry in a post-colonial context, however, West felt she had failed to meet Aryan expectations, regardless of how many laxatives she took, how many mountains she climbed, how many diets she followed, how many spas and sanatoriums and psychiatrists she tried. At the very point at which "she vacillates between her cousin and the student," she took "several Mensendieck courses" (1958, p. 247). Binswanger's translators offer a helpful gloss:

> Mrs. Mensendieck was a Swedish physician who developed a system of physical culture based on gymnastics and on certain weight-reducing devices. She opened many salons throughout Europe and even in California during the early part of [the twentieth] century. The popularity of her treatment program was at least in part a result of the increasing freedom for women and *the new trend of fashion toward a slim figure.*

> (p. 247, emphasis mine)

I read Mrs. Mensendieck as a kind of Jillian Michaels meets Martha Stewart for the Flapper generation. Bidart likens West's "fixed idea" with the desire to transcend the body to release the spirit of her creativity as a poet. By contrast, Binswanger connects West's "fixed idea" with the slim, blond Aryan body type represented by the student. To this end, Binswanger quotes from a West letter to her husband: "Ellen now compares her ideal, exemplified by her former fiancé, the student, with the ideal of being thin" (p. 250). Her experience of being "saddened when she looked at herself in the mirror, hating her body and often beating it with her fists" is, I would argue, expression of Jewish self-hatred (p. 248). She reads her body type as a signifier of an abject social position. Binswanger represents her on-the-rebound marriage to "her cousin" as a futile response to her rejection by the blond student. It is also an unsuccessful attempt at self-acceptance:

> She hopes after marrying her cousin to get rid of her "fixed idea," but only with a view to being able to remain thin, that she is subordinating every one of her actions to this end, and that this idea has gained a terrible power over her.

> (pp. 248–9)

Bidart omits West's ill-fated engagement with the blond student. He *does* quote, for the first time in his poem, from Binswanger (it appears later on page 249 of the English language version) a segment that picks up the story "at the beginning of West's thirty-second year." The selection, which describes her increased use of laxatives, examines her physical decline to the point where she "weighs only 92 pounds." In "Ellen West," Bidart is working with a collage technique indebted to High Modernists such as Eliot and Pound. In such a format, readers are encouraged to consider the semantic relation between juxtaposed segments of the text. To this end, Bidart places the passage concerning West's laxative use in her "thirty-second year" directly after a lyric segment in which she ponders the question of identity and its relation to gender and the body in ways comparable to Elizabeth Bishop's exploration of these themes in "In the Waiting Room" (1976). Where Bishop's childhood persona states, "But I felt: you are an *I*,/you are an *Elizabeth*,/you are one of *them*./*Why* should you be one, too?," Bidart's Ellen states:[9]

> Why am I a girl?
>
> I ask my doctors, and they tell me they
> don't know, that it is just "given."
>
> But it has such
> implications –;
>
>   and sometimes,
> I even feel like a girl.

(Bidart, 1990, pp. 109–10)

Juxtaposing West's interrogation of her "given" subject position as "a girl" with the poem's insertion of "found" discourse from

---

[9]A middle-length narrative poem composed of 99 short lines of about six syllables in length, "In the Waiting Room" is the story of a provincial little girl who loses confidence in the stability of the world around her when she hears her familial caretaker, Consuelo, cry in pain in a dentist's office. It is an incident through which Bishop, in modernist fashion, reflects on the metaphysical status of her identity by imagining her relationship to a dizzying series of ever-widening archetypal, intergenerational, and transnational categories of personhood. Observing the hands of the adults in the waiting room, and the naked breasts of African women in a *National Geographic* magazine, she comes to regard her own experience, name, gendered identity, and her own body as uncanny, and thus as so unbearably strange to her that she faints.

Binswanger, Bidart tilts the meaning of the quoted passage, and thus of the historical evidence we have of West's case history, in the direction of Bidart's metaphysical inquiry about the relationship of gender to identity. By so doing, Bidart removes the passage from the source text, which concerns West's deteriorating mental and physical condition after she feels she has failed to meet a "fixed idea," not because she has a body, as in Bidart, but because she lacks a very specific body type. As stated, we can historicize West's body issues according to the associations of blondness and thinness with an anti-Semitic discourse. This discourse connected the "bourgeois Jewish type" with an overemphasis on worldly pleasure and lack of control and linked the Aryan type with a quasi-Christian spirit through a willful control of embodied desire. Binswanger is upfront about these associations in his case history. For example: "The second analyst used the expression that for West slim 'meant' the higher intellectual type, fat the bourgeois Jewish type" (1958, pp. 290–1). And: "We shall come back to this in the next section. In contrast to the fat bourgeois Jewish type, the wife of the blond esthetic brother, with whom identification is naturally easy, is as mentioned above slim, blond, and artistically oriented" (p. 291). Or, to cite a third example: "The themes here to be considered are the 'equations' given by the second analyst: 1. Slender = spiritual (*geistig*); fat = Jewish bourgeois" (p. 315).

To return to the poem, Bidart places a long narrative passage, spoken in West's first person voice, after the "found" passage concerning her "thirty-second year." Once more, Bidart frames the Binswanger case study with a lyric monologue that explores the philosophical nature of West's body image crisis. The passage, regarding West's recollection from "[A]bout five years ago, [when] I was in a restaurant,/eating alone," recalls a scene in which two lovers feed each other in a way that "sickened me" (Bidart, 1990, p. 110). What "sickened" West, the poem implies, was her association of sharing food with the loss of authority as an independent self. The psychological struggle West is experiencing, according to Bidart, is, as in Bishop's "In the Waiting Room," a borderline personality disorder. In the restaurant example, the fragile ego is threatened by the site of one person inserting food, a symbol of a material good outside the self, into the mouth of another. In Bidart, the mouth becomes a symbol of the border representing the entrance into the interior realm that West struggles to protect through her regulation of eating. It is in the context of the restaurant scene that West declares, "I knew that to become a wife I would have to give up my ideal" (p. 112), The "ideal" would be to become a "self" not subject to any role imposed by another person, and, in the next segment, by mere being itself: "I shall *defeat* 'Nature'" (p. 112). By situating the restaurant narrative five years *before* the case study passage concerning West's thirty-second year, Bidart has placed West as "alone" at age 27, the period when she was, according to Binswanger, breaking with the blond student and engaging with the cousin. It is worth noting that in the passage Bidart does quote from Binswanger, he concludes before the paragraph's penultimate sentence, in which West states that she "is completely dominated by her 'overpowering idea, long since recognized as senseless'" (1958, p. 249). My point is that not only is the "overpowering idea" quite different in Bidart and Binswanger, but also that in Binswanger, West is already skeptical about the significance of her idealism, in this case copying the Aryan ideal.

The next section of Bidart's poem that includes material from Binswanger appears as a series of four diary entries, dated 16, 21 January and 8, 15 February. Bidart arranges these so as to represent the clinician's increasingly pessimistic observations about West's social activities, physical appearance, sexual proclivities, emotional reaction to her eating disorder, and the relationship of her feelings about having a body to the issue of the quality of her own poetry writing. He dates the four entries as if they were recorded by Binswanger within a relatively condensed temporal sequence—mid-January to mid-February—and as if these time frames occur fairly closely in time (about six weeks) to the highly controversial decision made by husband Karl, Binswanger, and two other psychologists (I will discuss the significance of the identity of these other men later) to "give in to the patient's demand for discharge" from the sanatorium. It is fair to say that Binswanger's decision to discharge West, who had attempted suicide many times, amounted to a green light for her to kill herself. In fact, three days after her release she ingested "a lethal dose of poison." As with his prior situation of the case history concerning West's idealism at age 32, Bidart places the chronological sequence from Binswanger in juxtaposition to two other lyric segments, each spoken in West's first person voice. Both lyric segments concern the metaphysical and aesthetic themes of nature, the body, "the History of Styles," and artistic production, in large part through the powerful set piece on Maria Callas.

An active reader and creative participant in the re-presentation of the West archive, Bidart regards West's narrative as a model to pattern his own displaced autobiographical reflection. By so doing, he distorts the archival record to make West's story fit his own semantic interests and to fulfill his aesthetic needs for lyric condensation and narrative flow. The January and February chronology of the clinician's observation diary of West is a case in point. West attended the Bellevue Sanatorium in Kreuzlingen from 14 January to 30 March of a year that is not specified in Binswanger's text, but was in fact 1921.[10] Bidart places the four entries within the time frame of West's final period of confinement in the sanatorium, but significantly alters the chronology. Most of the materials Bidart quotes from Binswanger appeared at earlier points in the West case history, often in the year *prior to* West's entry into the sanatorium. The 21 January entry in Bidart's poem, for example, is assigned the dates 18–19 November in Binswanger.

Why did Bidart adjust the dates of the clinical diary passages and what is the significance? One could argue that Bidart altered the entry date of one passage from November to January to facilitate narrative flow and lyric condensation, but the shift in dating the entries also influences our understanding of West's relationship to poetry writing, a key theme in Bidart's interpretation of her interests in the body, idealism, time, history, and creative expression as a mediation of body and spirit. In Bidart's rendering, West's physical decline and emotional upset can in part be traced to her failure to produce, in a comment that we may regard as an allusion to Harold Bloom's theory of poetic agon *après la lettre*, "strong" poetry. Bidart suggests that West believed any poetry she could write would become a sign of her being trapped in what West, in her account of Callas, calls a "history of styles." Bidart also relates West's worry about literary style to the problem of embodiment in nature.

---

[10] I should add here that one peculiarity of the Binswanger text is that he will often omit place names and years, as if to maintain the privacy of participants, but he exhibits no restraint at all in quoting from private forms of discourse such as letters between West and her husband or West's private diary entries.

Fearing mutability, West scorned "the 'natural' process of aging,"
or, in poetry terms, the problem of being overtaken by what T. S.
Eliot in "Tradition and Individual Talent" called "the really new."
In the 21 January entry, as recorded in Bidart, Binswanger quotes
from West's diary, where she writes that "art is the 'mutual perme-
ation' of the 'world of the body' and the 'world of the spirit'," and
adds that her own poems are 'hospital poems ... weak—without
skill or perseverance; only managing to beat their wings softly'"
(Bidart, 1990, p. 113). In the 15 February entry, the final selections
from Binswanger that Bidart quotes in this sequence prior to West's
monologue on Maria Callas, the clinician states, "Has entirely, for
the first time in years, stopped writing poetry" (p. 113). Recorded
in a different order and with significant editorial omissions of
passages that appear on pages 255 and 256 of the 1958 version
of Binswanger and associated with "small extracts" of poems that
Binswanger states "were written in the night of 18–19 November,"
Binswanger quotes West as writing:

> As soon as I close my eyes, there come poems, poems, poems. If
> I wanted to write them all down I should have to fill pages and
> pages – hospital poems ... weak and full of inner restraint. They
> only beat their wings softly; but at least something is *stirring*.
> God grant that it may grow!
>
> (1958, p. 255)

Binswanger represents West's mood in November, when she writes
these lines, as a period of emotional uplift that by no means
jibes with the themes of poetic failure and the problem of
aesthetic embodiment that drive Bidart's reading of her story.
Binswanger writes that, "Her notes and poems show new hope
and new courage" (p. 255). Here, and, throughout the case history,
Binswanger is what I would call a naïve reader of Ellen's poetry,
one who reads lyrics as if they were an unmediated reflection of
the writer's psychological state of mind. He quotes a quatrain of
a West lyric to suggest through a mixture of despair and cautious
optimism that a dark night of the soul may be passing:

> I see the golden stars and how they dance;
> It's night as yet, and chaos utterly.

Will with the early morn's clear countenance
Peace come to me at last, and harmony?

(p. 255)

I am reading West's poem in translation from the German to the
English, but the translators have reproduced her poem in the
strict and closed form of the rhymed iambic pentameter quatrain.
West displays formal skill in her creative rhyming of "dance" and
"countenance" and "utterly" and "harmony." It is clear that West
is engaged in "work" here and that her task is as much to conform
to formal expectations of rhyme, meter, and stanzaic convention as
to pour out her soul. Binswanger can be faulted for omitting the
complete texts from which he quotes, for the ethically problematic
freedom he takes in reading West's work, which appeared in private
diaries, and for his naïve strategy of reading her poems as windows
to her soul. To his credit, Binswanger acknowledges that "these
poems [are] reproduced here merely in small extracts"; he includes
the, presumably accurate, dates of composition; and he situates the
poems within a (in comparison to Bidart) relatively robust context
in which West is not satisfied with her poetry (which poet is?). In
Binswanger, West seems saturated with literary potential—"poems,
poems, poems." She is concerned about what she calls "inner
restraint," which seems to allude to the need to write in strict
forms that she likens to medical confinement ("hospital poems").
It is simply inaccurate to associate, as Bidart does with the Callas
story, West's stoppage of writing altogether with a desire to reach
a disembodied ideal. In fact, Binswanger reports that West is eating
"things she has not touched for years, such as soup, potatoes,
meat, sweet dishes, chocolate" (p. 255). Her weight is listed as
114 pounds. She is not at the time committed at Bellevue, but
rather is an outpatient who attends a "clinic," undergoes analysis,
and takes in lectures and the theater (p. 255). Bidart includes a
clinician's comment in a February 15th passage that "for the first
time in years, [she] stopped writing poetry." Binswanger does
quote 15 February clinical observation (on p. 263), but there is
no mention of West's poetry in the passage, and nothing about
her discontinuation of her writing. As far as I can tell, Binswanger
never states that West stopped writing poetry when she was under
his care. Bidart's contention appears to be an invention that

facilitates his desire to associate West's philosophy of art with the set piece on Callas that follows.

Bidart places West's comment that she "Has been reading *Faust* again" in the 21 January entry as a precedent to her statement about the weakness of her "hospital poems" and her failure to produce art that negotiates mind (or soul) and body (Bidart, 1990, p. 113). Bidart thus reads the information about West's interest in *Faust* as more evidence of an ontological crisis (one, as Bordo remarks, reflecting classical Western dualism as found in Plato, St. Augustine, and Kant) that motivates her anorexic behavior. By contrast to Bidart, the *Faust* comment in Binswanger appears in a 18 November passage on the page (1958, p. 256) that follows West's comments about her hospital poems. Bidart's placing of the *Faust* comment implies that, like the mythic figure who appeared most famously in German in Goethe's epic (and, later, in Thomas Mann's Nazi-era novel), Faust, for West, represents her life-threatening, all-or-nothing, sensibility. Like Faust or the syphilitic German composer Adrian Leverkühn from Mann's *Doctor Faustus* (1947), she is willing to relinquish an essential part of her self (in her case the body; in Faust's case, the soul) for the sake of extraor-dinary artistic achievement. In Binswanger, West's comments about *Faust* reveal she is open to growth and renewal. Her acceptance of life with only a partial understanding of its meaning contradicts Bidart's situation of the *Faust* comment in the context of West's artistic failure. Here is Binswanger's version of West's diary entry:

> I am reading *Faust* again. Now for the first time I am beginning to understand it. I am beginning: much will have to come, and many more heavy things in my life, before I may say, "I under-stand it. Yes, now I understand it." But I am not afraid of what is coming. It is sweet to fear and to suffer, to grow and to become.
>
> (1958, p. 256)

Bidart omits the historical context for West's maladies. Most troubling for me from an ethical perspective, however, is how he edits the January 16th passage, which does in fact occur on January 16th in Binswanger. Using ellipses to edit unsettling aspects of the racialist discourse that animates Binswanger's thinking about West's body type, and that animates the self-hatred of West's Jewish-encoded body, Bidart's version reads as follows:

The patient is allowed to eat in her room, but comes readily with her husband to afternoon coffee. Previously she had stoutly resisted this on the ground that she did not really eat but devoured like a wild animal. This she demonstrated with utmost realism ... Her physical examination showed nothing striking. Salivary glands are markedly enlarged on both sides.

(Bidart, 1990, p. 113)

Binswanger's text includes not only these sentences, but also other troubling descriptions of West. Omitted in Bidart, Binswanger includes accounts of the shape of her head and face, her skull, bone structure, and genitals. These observations appear in between the sentence "Her physical examination showed nothing striking" and the final sentence, which in Bidart appears to contradict the prior statement, that her "Salivary glands are markedly enlarged on both sides." Here is Binswanger's version:

Her physical examination showed nothing striking. She is a woman of medium height, adequately nourished, tending toward pyknic [thick] habitus, whose body build is characterized in the case record as boyish. However, signs of pronounced male stigmatization are missing. The skull is described in the case record as relatively large and massive, but otherwise no signs of acromegaly are present. Facial form oval and evenly modeled. Salivary glands are markedly enlarged on both sides. Thyroid gland not palpable. An earlier genealogical examination is said to have revealed "infantile genitalia."

(1958, pp. 261–2)[11]

Later, in his "Existential Analysis" section, Binswanger returns to this physical description of West, but with a somewhat different account of her relationship to "signs of acromegaly":

Our patient shows a body build which gives the definite,

---

[11] Etymology: Gk, *pyknos*, thick – describing a body structure characterized by short, round limbs; a full face with a broad head and thick shoulders; a short neck; stockiness; and a tendency to obesity. (*Mosby's Medical Dictionary*, 8th edition. © 2009, Elsevier.)

if not pronounced, impression of being pyknic. As to the endocrines, presumptive variations to be mentioned are the slightly acromegalic skull, the thickening of the salivary glands, which was traced by the internist back to an endocrine disturbance, the infantile genitalia reported by a gynecologist, and the absence of menstruation for years.

(1958, p. 360)

What is "acromegaly" and why would it be an important dimension of Binswanger's observation of West, a suicidal anorexic patient? According to the Mayo Clinic:

Acromegaly (ak-roh-MEG-uh-lee) is a rare hormonal disorder that develops when your pituitary gland produces too much growth hormone, nearly always as a result of a noncancerous (benign) tumor. The excess hormone causes swelling, skin thickening, tissue growth and bone enlargement, especially in your face, hands and feet.

Think Andre the Giant and Jaws from the James Bond movies when you think of contemporary figures who suffered from this rare affliction. Given the unlikely possibility that West had symptoms of this rare disease, we are left to think the clinicians' emphasis on skull size, "facial form," "infantile genitalia," lack of menstruation, and "boyish" features conspire to create an impression of her as freakish, abjected, Other. The clinicians regard her as a misfit who fails to perform the role of child bearer, who upsets generic distinctions, but who, like her father, on the surface *almost* appears to be able to pass as a mainstream Germanic type.

Bidart quotes as a 30 March entry a portion of a 24 March entry in Binswanger. In it, Bidart omits a section from the case study that offers a Doctor Bleuler's diagnosis that "schizophrenia is indubitable" (1958, p. 266). Bidart represents the passage about the "Result of the consultation" with "Both gentlemen [who] agree completely with my prognosis and doubt any therapeutic usefulness of commitment even more emphatically than I" (Bidart, 1990, p. 118). This decision leads a few days later to West's suicide. Of great ethical concern is that one of these two "gentlemen" was Alfred Hoche, the author of a study in favor of euthanasia that greatly influenced Nazi policies (Akavia, 2008, p. 128). According to West's husband's diary from 10 March 1921, "[Binswanger] did not appear to be opposed to euthanasia in principle" (Akavia, 2008, p. 127). One reason Binswanger selected Hoche for the case, Naamah Akavia surmises, is that Hoche had in 1920:

> [P]ublished a short booklet, entitled "The permission to annihilate lives unworthy-of-being lived"..., which advocated the euthanasia of terminally ill, but also of mentally disabled and mentally ill patients. To justify the annihilation of those they called "mentally dead"..., "empty human shells," or of "burdensome existence," Hoche and [his co-author] Binding appealed to cost-benefit reasoning, as well as to eugenic motivations ... In hindsight, this booklet has frequently been seen as the theoretical and ethical text that prefigured and supported the Nazi mass-exterminations of the mentally retarded and ill, beginning in 1939.
>
> (p. 128)

Especially relevant in this context is Hoche's comment that, in the case of suicidal patients, it is particularly tempting to "let fate take its course."

Bidart is widely regarded as an idea-oriented, highly intellectual member of the post-confessional generation of American poets that includes his former Wellesley College colleague Robert Pinsky. Like Pinsky, in his various long "essay" poems (on psychiatrists, on America), Bidart attempted to bring what Pinsky in *The Situation of Poetry* calls "the discursive aspects of poetry" (Pinsky, quoted in Williamson, 1984, p. 166). "Ellen West" is a "discursive" poem, but by no means is Bidart a research scholar. His goal is not to set the record straight about the death of West, or to determine the quality of care and advice given to her by Lionel Binswanger, or to rehearse the Nazi racialist policies that surrounded the assessments of her body type by anti-Semitic pseudo-scientists, as is the project of a scholar such as Naamah Akavia. One could argue that Bidart omits disturbing features of the case history because they are distasteful and simply irrelevant to the story he is trying to tell about a thirty-something female poet who committed suicide because she could not write poetry in a way that would reconcile body and spirit. I do not consider poems about historical figures caught up in experiences related to the Holocaust to be special cases requiring a fidelity to facts that I would not expect of other poems set in a documentary mode concerning other tragic pasts. And yet I wonder if Bidart is violating a trust when writing about a person who represents a vulnerable group such as European Jews in the 1930s. Can a poet simply take any piece of history and use it in whatever way suits his or her project? How much artistic license is morally defensible? Is a poet expected to inquire into the historical contexts that led Binswanger to consult a "foreign psychiatrist" whose on-the-record affirmation of euthanasia policies enabled Binswanger to take solace that his inability to help West with his brand of existential psychology stemmed from the fact that she was beyond help, and therefore could be released from treatment and sent towards near certain death? Other leading twentieth-century American poets such as Muriel Rukeyser in "The Book of the Dead" from *U.S. 1* (1938 in Rukeyser, 2005) and Charles Reznikoff, in *Testimony: The United States (1885–1915)*, have written long works based on documentary research and legal testimony of historical events. Rukeyser's long poem documented the Gauley Bridge, West Virginia, "industrial disaster that left hundreds of minders dead and disabled for silicosis" (Hartman, 1999, p. 209). Reznikoff focused on race issues in the United States around the turn of the 20th Century. I am not sure that we can ask of a literary poet such as Bidart the level of research found in politically-oriented poets such as Reznikoff and Rukeyser, but I am arguing that if poets do use historical figures, they have an obligation to do justice to that history. Even if they take some artistic liberties, these may be poetic but should not grossly distort or ignore history.

In assessing how Reznikoff in *Testimony* and Bidart in "Ellen West" work with historical materials, we cannot say the difference between them is a case of editing the documentary record. Both authors do so in a highly selective manner. Following Michael Davidson's (1997) analysis of Reznikoff's *Testimony*, however, I do think we can distinguish the two poets by assessing their motives in turning to the documentary record. We can also notice how each author relates (or does not relate) the materials as they appear in his poem to a social and historical context, and we can consider how each author frames the material he chooses to shape into the poem. According to Davidson, Reznikoff's *Testimony* was of what he calls a "documentary character" because of its strict reliance on "a public record and the institutions that support and uphold that record" (Davidson, 1997, unpaginated). For Davidson, Reznikoff's *Testimony*, with its representation of transcribed court testimony that the poet came across while working for *Corpus Juris*, a legal encyclopedia, in the early 1930s, became the poet's way to move poetry away from lyric subjectivity and towards what Davidson refers to as "the system of jurisprudence that mediates relations between individuals under the law" (1997, unpaginated). Of course, as is the case with Bidart and the Ellen West archive, Reznikoff found personal meaning in his selections from the legal records, but his selection process emphasized what Reznikoff himself called seeing "in the facts of a case details of the time and place" and "out of such material the century and a half during which the U.S. has been a nation could be written up." As Davidson argues, such an emphasis on racial and labor history in a national context places Reznikoff as a socially-oriented author engaged in "exposing the institutional venues through which history is written" (1997, unpaginated). By contrast, I have tried to show that while Bidart, like Reznikoff, created a hybrid text that blended lyric and documentary modes, Bidart's emphasis in using testimony in "Ellen West" is in a tradition that Davidson describes as a form of lyric storytelling that "confirms the authority of a reflective consciousness at odds with modern materialism." My point is that it is Bidart's "reflective consciousness" that is displayed in and through the story of Ellen West and that the national history that, I argue, so motivated Ellen's body troubles, was erased and ignored in "Ellen West." Bidart is not doing justice to the historical record in the case of Ellen West—that is, he's not "seeing in the facts of a case details of the time and place."

I remain troubled by Bidart's exclusion of materials from the West case history that he *does* quote calling attention to a cultural context and a case history in which the "Jewish bourgeois body" was coded as inferior to the "thin," "blond," and "Aryan" one associated with spirituality, intellectualism, and aesthetic prowess. In a poem represented as based on a case history, I remain disturbed by Bidart's treatment of a personal narrative that is so closely linked with racist and anti-Semitic tropes, but that in his rendering is virtually devoid of these dimensions in his account of her death. As I have argued, I understand Bidart's erasure of West's Jewish difference as the result of *literary* historical concerns. These concerns motivated him to veer away from poets of a prior generation as well as from contemporary multiculturalists by not invoking the Jew as a signifier of difference. Bidart distances himself from West's Jewishly encoded body because, ironically (since for the prior generation, Jewishness signified difference), he wants to imagine a lyric voice that is not based on a speaker's embodiment, and therefore not based on the establishment of the difference between self and other or the cultural specificity of the lyric speaker. Trying to find a way out of the conundrum of the limited vocal possibilities of the domestic monologic lyric, Bidart is attracted to West's narrative because it concerns a poet who had body troubles. But in order to make West's narrative serve his literary purposes, Bidart must erase the very cultural marker—West's Jewish difference—that animates her desire to be released from her body. Critiquing rather than embracing the value of the specificity of her difference from normative images of female personhood, Bidart in "Ellen West" goes against the grain of the multiculturalist celebration of identity as acknowledging the embodied presence of the Other in all her dimensions (gender, sexuality, ethnicity, national origin, linguistic disposition, familial and educational background, geographical location). He does so by imagining Ellen West as, ironically, an idealist who is resistant to any designation of her self as contingent upon what he describes as her "fate." By "fate," Bidart is referring to her embodied presence in the physical world as well as to the symbolic assignment of any subject positionality (including gender) that from her point of view would inhibit her desire for a platonic (what she calls "true" or "ideal" or "spirit") version of self. West's wish, as Bidart imagines it in his poem, would be quite literally to transcend any instantiation of "Ellen West" within the cultural imaginary, which is understood as a space of confinement.

    In order to create an ethically valid dialogic situation, whether viewed through Bakhtin's emphasis on the singularity of the authorial perspective and the concept of "answerability" or from the Levinasian view of the infinite alterity of the other persons to whom the self is responsible, contemporary views of ethical relationships demand acknowledgment of the different positions of the two persons involved in any communicative encounter. In short, a contemporary ethics demands a respect for the border that distinguishes self from other. As Augusto Ponzio writes:

> What unites especially Bakhtin and Levinas is their both having identified otherness within the sphere of the self, which does not lead to its assimilation, but quite on the contrary, gives rise to a constitutive impediment to the integrity and closure of self.
>
> (quoted in Nealon, 1997, p. 133)

Bidart entitles his poem "Ellen West," but I argue that his ventriloquization of West's "I" exceeds the demands of respect for her alterity.

In "In the Waiting Room" (1976), Elizabeth Bishop explored the unstable border between self and other when the little girl realizes that the "cry of pain" she assumed was coming from "inside" the dentist's office work area where her Aunt Consuelo was being operated upon, and, therefore, "outside" the speaker's "inside" (or emotional life), was in fact coming from "inside" her own mouth. Bishop's confusion about the relationship of "my voice, in my mouth" to her vertiginous "surprise" that "it was *me*" and yet that she, at least at first, associates with another—her Aunt—speaks to the complex relationship Bidart explores between the poet's "inside" "voice" and that assigned to a historical person who exists "outside" the authorial self, Ellen West. As I have noted, Bidart's blurring of the difference between his own perspective and the always already mediated version of Ellen West speaks to the complex ethics of Bidart's poetics. On the one hand, like Bishop in "In the Waiting Room," Bidart's dramatization of West's narrative extends the reach of lyric subjectivity, and thus answers the concomitant critique leveled against it as a solipsistic genre that is guilty of what Mark Jeffreys calls a "programmatic exclusion of otherness or difference" (Jeffreys, 1995, p. 197). On the other hand, Bidart's poem, like Bishop's, foregrounds the generic crisis of the status of the lyric voice as a respectful way to imagine the life (and, in West's case, death) of another person. Does Bidart respect, in Levinasian parlance, West's "irreducible alterity" or does her story, as mediated by her husband, Binswanger, and the art of translation, merely become an impersonal text through which Bidart can explore his own personal and professional concerns? If Bidart does not exclude the other, as a stereotypical reading of solipsistic post-modern lyrics implies, does he not, in Modernist fashion, erase difference by absorbing the trace of an other author (West) into his own excessive poetics?

8

Narrative and Survival in *The Delicacy and Strength of Lace*

I

A brilliant, loving exchange of letters between the poet James Wright (1927–80), and Leslie Marmon Silko (1948–), a Native American poet and novelist, makes use of the Laguna view of narrative's ability to communally contextualize individual stories, in this instance with Wright's struggle with death. The exchange took place between 1978 and Wright's death from cancer in 1980 and was published in edited form as *The Delicacy and Strength of Lace* in 1986. Silko explores how language forms and situates humans and also shows how narrative and narrative forms of poetry can serve a pragmatic, therapeutic function. In an essay called "On Nonfiction Prose," Silko explains the letters as a means of personal survival, describing them as a "lifeline to me ... at a time when I was very much isolated after my move to Tucson" (1996c, p. 193). Wright described the letters as "one of the finest things I have ever had anything to do with in my life" (Silko and Wright, 1986, p. 79).

In this chapter I pay special attention to three poems Silko included in her second letter to Wright. I call this letter the "rooster letter" because its preliminary subject matter is the activity of a rooster who carries on its existence outside Silko's front door in Tucson. The rooster's death by coyote attack mid-way through the correspondence leads Silko to observe how ordinary and virtually unlovable aspects of nature may be situated and formed in narrative. The "rooster letter," a mosaic of poems, personal anecdotes, as well as Native American cultural lore about the ritual deer dance, allows me to focus on the semantic, or referential, nature of representation as Silko understands it. I can also discuss the pragmatic function of poetry, or the relation of the sign to the participants in its communication. Silko emphatically does not identify her stories and poetry with the culture of the white West. She offers them to Wright as an alternative, a non-tragic model of "presence" that will provide him comfort as he faces death by cancer in 1980. As opposed to the Western ideal of writing based on the principle of difference signified by individual style, Silko's female-centered perspective understands narrative as a collective activity. Storytelling is for her a matter of translating oral myths and history to new audiences by way of non-traditional media such as the printed text and film. She had argued elsewhere that Laguna narratives recontextualized individual trauma as "part of the village's eternal narratives about loss and failure, narratives that identify the village and that tell the people who they are" (1996d, p. 91). In the rooster anecdote, the "Note on the Deer Dance," and the poems she included in her letters to Wright, Silko linked personal being to communitarian belonging through narrative intervention.

Wright and Silko perceived themselves as figures on the margin between distinct literary and social communities and each of them perceived their work as a link between persons at critical inter-sections within the American experience. Wright's initiation of a correspondence with Silko upon reading her novel *Ceremony* (1977) is in line with the attention he paid throughout his career to literary models that challenged traditional English forms. In the 1950s, when the urbane voices of W. H. Auden and T. S. Eliot became the examples for much academic American poetry, Wright modeled his first two books after Robert Frost and Edwin Arlington Robinson. In the early 1960s, he renewed his style by publishing translations of South American poets Pablo Neruda and Cesar Vallejo and the Austrian poet Georg Trakl and then incorporating their practice of suppressing the continuities between images into his own poetry in the groundbreaking volumes *The Branch Will Not Break* (1963) and *Shall We Gather at the River?* (1968). Many critics have noted that Wright's poems were also distinguished by their empathetic treatment of unconventional subject matter. In poems such as "Hook," "Gambling at Stateline Nevada," "To a Fugitive," and "A Poem Written under an Archway in a Discontinued Railroad Station, Fargo, North Dakota," he represented himself at the crossroads where persons from unlike backgrounds exchanged news of grief and cultural dispossession. The archetypal location of engagement in Wright's poetry can be found in "Hook" (1977) where the speaker acknowledges his isolation on a cold night while awaiting a late bus to Saint Paul, Minnesota, with a handicapped Sioux Indian. As Peter Stitt has written, "Wright seems always to empathize most strongly with those who are victims of large and seemingly impersonal forces—politics, economics, the dictates of society in general" (1990, p. 2). At the Michigan Writers Conference where Silko met Wright briefly in 1975, she heard him read in his characteristic "no frills" style that reflected the content of his poems, and, she felt, his temperament:

> (I feel so much an outsider and alien to mainstream poetic style). Your directness and leanness I could understand in the way that the old people at home talked … I know Shakespeare's histories but I know so little of Pound or even Lowell. But when I heard you I thought well maybe academic background only runs so far, and then finally it is simple guts and heart.
>
> (Silko and Wright, 1986, p. 4)

Silko characterized Wright's poetry as literally stemming from the organs of his body, the guts and heart, organs associated with feeling, not mind. Her reading of his poetry as bodily manifestation replaces an allusive and, therefore, exclusive, canonical modernist genealogy— "Pound or even Lowell"—as definitive criteria for interpreting poetic value. Just as she will argue that in the Laguna tradition there is no outside to representation, which makes the world apparent and the persons in it visible, she perceives Wright as if his poetry were the site of his identity. Based on his persona as a border figure in poems such as "Hook" and on the poems she heard him deliver in a "flat voice" at the Michigan conference, Silko interpreted Wright as a split figure in American letters who was interested in making the difficult journey away from familiar and fixed values.

In a 1972 interview, Wright said he "wanted to make the poems say something humanly important instead of just showing off with language" (in Elliott, 1991, p, 1806). His understanding of poetry as a pragmatic act of communication between isolated persons can be applied to Silko's project of sending Wright poetry that helped him reconfigure his experience. In her opening response to Wright's letter of appreciation for *Ceremony*, Silko asserted that representation provided healing in the face of grief over loss and pain:

> Your letter came at a time when I needed it most. So many sad things have happened with my marriage and my children—it is good to know that my work means something ... I remember you well from the Michigan time—because you had been ill and you reminded me of my grandfather though I know you are a much younger man—grandfather in the sense that I grew up with.
>
> (Silko and Wright, 1986, p. 4)

Wright's letters affirm her point about the therapeutic value of representation, and the poet reminds her of Robert G. Marmon, her paternal great-grandfather, a white man and Civil War veteran from Ohio. According to Silko, Marmon had been portrayed by some anthropologists as an "instigator or meddler" but "people at Laguna remember him ... as a gentle, quiet man" (1996a, p. 104). Her intuitive link of Wright with Marmon, who, Silko had written,was "adopted by his [Laguna] wife's family and clans," suggests her attempt to go, in Werner Sollors's term, "beyond ethnicity," to create a symbolic or willfully chosen genealogy between herself and Wright based on sentiment (1996a, p. 103). By restating Wright's identity as a contemporary version of the great-grandfather she had heard about from her Aunt Susie's oral legends, Silko created an identification with Wright that privileged Laguna storytelling practices, and in this sense she asserted her distinct ethnic heritage and aesthetic tradition. Symbolic identification within the realm of Laguna narrative, however, allowed Silko and Wright to access shared experiences of interpersonal crises, such as divorce, a runaway child, and the disagreement of the body with itself: the body in pain. Silko told an interviewer in 1986:

I think that it's possible that the most deeply felt emotions, like the deepest kind of fear or loss or bereavement or ecstasy of joy, those kinds of deep, deep, deep level feelings and emotions, are common in all human beings.

(Barnes, 1993, pp. 52–3)

In spite of her optimism about sharing "deep level feeling and emotions" with "all human beings," Silko's opening address to Wright in the "rooster letter" expressed her ambivalent relationship to university-sanctioned literary authority and her wariness about trusting Wright's status as outcast and academic insider. She registered her ambivalence through the split form of her address to him: "Dear Mr. Wright, Dear Jim." Her decision to open her letter with a colorful anecdote about her yard rooster suggests her desire to construct a discursive space that provided a shared experience if not a shared interpretation:

Dear Mr. Wright, Dear Jim,
I just fed the rooster a blackened banana I found in the refrigerator ... [H]e is the rooster out of all the rooster stories my grandmother ever told me—the rooster who waited inside the barn on winter mornings when it was still dark and my grandma was just married and going to milk her father-in-law's cow ... [My great-grandfather] was an old man by then, the white man who came from Ohio and married my great-grandmother from Paguate village north of Laguna ... They tell me that my great-grandfather was a gentle person ... There are all kinds of other rooster stories that one is apt to hear. I am glad I have this rooster because I never quite believed roosters so consistently *were* as the stories tell us they are.

(Silko and Wright, 1986, p. 6)

Silko's concern for literary detailing was a form of self-invention through the dialogic engagement. In the process of inscribing her world for Wright, she was also inventing her place in it for herself: "I never know what will happen when I write a letter. Certain persons bring out certain things in me. I hadn't intended to go off with rooster stories ..." (p. 7). The anecdote enabled Wright to perceive her immediate surroundings in Tucson through vivid description. By feeding the rooster, she exhibited her definitive connection to nature and to the animal world. By remarking that she was "afraid [the rooster] isn't getting enough to eat," she also disclosed her own harsh economic circumstances as a divorced single parent from a historically oppressed group. Given the rooster is a common phallic symbol, we sense Silko is also engaging in flirtatious discourse. Wright, in subsequent letters, responded to Silko's economic insecurity by offering practical support and advice to alleviate her hardship. He sponsored her for a Guggenheim Fellowship and offered her, albeit paternalistic, information about teaching positions and other literary grants. The opening anecdote revealed a part of Silko's world to Wright, but it also displayed her literary restraint. She understood the correspondence as a literary negotiation, a performance that recognized two distinct identities bound together through mimesis.

Silko's comments on the rooster enhanced her sense of place through rich and thick description and demonstrated her views about the meeting of narrative and reality, including the way stories connect the present to the past: "I am glad I have this rooster because I never quite believed roosters so consistently *were* as the stories tell us they are" (p. 6). Connecting the rooster to legendary stories also returned her to stories about Robert Marmon, the great-grandfather from Ohio who was, in Silko's imagination, "a gentle person" related in temperament to her new correspondent. Silko's assertion of Wright's "gentleness" provided the link between him and a founding member of her own family. Registering Wright's temperament enables Silko to inscribe Wright in the Laguna story tradition. Discovering shared aspects of feeling, rather than negotiating individuated domains in a contractual sense, allows Silko to lift Wright's significance out of a fatal quotidian of mere accident and enter it into an undying story tradition.

From the initial "rooster letter" until the end of the correspondence in March, 1980, news about the rooster marked the development of the literary relationship. Most important, the rooster became a site for Silko to mix traditional legends with stories about contemporary life in such a way that representation became an extension of, rather than a replacement for, lived experience. Her confidence in the conservational value of stories about a lost object of affection came to a head mid-way through the exchange when she reported from Tucson that the rooster and white hens had been killed by coyotes:

> Coyotes waste nothing and so it is as if the white hens were never here; the rooster, on the other hand, was always a strange creature. A number of times I would be talking to Denny and would feel as if we were not alone; when I looked out the open window I'd find the rooster listening outside like a being out of some Haitian voodoo story. Now when the wind blows I find feathers, every time thinking that surely now I am seeing them for the last time, but finding them again and again. What is remarkable though are the colors of the feathers, which is as glossy as if they had only just fallen from him; and all this after weeks of the feathers blowing around the ground in dust and rain.

> (p. 41)

Silko perceived the "strange creature" before its death by coyote attack as a textual artifact, "a being out of some Haitian voodoo story," a figure in a narrative tradition characterized by charms, fetishes, spells, or curses believed by followers to hold magic power. After the rooster's death, she conserved the rooster image by representing it to Wright as part of a story tradition that reflected testimonies by Silko's ancestors: "[H]e is the rooster out of all the rooster stories my grandmother ever told me—the rooster who waited inside the barn on winter mornings when it was still dark and my grandma was just married and going to milk her father-in-law's cow." The maintenance of the rooster image through narrative repetition echoed Silko's revision in *Storyteller* and *The Delicacy and Strength of Lace* of an Aunt Susie legend about the little girl who ran away from home and jumped off a cliff because her mother did not feed her a cornmeal mush:

> The mother is very sad, and when she returns to Acoma mesa, she stands on the cliff and throws the *yastoah* [cornmeal mush] and the little girl's clothing over the edge—she throws them off, but as they fall they become the most beautiful butterflies of all colors—blue ones, yellow ones and white ones. And so they say

that's why you still find such beautiful butterflies around the
Acoma area.

(Silko and Wright, 1986, p. 71)

The little girl's image is conserved through the transformation
of her clothing into "beautiful butterflies" and the rooster image
remains visible at the edge of any sign of its physical appearance
through Silko's invocation of collective narrative resources that
fold incident into archetype: "[H]e is the rooster out of all the
rooster stories my grandmother ever told me." Her literary interest
has been informed by her philosophy of universal empathy. As
Silko argued elsewhere, "the ancient Pueblo vision of the world
was inclusive. The impulse was to leave nothing out ... Otherwise,
the collective knowledge and beliefs comprising ancient Pueblo
culture would have been incomplete" (1996b, p. 31). When the
rooster is killed by the coyote attack, she expresses her refusal to
base representational value on the selective principle of beauty:

> He was a mean and dirty bird but we loved him in a strange sort
> of way. Our friends who had been pursued or jumped by rooster
> find it difficult to appreciate our loss. I guess I am still surprised
> at the feeling we had for him—to realize that without wanting
> to, without any reason to, he had been dear to us. We are told
> we should love only the good and the beautiful, and these are
> defined for us so narrowly.

(Silko and Wright, 1986, p. 41)

Her policy of boundless affection became the philosophical
underpinning to a democratic aesthetic that, like the poetry of
Walt Whitman and Gertrude Stein, attempted to reduce the
violence of writing by leaving nothing out of the text. Since in
the Laguna Pueblo tradition, representation and reality were
indelibly bound, no part of the world could be omitted from
story if the world was to remain whole. Her inclusive literary
vision was shared by Wright in his poetry as well as in his
description of a lesson he acquired by reading the seventeenth-
century Dutch philosopher Baruch Spinoza's *Ethics*: "Spinoza says
that the human being is a miraculous creature, and his miracle
consists in his capacity for love. He can love anything, from an

atom all the way to God" (pp. 45–6). Wright's poetry of mourning for such despicable persons as the murderers George Doty ("At the Executed Murderer's Grave") and Caryl Chessman ("American Twilights, 1957"), and for such figures of political incompetence as Warren G. Harding ("Two Poems about President Harding"), becomes sensible within the context of Silko's version of the Laguna philosophy of indiscriminate compassion.

II

The rooster anecdote illustrates that narrative can be viewed as a pragmatic act when there is common agreement that stories are related to visibility. "Note on the Deer Dance" functions metadiscursively in relation to the "rooster letter." It is a gloss on how narrative is implicated in personal and communitarian survival. Silko's "Note" comments on the value of representation beyond ornament or entertainment as the deer dance is a theatrical performance of the hunt and is itself an expression that ensures the hunt's success:

> In the fall the Laguna hunters go to the hills and mountains around Laguna Pueblo to bring back the deer. The people think of the deer as coming to give themselves to the hunters so that the people will have meat through the winter. Late in the winter the Deer Dance is performed to honor and pay thanks to the deer spirits who've come home with the hunters that year. Only when this has been properly done will the spirits be able to return to the mountain and be reborn into more deer who will, remembering the reverence and appreciation of the people, once more come home with the hunter.
>
> (Silko and Wright, 1986, pp. 9–10)

Following Silko's comments on the rooster's conservation through literary resources—"Now when the wind blows I find feathers, every time thinking that surely now I am seeing them for the last time, but finding them again and again"—I contend that she offered the "Note" to illustrate how representation provides guidance at events crucial to personal and collective survival. Like the poems about bear and deer hunts that follow in the letter, the dance represents the hunt and is a performance that convinces the deer to return. In "Interior and Exterior Landscapes," Silko expressed how representation supported the hunters' survival:

> [H]unting stories were not merely after-dinner entertainment. These accounts contained information of critical importance about the behavior and migration patterns of mule deer. Hunting stories carefully described key landmarks and locations of fresh water. Thus, a deer-hunt story might also serve as a map. Lost travelers and lost pinon-nut gatherers have been saved by sighting a rock formation they recognize only because they once heard a hunting story describing this rock formation.
>
> (1996b, p. 32)

Silko asserted that Laguna narratives never were intended merely as ornaments, but were valued because they helped insure community survival, if only because language was a necessary means of guiding the hunter in unfamiliar territory. For Silko, the world can become recognizable and negotiable through discourse in the way that verbal and graphic representations are combined to produce an image of reality on a map. By contrast to Silko's tendency to value language for its ability to inform persons about the world around them, Wright tended toward a Kantian formalism. He regarded everyday scenes of writing, such as the notes referred to in the poem "A Note Left in Jimmy Leonard's Shack" (1959), as practical communications while reserving for the fine arts the status of beauty and transcendence of time and place. Discussing a Praxiteles sculpture he saw on his last trip to Italy in 1979, Wright maintained that art could be evaluated outside the historical moment:

> Tarento is one of those strategically important places that have been raked over and bombed over and massacred over by everyone from the barbarians to the Saracens to the Turks to the Germans to the Americans to God knows who else. But other things, other things fully as true: Lysippis and Praxiteles worked here long ago, and the latter left an incredibly beautiful girl's face. Pythagoras, our old high school chum, came here and walked in the groves, pondering the right

triangles in mid-air. And, believe it or not, Plato came here for visits.

(Wright, 1990, p. 49)

For him, art maintained its ultimate value outside the ravages of time and the history of political and military conflict. Art provided the community with a stay against deterioration and, therefore, Wright viewed art as a quasi-religious means toward transcendence. Silko was more pragmatic than Wright about the use of representation and less concerned than he was about maintaining the distinction between utilitarian communications and aesthetic designs. For her, stories and poems are ways to place temporal events in terms of collective memory.

For Silko, stories negotiated crisis points in human experience. In "Note on the Deer Dance," and in poems about the deer hunt and a hunter lost in bear country, stories mediate life and death interactions between human and animal and between the world of the body and the world of the spirit. In Silko, stories about crossings by Laguna women who risked entering wild zones outside Laguna Pueblo have as outcome the perpetuation of the group through the replenishment of its sources of strength and creativity. In the "Yellow Woman" legend as told by Silko, a Pueblo woman is abducted by a figure named Silva who represents in anthropomorphic terms the generative nature of the wild. The outcome to the abduction in the tale was the appearance of two male babies who signified the perpetuation of the tribe.[1] Silko noted that of the old Laguna stories, "Yellow Woman" was her favorite,

---

[1]Paula Gunn Allen has discussed the culturally productive value of female sexual adventures and transgressions upon communal expectations in "Yellow Woman" tales in her essay "Kochinnenako in Academe":

> Kochinnenako is a role model ... [whose] very difference [from communal expectations and norms] makes her special adventures possible, and these adventures often have happy outcomes for Kochinnenako and for her people. This is significant among a people who value conformity and propriety ... It suggests that the behavior of women, at least at certain times or under certain circumstances, must be improper or nonconformist for the greater good of the whole.

> (1993, pp. 88–9)

because she dares to cross traditional boundaries of ordinary behavior during times of crisis in order to save the Pueblo; her power lies in her courage and in her uninhibited sexuality, which the old-time Pueblo stories celebrate again and again because fertility was so highly valued.

(1996e, p. 70)[2]

To illustrate to Wright how she has translated into poetry the pragmatic message of the "Note on the Deer Dance," Silko included poems that she would also include in *Storyteller* (1981). "Deer Dance/For Your Return" is an elegiac love lyric spoken by a deer hunter. The eroticized prayer is not addressed to a human beloved, but to the departing spirit of a recently killed or dying deer. By addressing the deer with love and erotic longing, the speaker wishes to insure the deer's voluntary return the next season:

If this
will hasten your return
then I will hold myself above you all night
blowing softly
down-feathered clouds
that drift about the spruce
and hide your eyes
as you are borne back to the mountain.

(p. 10)

As in her description of the rooster and its relationship to earlier stories, and as in her perception of Wright as related by sentiment to a founding member of her family, the lyric about the deer hunt shows how language negotiates the crossing

---

[2]Elaine A. Jahner has written that:

> [Silko's] stories dramatize how desire, need, and sexuality are all variations of the same psychic dynamics feeding the wellsprings of life, consciousness, and culture. Silko brings the reader close to the moments when sexuality and storytelling participate in the same gestures of becoming.
>
> (1994, p. 505)

between life and death by creating a pattern that links the present to the past. The poem relieves anxiety about communal survival by yoking the hunt to a narrative that reconfigures the relationship between human and animal on humanistic terms as a tragic love story based in longing for an absent beloved. As in the "Yellow Woman" legend, in the "Deer hunt" poem, Silko depicted nature as a site of human desire: "we have missed you/I have longed for you./Losses are certain/in the pattern of this dance" (p. 11).[3] The classic Western lyrical theme of longing for a departed beloved was reinscribed as a magical charm that helped the community—the "we"—deal with its need to sacrifice animal life to survive: "I will walk these hills and/ pray you will come again/I will go with a heart full for you/to wait your return" (p. 12). The poem exists between the Western lyrical tradition of the love poem based on tragic conceptions of representation as the compensation for experiential loss and the Pueblo sense of the poem as ceremonial incantation or magic charm. The poem negotiates the crossing between human and animal world, temporal and spatial understandings of poetry, animate and inanimate states of being, as well as (white) Western and Laguna conceptions of story.

"Story from Bear Country," a second narrative poem Silko included in the "rooster letter," was also set at the intersection between the human and animal worlds. The poem maintained human appearance by retracing in language the steps made by a hunter who entered bear country, but lost his way home. To return from his disfiguring journey, the hunter needed to follow the speaker's words and to hear the speech of shaman figures whose voices were predicted in the poem:

It is difficult to explain
how they call you.
All but a few who went to them
left behind families

---

[3] At the end of the Buffalo Story, similarly, Silko noted that "the people have been starving, and the buffalo says, 'We will give up our spirits, we will come and die for these people because we are related to them. Kockininako is our sister-in-law'" (Barnes, 1993, p. 57).

grandparents
and sons
a good life.

The problem is
you will never want to return.
their beauty will overcome your memory ...

And you will remain with them
locked forever inside yourself
your eyes will see you
dark shaggy thick.

                                                        (p. 13)

Silko effectively uses lineation, a fundamental graphic feature of
poetry, to enhance the mimetic aspect of her poem, placing on
separate lines the loved ones the hunter had left behind: "families/
grandparents/and sons." The poem is concerned with the exotic
worlds of spirit, nature, and states of extreme feeling and perception,
but the tone of address is calm as the speaker guides the hunter from
the mountains to the pueblo. The speaker is a humanistic version of a
shaman, similar in character to Betonie, from *Ceremony*, who devises
the plot for Tayo to rescue Uncle Josiah's stolen cattle. In the novel,
Betonie's quest narrative enabled Tayo, the shell-shocked prisoner of
the war on the Pacific Rim, to recover from trauma figured as the white
shroud of invisibility he experienced in the Veterans Administration
Hospital in California. By enacting Betonie's narrative plan, Tayo
gained a renewed sensual awareness of his homeland, his sexuality,
and his community. The speaker of "Story from Bear Country" was,
like Betonie, a narratologist rewriting a story that would otherwise
end with the splitting of community and the distorting of personal
identity. Speaking in the third person on behalf of the community,
the voice directs the hunter to other rhetoricians of personal healing,
"bear priests" whose "beautiful songs" counteracted the seductive
influence of natural beauty:

We can send bear priests
loping after you
their medicine bags

bouncing against their chests.
Naked legs painted black ...
They will follow your trail
into the narrow canyon ...
where you stopped to look back
and saw only bear tracks
behind you.

(pp. 13–14)

The poem revised the hunter's perception of himself through a collective discourse that was ceremonial as well as lyrical. Because the poem also mentioned the words of "bear priests" that supplemented the speaker's words, "Story from Bear Country" served a practical function by reconfiguring the hunter's identity as well as a literary function by pointing toward other ritual uses of language:

When they call,
faint memories
will writhe around your heart
and startle you with their distance.
But the others will listen
because bear priests sing
beautiful songs.
They must
if they are ever to call you back.

(p. 14)

The priests' strategy for coaxing the hunter to break the natural seduction was to activate his longing for home through seductive rhetoric, beautiful song. Recovering his image by way of the communal voice proved to be a painful method of recuperation, however. Situated between two worlds, the hunter became aware of his difference from nature and from the community he had abandoned. Caught between the wish to return home and the allure of nature, the hunter experienced as painful the "faint memories" of community in the region of feeling, the heart. Beautiful words served a practical, guiding function, however painful the logic of recuperation. The art of singing allowed the hunter to recover his place in community through language:

They will try to bring you
step by step
back to the place you stopped
and found only bear prints in the sand
where your feet had been.

The poem is a quasi-religious form of discourse that I have compared
to a magic charm, but the cultural work it performs is quotidian, not
esoteric or mystical. The poem is designed to return the hunter to his
community, to his family, and to recognition of his humanity in an
embrace of ordinary events by way of the communal or "we" voice:

Whose voice is this?
You may wonder
hearing this story when
after all
you are alone
hiking in these canyons and hills
while your wife and sons are waiting
back at the car for you.

The integrated version of the instruction from the "I" to the "you"
allowed the hunter to endure the isolation from community indicated
by his journey into bear country. The hunter could survive in the
wild at a moment of visual crisis so long as he heard another voice
describing a common reality. The poem took place at sundown, the
crepuscular moment, a figure for the hunter's loss of the natural
means to see enough to return without a textual mediation:

See, the sun is going down now
the sandrock is washed in its colors.
Don't be afraid
we love you
we've been calling you
all this time.
Go ahead
turn around
see the shape
of your footprints
in the sand.

The poem helped the hunter return by convincing him that someone waited on the other side of bear country to recognize him, to greet him, and to reintroduce him to community. "Story from Bear Country" converted the hunter toward a recognition of his own humanity: "turn around/see the shape/of your footprints/ in the sand."

"Skeleton Fixer's Story," a third poem Silko included with her "rooster letter," was also concerned with reconfiguring the human image through words spoken by a poet who functioned like the shaman of *Ceremony*, Betonie. Silko did not present the poem as an "original" work, but as a revision of an oral Laguna legend based on a written version by Simon J. Ortiz in *A Bigger Story They Tell Around Laguna and Acoma*. The shaman, called Old Badger Man, like the poet who describes his actions, recovered the body of a woman through knowledge of how poetic structures relate to human appearance: "He took great care with the ribs/marveling at the structure/which had contained the lungs and heart" (Silko and Wright, 1986, p. 19). The Skeleton Fixer's words revived and reconstructed the dead matter, bones, that had been "scattered all over the place" (p. 18). In their close proximity to language forms—as in N. Scott Momaday's paraphrase of the title of a Wallace Stevens poem for his essay "The Man Made of Words"—the bones were explicitly related to Silko's contention that human presence was bound to communal discourse. Personal identity was obtained by entering the body into language, where the person could be made knowable to others. Through the Old Badger Man's concern for how words related to human presence, bodies were recuperated and departed spirits were called to mind:

"Oh poor dear one who left your bones here
I wonder who you are?"
Old Skeleton Fixer spoke to the bones
because things don't die—
they fall to pieces maybe,
get scattered or separate,
but Old Badger Man can tell
how they once fit together.

(p. 19)

As in "Story from Bear Country," "Skeleton Fixer's Story" existed as an intermediate utterance. It pointed toward the Old Badger Man's knowledge of how to recover the body in language and the poem set forth that act. The Old Badger Man's act was described as a pragmatic event that placed the ability to revive the bones into the hands of the literary creator: "A'moo'ooh, my dear one/ these words are your bones" (p. 21).[4] The Skeleton Fixer's ability to revive the woman in the poem seems to be related to a prior story of transformation that Silko knew from her aunt, the story of the little girl whose clothes were transformed into butterflies. The Old Badger Man's construction of persons out of words is enabled by his knowledge of a reservoir of stories in which there is a transformation of loss into, in the case of the little girl and the butterflies, a metamorphic beauty. "These words" that Old Badger Man speaks to revive A'moo'ooh were not his singular possession—they were not marked by his stylistic difference from prior language users—but were the fundamental linguistic resource of a community. The Old Badger Man was not a poet in a Western Romantic sense, but he was a custodian of a principle of language resources necessary to maintain personal visibility across time and change.

"Skeleton Fixer's Story" illustrated Silko's persistent message to Wright: there existed a correspondence between collective representation and personal identification. In the last part of the correspondence, the message of the skeleton fixer poem would provide Wright a significant degree of comfort. In such poems where textual identity authorizes the lived reality of the Old Coyote Woman, the border between the material life and death of the body, a border that Wright experienced through his struggle with cancer, was interpreted by Silko as a comparatively inconsequential fact.

---

[4]Allen Grossman has noted in conversation that since A'moo'ooh is a name for Aunt Susie, she is the person whom we see named by the Skeleton Fixer as brought back to life in the form of the words of which she was the master. The Skeleton Fixer is the story process which continuously reconstructs the human form of the old woman, A'moo'ooh, who is the principle of the story.

III

In the poems I have discussed, the woven texture of the Laguna community's collected narratological wisdom about what happens to persons became an indispensable human enactment of an impersonal structure. The literary structure was useful to classify general categories of human trauma so the individual could share his or her pain through prior accounts. In the deer hunt poem, the speaker provided the community with assurance that the seasonal crisis would be overcome through a beautiful song. In the bear country poem, the speaker's voice guided the hunter back to human form. In the Skeleton Fixer poem, the Old Badger Man's knowledge of how words related to presence allowed him to recuperate A'moo'ooh's inert and shattered body. Discussing her great-grandfather from Ohio, Robert Marmon, Silko again stressed the congruence between representation and personal appearance. She asserted that the contemporary story could best be understood in the context of prior stories about related subject matter. In the course of her discussion about Marmon, as in her discussion of the yard rooster, Silko realized that persons became visible and memorable through oral storytelling and photographic snapshots.

Silko told Wright she assumed that throughout her childhood she had been in the presence of Robert Marmon. In an epiphanic and uncanny moment occurring mid-way through the correspondence, however, she realized a consequential fact about how she knew him:

> The photographs were taken by my father and my grandfather and go back to the 1890s in the Laguna Pueblo area. After I began considering using the photographs [for the *Storyteller* collection] I realized that all I've ever known about my great-grandpa Marmon is the stories I've heard and the old photographs we have of him; and yet I feel as if I was alive when he was, though of course I was not. At least part of this sense of him, I see now, comes from these old photographs.
>
> (Silko and Wright, 1986, p. 62)

Silko's realization that Marmon's presence was doubly mediated through photography and oral stories led her to remember that how she knew Marmon was in line with how she knew other members of her family and community, as well as how she gained access to her sense of place:

> [M]uch of what I "remember" of places and people is actually a memory of the photograph of the place and person, but that I had forgotten the photograph and remembered it as if I had been told about it. There were always many stories that accompanied the evening we spent with the tall Hopi basket full of photographs. We would ask Grandpa or Grandma to identify people we did not recognize, and usually we would get a story of some sort along with the person's name. I suppose that may be why I have remembered these old photographs *not* as visual images but as the words that accompanied them; in one sense, of course, the old snapshots are boring or meaningless if one doesn't have an identity of sorts for the person or places in them ... Strange to think that you heard something—that you *heard* someone describe a place or a scene when in fact you saw a picture of it, saw it with your own eyes.

(p. 65)

Silko's revelation about her epistemic relationship to Marmon and to other close relatives at the Laguna village had profound consequences for the narrative theory she developed in dialogue with Wright. Based on the uncanny recollection of her great-grandfather, her theory also had consequences for how she performed through narrative a type of healing as Wright confronted news of his throat cancer. By locating the class of Wright's temperament with her uncanny synaesthetic experience of Marmon, whom she had forgotten she had always known through the filters of representation, Silko could place Wright into a collective story tradition. She could in effect restate the significance of Wright's dying body within a narrative pattern that perceived no difference between presence and textual manifestation. By restating his mutable form inside a collective account, Wright was said to embody a spirit of feeling that had already been and in fact *had always been* a textual matter.

For Wright and Silko, the use-function of poetry and story had to do with how texts translate voice, body, and the personality of the writer into artifacts. From Silko's point of view, artifactual appearance is the residence of personal identity. Her project in the correspondence, her gift to Wright, was to articulate his visibility within her Laguna (Navajo) tradition of stories—an alternative narrative reality that contains within it the personal experiences of all members of the Laguna people, and maybe somehow all persons, because Silko presents sharing stories as a way of making sense or at least making bearable the inevitable pain and loss of all personal life:

> [T]hrough stories from each other we can feel that we are not alone, that we are not the first and the last to confront losses … At Laguna, whenever something happens (happy or sad or strange), that vast body of remembered stories is brought forth by people who have been listening to the account of this recent incident. Immediately the listeners, in turn, begin telling stories about the other times and other people from the area who have enjoyed or suffered the same luck, and by the time people get done telling you about all the others who have lost wagons and whole teams of horses in the quicksand, you aren't feeling nearly so bad about spending an entire Saturday digging your bay mares out of quicksand. "The word gets around," as they say, and so it all becomes a matter of community knowledge and concern. If something very sad and difficult comes to you, you know that it will take its place with the other stories and that somehow, as a story, it will, from that time on, be remembered and told to others who have suffered losses
>
> (p. 68)

Besides imagining the relationship between personal "presence" and narrative appearance, Silko also imagines the next world in the Laguna tradition. When she talks to Wright about her ancient legend-laden Aunt Susie, the storyteller who is 106 years old, going over to the "Cliff House," the Laguna place of the dead, it is as if Aunt Susie is just traveling to another town down the way, another pueblo, in Arizona or New Mexico. The blurring of the line between the living Laguna Pueblo community and the place of the dead, Cliff House, speaks to a sense of no difference, or a difference that is equivocal, blurred or hazy, between life and death. For Silko, no bright eschatological line exists between life and death. Like Cliff House, narrative space is understood as the residence of persons, not merely the space of restoration for paradigmatic figures as in Shakespeare and Homer. Stories are a place for the residence of all persons in a community. Silko does not view specific storytelling forms, such as the Laguna oral tradition, as sacred. She does, however, conceive of their ultimate use-function, the preservation of the story of the person in community, as residing without alternative in the maintenance of storytelling as an idealist abstraction. She perceives herself as a narrative technician who bridges the experience of more than one interpretive community by devising ways to share stories across cultural boundaries through new media forms.

9

Before and After the Fall: Tribalism, Individualism, and Multicultural Poetics in Sherman Alexie

In *After the Fall*, a study of post-9/11 literature, Richard Gray critiques texts that withdraw "into the domestic and the security fortress of America" (2011, p. 17). Gray applauds writers who "get it right ... thanks to a strategy of convergence, rooted in the conviction that the hybrid is the only space in which the location of cultures and the bearing witness to trauma can really occur" (p. 17). Gray's prescription for a post-9/11 literature that foregrounds dialogism and hybridity is apparent in the later works of Sherman Alexie (b. 1966), the multi-talented poet, fiction writer, filmmaker, stand-up comedian, Poetry Slam performer, and public intellectual. A Spokane/Coeur d'Alene Indian, Alexie grew up on the Spokane Indian Reservation in Wellpinit, WA, about 50 miles northwest of Spokane, WA. What makes Alexie's case peculiar, as well as potentially instructive to our imagining of representation in a post-9/11 environment, is that, prior to the Fall described by Gray, he imagined himself as an anti-white, Native American nationalist who, in "On the Amtrak from Boston to New York City" (1993), "as all Indians have done/since this war began, made plans/for what I could do and say the next time/somebody from the enemy thought I was one of their own." In contrast to the threatening discourse from the 1993 poem, Alexie, in a *Time* magazine essay on Sacagawea from 2002, in his National Book Award winning, semi-autobiographical novel *The Absolutely True Diary of a Part-Time Indian* (2007), in his visionary historical novel, *Flight* (2007), and in *Face*, a book of poems published in 2009, self-consciously re-imagines his relationship to American culture in a post-9/11 context in which, in Gray's terms, "Americans find themselves living in an interstitial space, a locus of interaction between contending national and cultural constituencies" (2011, p. 18).

In the post-9/11 texts, Alexie comes to regard the binary thinking about issues of ethnicity, history, and citizenship that animated "On the Amtrak" as constitutive elements of the mindset that prompted the 9/11 attacks. In "On the Amtrak," Alexie partici-pates in a terrorist's imagination of the United States as an Evil Empire responsible for the suppression of native experience. He also regards himself as a humanistic individualist, found via multi-culturalism rather than strictly through the European tradition. In the later works, Alexie revises his understanding of the authorial self by taking into account how identity is created in dialogue with other lives, including white folk whose perspective he dismissed in "On the Amtrak." Overall, Alexie takes an individualist journey of self-creation that accounts for, but is not superseded by, a multi-plicity of more fixed, nationalist identities.

"On the Amtrak from Boston to New York City"

Contra the once New Criticism, literary theorist William Waters argues that post-Romantic lyric poetry may be considered less a "monologic genre" than one that highlights the "ways a poem resembles ordinary communication" (2003, p. 3). Alexie's "On the Amtrak" (1993)—from *The First Indian on the Moon*—is, at first glance, one of these poems. "On the Amtrak" sets up a dialogic situation between the authorial persona and "the white woman" who sits across from him on a passenger car. In the poem, however, Alexie's persona turns inward. Withdrawing from Waters's "ordinary communication," he enters the Romantic lyric mode even as his blatant politics differs from what we ordinarily conceive of as the Romantic persona. Alexie enters the Romantic lyric mode in the sense J. S. Mill theorized: his mode represents "feeling confessing itself to itself, in moments of solitude" (quoted in Waters, 2003, p. 4).

In Waters's terms, Alexie's poem belongs to a set of lyrics in which the speakers "can withdraw so decisively from their addressees that they exclude them from hearing the poem at all" (p. 38).[1] Alexie refuses to imagine poetry as a forum for summoning another person from a different subject position into what Mary Louise Pratt referred to as a "contact zone," defined as a "social space ... where cultures meet, clash, and grapple with each other, often in contexts of highly asymmetrical relations of power, such as colonialism, slavery, or their aftermaths as they are lived out in many parts of the world today" (1992). Rather, Alexie's persona asserts his acute dissimilarity from the woman on the train from Boston to New York. Dissociating himself from citizenship in a nation that he interprets as populated by "enemies" in an undeclared civil war, Alexie's persona speaks in what T. S. Eliot in "The Three Voices of Poetry" called lyric's "'meditative' mode ... the voice of the poet talking to himself or to nobody" (quoted in Waters, 2003, p. 18). He recoils from what Eliot called the "second voice" of poetry, "or the poet speaking to other people," which regards poetic discourse as a form of communication. Ironically, Alexie represents the white woman as a willing interlocutor. She calls him to "look" at the historically-inflected landscape outside the train's window frame, but Alexie's persona, rigid and judgmental, refuses to answer. Avoiding the "contact zone," he turns away from a scene of instruction with her about history, time, citizenship, and place as each travels from the center of intellectual to financial power on the Northeast seaboard on the ironically-titled Amtrak—only provisionally America's train (2003, p. 18).

---

[1] Waters locates:

> A small subgenre of modern poetry centers on this paradoxical thwarting of the communicative gesture. Often the marked refusal or retraction of effective address only sharpens, in such works, the palpability of the "other" with whom the poem shows itself preoccupied, as if negation and absence generated a peculiarly potent virtual presence.

> (2003, p. 38)

A liminal figure from his teenage years, Alexie was raised on a reservation outside of Spokane, Washington, but he was educated at an otherwise exclusively white, German-American sponsored high school, Reardan, outside the reservation, the subject of his National Book Award winning quasi-autobiographical novel, *The Absolutely True Diary of a Part-Time Indian* (2007). After Reardan, Alexie attended the Jesuit college Gonzaga, and later Washington State University, where he was encouraged to pursue creative writing. In the poem, Alexie sets his persona as an outsider in a liminal area between two iconic East Coast American cities. "Boston" commonly signifies American Exceptionalism in terms of religious and political independence from Imperial control. It is the quasi-biblical "City shining on a hill" John Winthrop speaks of in his sermon from 1630. One senses this is in fact how "the white woman" interprets "Boston" and nearby Walden Pond. Considered by some as the "cradle of the Revolution," New England does not, from Alexie's point of view, represent the original site of "freedom," "independence," and "liberty for all" from English imperial dominion. Instead, "Boston" signifies the inauguration of his people's displacement from native ground by a *New* English Empire. "New York City"—like New England, a signifier of white European control over Indian territory—now represents, not the archetypal site of immigrant possibility, but America's economic, cultural, and architectural preeminence in the twentieth-century. Alexie's persona refuses to discuss American history with the white woman, but he experiences contemporary America as the direct opposite of what it means to her. Blurring present and past in a manner that post-Freudian theorists such as Cathy Caruth and Dominick LaCapra would read as signifiers of a traumatic discourse, he travels on a means of transportation—the train—associated not with late twentieth-century America, but with westward expansion and manifest destiny. "Amtrak," of course, literally refers to the federal passenger rail system, founded in 1971, but in the poem symbolizes America's dominance of the continental United States from East to West, the path connected by rail in Utah in 1869.

In her landmark study *Resistance Literature* (1987), Barbara Harlow has explained that resistance poems, "actively engage in the historical process of struggle against the cultural oppression of imperialism" (quoted in DeShazer, 1994, p. 1). "Poetry," Harlow continues, "as part of the cultural institutions and historical existence of a people, is itself an arena of struggle" (DeShazer, 1994, p. 9). Alexie's poem is certainly resistant to the "white woman's" call to respond to her interpretation of American history. His disingenuous assertion that politeness is a sign of respect for her is another example of his resistance towards imagining her as more than a ventriloquist rehearsing a legacy of imperial oppression. But Harlow and fellow scholar Mary K. DeShazer in *A Poetics of Resistance* also emphasize that resistant poetry should foster "a commitment to dialogue as a tool for exploring differences, and an ethic of empathy" (1994, p. 10). This Alexie does not do. By shifting from Eliot's "second voice" of poetry, "or the poet speaking to other people," to the "'meditative' mode ... the voice of the poet talking to himself or to nobody," he fails to combine the "blend of caring and confrontation" that DeShazer defines as key elements of resistant poetry (1994, p. 10). His final response to the "white woman" in "On the Amtrak" is woefully inadequate because it resists a figure of the oppressor, but does not resist the violence spawned by oppression. By its concluding stanzas, "On the Amtrak" "advocates revolutionary change." Because Alexie's persona fails to transmit history to "the white woman," a figure for the poem's primary intended audience, however, the poem fails to perform a central task of resistance poetry, although it might do so to those reading it in showing the submerged anger of Native Americans (DeShazer, 1994, p. 13).

In "On the Amtrak," Alexie's persona becomes a metonym for the return of an erased part of American history. Symbolically, he carries the traumatic aspects of Native American attitudes, values, and beliefs from West to East. The speaker then travels from North to South—Boston to New York—to protest though silence the woman's interpretation of the meaning of place. Poet and activist Carolyn Forché, editor of *Against Forgetting: Twentieth-Century Poetry of Witness* (1993), asserted that, "vision is always ideologically charged; perceptions are shaped a priori by our assumptions and sensibility formed by consciousness at once social, historical, and esthetic" (Forché, quoted in DeShazer, 1994, p. 16). Alexie brings Forché's insight into his reading of the relation between private perception and public witness in "On the Amtrak." He interprets the woman's way of seeing the landscape as an "ideologically charged" account of a nation's foundation. Alexie imagines the train windows as a moving picture plane. The windows frame the geography of the Northeast corridor, but more pointedly,

Alexie suggests the viewer's subject position frames how history is inscribed into the landscape. Midway through the poem, Alexie's persona allows readers to overhear what "I could have told her" about American history (line 18). Nowhere in the poem, however, does he share his perspective with the woman, even as the author shares his suppressed rage with us in the lyric.

In an interview from 2000, Jessica Chapel asked Alexie if he thinks "white Americans have a different sense of history—both of events, and the significance of those events in contemporary culture—than American Indians?" (Peterson, 2009, p. 99):

> White Americans have a short memory. This country really hasn't entered puberty yet—white Americans' political thoughts are really young, and the culture is really young. The one general statement you can make about America is it's young, and wildly immature, and incredibly talented. Like some twelve-year-old kid who really pisses you off, because he's really good at everything and he knows it.
>
> (Peterson, 2009, p. 99)

In the interview, Alexie goes on to state that he believes "in fighting conservatism." He sees the United States as "getting better and better" in terms of social progress for women, blacks, and native persons. In "On the Amtrak," by contrast, Alexie's persona does not contest the white woman's "short memory" displayed by her comments on place, history, and Native American/European relations. We may read Alexie's interview as the first part of a dialogic, which he continues in his later work.

In the surreal poem "Evolution," Alexie describes how a character named Buffalo Bill "paints a new sign over the old" one for a pawn shop in which he exploited alcoholic native peoples "on the reservation." He "calls his venture THE MUSEUM OF NATIVE AMERICAN CULTURES/charges the Indians five bucks a head to enter" to see the actual body parts the Indians have pawned. As in "Evolution," Alexie in "On the Amtrak" critiques museum culture—figured in the image of Walden Pond—as contributing to Indian dispossession. He notes the woman's gushing excitement upon seeing a New England house as if it were a museum signifying colonial American history:

"Look,
look at all the history, that house
on the hill there is over two hundred years old,"
as she points out the window past me

into what she has been taught.

Alexie perceives her excitement as a sign of her ignorance that the
land upon which that house was built had been the site of "tribal
stories/whose architecture is 15,000 years older/than the corners of
the house that sits/museumed on the hill." In "On the Amtrak,"
museums, mocked in "Evolution," authorize an official version of
American history at the expense of the erasure of Indian narratives,
the "tribal stories" that Alexie states are "15,000 years older" than
the colonial house on the hill. Museums, like history textbooks, are
for Alexie merely the ideological wing of state control.

It is not difficult to imagine Alexie's persona reciting the phrase
"what she has been taught" in a cynical tone that reflects his
disdain for how American history is taught in public schools.[2]

---

[2]In the much-anthologized short story, "The Lone Ranger and Tonto Fistfight in
Heaven," (1993) Alexie's main character—as in "On the Amtrak," a figure for the
author—struggles with how white people stereotype him with little more to go on
than hackneyed images from radio and television programs. Alexie proposes that
images in a postmodern media culture have saturated his urbane white girlfriend's
mind so that she cannot separate his identity from representations of Indians in
popular culture. In another scene, a police officer stops Alexie's persona after he
drives into an affluent white neighborhood:

"Well, you should be more careful where you drive," the officer said. "You're
making people nervous. You don't fit the profile of the neighborhood."
I wanted to tell him that I didn't really fit the profile of the country, but I knew
it would just get me into trouble.

I empathize with the character's decision to avoid "trouble" by refraining from
mocking the officer. But, as we will see, Alexie's persona in "On the Amtrak" has the
same impulse to speak back to someone he perceives to be a representative of white
power, but refrains. Alexie's inability to recognize the difference between chiding a
police officer in "Tonto and the Lone Ranger" and discussing history with a white
woman in "On the Amtrak," speaks to his inability to appreciate differences among
potential white interlocutors. He is lumping, rather than splitting, white persons
into pre-arranged categories.

In a 1993 interview, Alexie was asked about the "sketchy at best" nature of his representations of white characters. In typical tongue-in-cheek fashion, Alexie considers whether stereotyping makes him "uncomfortable":

> No, I have fun making them sketchy. Because Indians have been sketchy for a long time. I enjoy playing with them as one-dimensional characters. That's on purpose. They're flat cardboard cut-outs, the kind you get your photograph taken with at Disneyland [*Laughter.*] The whole idea gets my mind working. It'll probably even end up in a story now. White people cut-outs at the trading post:
> "Come get your photo taken with a white person. Only a dollar fifty!"
>
> (1993, p. 11)

In the poem, his designation of "the white woman," with its use of the definite article, implies that he sees a type, not an individual. Deciding against challenging her enthusiastic response to the colonial architecture, he asserts, "I respect elders/of every color." By this late stage of the poem, however, he is grafting old resentments onto current conditions even as he denies his contempt for her under the guise of politeness.

Alexie's persona holds strong views about history, place, nation, and education, but he refrains from sharing them with the woman in a poem, ironically, partly about a socially enforced silence that the poem intends to break. He tells us, rather disingenuously, "I don't have a cruel enough heart to break/her own." From what we learn in the poem, should he consider her to be too emotionally fragile to learn from him? No. I say this because she demonstrates open-mindedness, fascination with history and education, and willingness to take risks, as her decision to travel alone to New York City suggests. She might enjoy widening her temporal and historical perspective to include the "15,000 years" of "tribal stories" that Alexie states existed in the area now known as Walden Pond. I say this because it is unusual for one passenger to shout to another "across the aisle" to engage him in an act of historical appreciation: "'Look,/look at all the history, that house/on the hill there is over two hundred years old." His comment that what she sees reflects, "what she has been taught," implies he does not believe she can interpret what she sees for herself. He interprets the woman's gesture of "pointing out the window past me" as a literalization of the historical erasures of Native Americans. Instead of viewing the woman as a life-long learner open to his narrative, he treats her as a feeble-minded grandmother who could not handle his criticism of her point of view and whose perspective contributes to the historical erasure he laments. "I didn't say a word to the woman about Walden/Pond because she smiled so much and seemed delighted/that I thought to bring her an orange juice back from the food car. I respect elders/of every color." Interpreting subject positions as fixed, Alexie's persona suppresses his anger, taking comfort in depriving himself of a companion. He perceives himself as an intellectual terrorist, an alien revolutionary who could never feel at home in America's commodified postmodern society:

All I really did was eat
my tasteless sandwich, drink my Diet Pepsi
and nod my head whenever the woman pointed out

another little piece of her country's history
while I, as all Indians have done
since this war began, made plans
for what I could do and say the next time

somebody from the enemy thought I was one of their own.

Alexie's persona quite literally sublimates his rage by stuffing his mouth with commodities. The prepackaged sandwich and diet soda signify his displacement from traditional Indian folkways such as the Fry Bread and hand-woven blankets that Alexie often discusses in his work. His cursory acceptance of Amtrak's food, drink, and the woman's interpretation of history speak to Alexie's opinion that his character's identity is split. On the one hand, he displays a public self that is cordial and integrated as he travels, eats, and smiles on America's train. On the other hand, his persona is not an engaged citizen in a multicultural environment, but rather a resident alien who believes his resentments at past misdeeds entitle him to imagine himself as a victim with a license to dismiss the perspectives of others, however limited these perspectives may be. Acting out, rather than working through trauma, he is a proto-terrorist engaged in a practice of cordiality that will enable him to go under cover to gain more evidence of white America's ideological blindness to a native person's point of view. Alexie's persona sees himself at "war," the woman is "an enemy," and the United States as not his nation.

Alexie critiques how the woman has been taught, but his own version of American history deliberately rejects how individuals may resist hegemony through counter-cultural behaviors. Critiquing Henry David Thoreau and Don Henley, the California pop star who devoted himself to preserving Walden Pond, Alexie deliberately picks on well-known, even radical, targets to show that even they participate in the crossing out of native history. Lumping all white Americans together as "an enemy," Alexie's persona fails to distinguish between constructive versus destructive personages, places, and events in the ambivalent story of American racial and ethnic relations. I can empathize with Alexie's lyric rant when I regard it as a traumatic discourse that registers his resentment at the historical mistreatment of Native American peoples. But I resist his disregard of attempts by persons ranging from "the white woman" to "Walden" (Thoreau) to the pop musician and ecological activist he refers to as "Don-fucking-Henley" to learn from native cultures and to protest America's misdeeds. It is difficult for me to read Thoreau as merely another "enemy" bent on deleting the ancient narratives of native peoples. Everything about the Alexie persona's view of Thoreau and his experiment in simple living at Walden Pond in the 1840s lacks subtlety and sound judgment. One could argue that he, unlike Alexie, had the ability to choose to be an outcast—as did the beatniks and hippies—but Thoreau has much in common with the contemporary Native American author. Both identify themselves as marginalized figures who nonetheless remained connected to mainstream American culture. Although himself an urban Indian, Alexie, in poems such as "Reservation Love Song," imagines prior generations of native peoples as connected to the land in a spiritually meaningful way that has been compromised by the interference of an alphabet soup of government programs and commodity culture. Thoreau, too, wished to isolate himself from village life in Concord because he considered industrialism and modernism obstacles to his communion with nature. In his words,

I went to the woods because I wished to live deliberately, to front only the essential facts of life, and see if I could not learn what it had to teach, and not, when I came to die, discover that I had not lived.

Alexie declares his independence from America—his persona says he is not a citizen. So too did Thoreau face arrest for refusing to pay federal taxes to protest the government's relation to the slave trade. Famously lauding those who beat to their own drummer, Thoreau was anti-business, anti-consumerist, on the side of nature and animals. He was no fan of the very railroad tracks upon which Alexie travels in "On the Amtrak." Thoreau's essay "Civil Disobedience" became a seminal text for non-violent protest on behalf of major twentieth-century progressive social movements set forth by Gandhi in India and in the American South by Dr. Martin Luther King.

While Alexie's purposeful tactic is to confront white liberals, only the most cynical observer could view Thoreau's experiment in his tiny cabin outside Concord as promoting a white hegemony that contributed to the destruction of native peoples. I suppose it is possible to feel that contemporary white members of the ecocritical community who spend their time, money, and cultural capital fighting for the preservation of natural lands against commercial development are in it for self-aggrandizement. The Alexie persona's curse-filled rant against Don Henley's efforts, beginning in 1990, to translate his fame as a member of the California soft rock group, The Eagles, into a movement to protect Walden Pond from development, however, merely repeats the speaker's refusal to distinguish whites who resisted hegemony from those who committed atrocities against native peoples.

"What Sacagawea Means to Me (and Perhaps to You)" and *The Absolutely True Diary of a Part-Time Indian*

Alexie published "On the Amtrak" early in his career. It appeared in his second book of poems, in 1993, when still in his twenties. One may read the poem as testimony from an angry young man whose outrage over past atrocities leads him into absolutist reasoning. The poem is a statement of his wish to resist assimilation when his identity is threatened by confrontation with other Americans in the unfamiliar environment of an Amtrak train traveling on the East Coast thousands of miles away from his tribe in Spokane. We do not associate youthful thinking with the gray zone of ambivalence and contradiction. Alexie's speaker remains distant from a greater understanding of the white woman in 1993. By contrast, Alexie moves toward a complex vision of white/native relations in an essay commemorating Sacagawea published in *Time* magazine in 2002.

The twenty-something version of Alexie as Angry Young Man refused to discuss history with the white woman in "On the Amtrak." In his mid-thirties, Alexie begrudgingly acknowledges the contradictory, messy, and multiculturally interactive quality of key elements of American history in his essay on Sacagawea. His focus, ironically enough, concerns the quintessential journey associated with expansionism that confined native peoples to reservations—the expedition of Lewis and Clark (1804–6). Alexie begins his *Time* essay in flippant tones that suggest his thesis will argue American history has been transformed into a postmodern commodity that masks Indian trauma. In Warholian fashion, he imagines Sacagawea as an icon at a theme park whom "every U.S. citizen will get to be ... for 15 minutes." In the second paragraph he flirts with the belief that Sacagawea's death by a "mysterious illness" in her early twenties might have been a colonial "murder."

> I suspect that Sacagawea's indigenous immune system was defenseless against an immigrant virus. Perhaps Lewis and Clark infected Sacagawea. If true, then certain postcolonial historians would argue that she was murdered not by germs but by colonists who carried those germs.

At first, the *Time* essay rehearses the thesis that Lewis and Clark could be accused of genocidal terrorism through germ warfare, but the essay shifts to confront the history of Sacagawea's affiliation with Lewis and Clark. Contra his claims in "On the Amtrak" that "all Indians" have been at "war" with the "enemy"—the United States and, more broadly, European colonialism—Alexie acknowledges that Sacagawea assisted Lewis and Clark as if she were their diplomat. Alexie revises his desire to ignore Sacagawea's quite literal acceptance of being "in the same boat" with a multicultural and dual-gender mélange of persons who cooperated with Lewis and Clark's government-funded expedition of the territory Jefferson has recently acquired from France. In Whitman fashion, Alexie acknowledges the "contradictions" within an American multicultural environment that is at once inclusive and supremacist.

> As a Native American, I want to hate this country and its contradictions. I want to believe that Sacagawea hated this country and its contradictions. But this country exists, in whole and in part, because Sacagawea helped Lewis and Clark. In the land that came to be called Idaho, she acted as diplomat between her long-lost brother and the Lewis and Clark party. Why wouldn't she ask her brother and her tribe to take revenge against the men who had enslaved her? Sacagawea is a contradiction. Here in Seattle, I exist, in whole and in part, because a half-white man named James Cox fell in love with a Spokane Indian woman named Etta Adams and gave birth to my mother. I am a contradiction; I am Sacagawea.

If Alexie had distanced himself "across the aisle" from the woman on America's train, in the *Time* essay, he discloses his own multi-ethnic family background. In an extraordinary act of imaginative empathy that is baffling in its generosity towards key figures in U.S. conquest of native lands, Alexie goes on "to wonder if colonization might somehow be magical"! Replacing the us-versus-them thinking that characterized "On the Amtrak," Alexie considers the Lewis and Clark expedition as a multicultural parade involving "approximately 45 nameless and faceless first- and second-generation European Americans who joined the journey." Ironically overstating his point here to dramatize the irony—and perhaps to make fun of the extremism of his earlier position, Lewis and Clark no longer only represent the leaders of a journey that enabled the United States to map, and, in time, to dominate the Pacific Northwest. They also led an expedition that was diverse and inclusive:

> The Lewis and Clark Expedition was exactly the kind of multicultural, trigenerational, bigendered, animal-friendly,

government-supported, partly French-Canadian project that should rightly be celebrated by liberals and castigated by conservatives.

In a 2007 interview with Tanita Davis and Sarah Stevenson, we notice how Alexie is moving toward an inextricably multicultural America in which all our destinies are one. In the interview, Alexie discusses his recently published young adult novel *The Absolutely True Diary of a Part-Time Indian*. In it, the main character, Arnold Spirit, in Alexie's terms, "is struggling to reconcile two identities (rez Indian and off-rez Indian)" (2007a p. 188). As with Alexie, who grew up between the "rez" and the all-white Reardan school, Spirit discovers that he "belongs to more than one tribe" (p. 190). Asked about Spirit's "transition between 'worlds'" (p. 190), Alexie, with winning humor, aligns the dangers of binary thinking, which animated "On the Amtrak," with the fundamentalism that led to 9/11:

> For many years, I've said that my two strongest tribal affilia-
> tions are not racially based. My strongest tribes are book nerds
> and basketball players, and those tribes are racially, culturally,
> economically, and spiritually diverse. And, like Arnold, I also
> belong to a hundred other tribes, based on the things I love to
> read, watch, do. Ever since 9/11, I have worked hard to be very
> public about my multi-racial identity. I think fundamentalism is
> the mistaken belief that one belongs to only one tribe; I am the
> opposite of that.
>
> (interview, 2007, p. 190)

Alexie, in effect, associates his refusal in "On the Amtrak" to accept his participation in many "tribes" as a cause for terrorism in a "war" against an "enemy" with the ideology that produced the 9/11 attacks in New York City. Paradoxically, this is the very city—and very multicultural city—to which the Alexie persona and the white woman are traveling in "On the Amtrak."

Imaginatively returning to his 16-year-old persona as the only Wellpinit Indian at Reardan, located in a small farming town outside the Spokane Reservation, Alexie represents Arnold Spirit in *The Absolutely True Diary of a Part-Time Indian* learning from white teachers and students. Spirit rages at the outdated textbooks used in the rez school by throwing one of them at a white teacher, Mr. P. Spirit is suspended from the rez school, but Alexie represents Mr. P., who lives in a trailer on the reservation, as a sympathetic character. Instead of condemning Spirit for injuring his nose with the book, Mr. P. appears at Sprit's home to call him, "a bright and shining star" (2007a, p. 40), explaining "I don't want you to fail. I don't want you to fade away" (p. 40). He tells Spirit that when he started teaching, "We were trying to kill Indian culture" (p. 35) by demanding Indian students embrace a Eurocentric perspective that dismissed the value of "Your songs and stories and language and dancing" (p. 35).

> You were right to throw that book at me. I deserved to get smashed in the face for what I've done to Indians. Every white person on this rez should get smashed in the face. But let me tell you this. All the Indians should get smashed in the face, too.
>
> (p. 42)

His final comment that "Indians should get smashed in the face" signals his belief that pain is necessary to awaken people to their situation. He interprets Spirit's act of throwing the book at him as a positive development because the young man has not suppressed his rage: "somewhere inside you refuse to give up" (p. 43). Rage is dangerous, as it leads to events like 9/11, but Mr. P. emphasizes the therapeutic side to fury—it's necessary to acknowledge and it acts to motivate. Formerly misguided, he repents, encouraging Spirit not to "fight us forever," but rather to find "hope" outside the reservation. Taking responsibility for the defeat and hopelessness that characterize the emotional life of many rez folk, Mr. P. encourages Spirit to leave. One may contrast this emotional portrait of Mr. P. as a symbolic father to Spirit, who decides to transfer to Reardan in the following chapter, with Alexie's dismissal of white activists such as Thoreau and Henley in "On the Amtrak."

At first physically bullied and the victim of racist slurs at Reardan, Spirit finds a learning companion in Gordy, whom Spirit refers to as the smartest person he has ever met. Alexie's persona had refused to discuss history with "the white woman," but Spirit learns to confront his past via a white mentor by learning to read books as historical documents from Gordy. "The second time you read a book, you read it for its history. For its knowledge of history. You think about the meaning of each word, and where that word came from" (p. 95), Gordy tells Spirit, who now affiliates along lines other than race or ethnicity. Moving his identity away from tribal affiliation and towards a humanistic individualism, Spirit partners with Gordy as a fellow "freak" intellectual who gets "boners" when reading books. Gordy's interpretation of his captivation with Reardan's small library as a sign that, "even the smallest parts of it, is filled with things you don't know" (p. 97), leads Spirit to acknowledge the mysterious significance of Wellpinit. "Any town, even one as small as Reardan, was a place of mystery. And that meant that Wellpinit, that smaller, Indian town, was also a place of mystery" (p. 97). "Traveling between Reardan and Wellpinit, between the little white town and the reservation, I always felt like a stranger," Spirit writes. Alexie's persona took a literal train journey between Boston and New York, but he did not draw closer to the white woman. He also did not come to terms with his identity as a cosmopolitan, hyphenated American who lives and works on two coasts, and who was educated at Indian and white schools. By contrast, Arnold Spirit acknowledges that his self-definition as an angry, dispossessed Indian—embodied in the rez buddy Rowdy and Alexie's persona in "On the Amtrak"—requires *less* courage, and is *less* challenging to one's sense of identity, than living in between the rez and Reardan. "I felt like somebody had shoved me into a rocket ship and blasted me to a new planet. I was a freaky alien and there was absolutely no way to get home" (p. 66).

Spirit's identity confusion and complex tribal affiliations come to a head in the final showdown basketball game between Spirit and the Reardan team and Rowdy and the Wellpinit team. Spirit plays the game of his life, rising to block Rowdy's shots, and then faking his former best friend to hit a three-pointer that crushes Wellpinit's will. At first, Spirit identifies himself with Reardan, and sees himself as a David representing an oppressed minority population: "We had defeated the enemy! We had defeated the champions! We were David who'd thrown a stone into the brain of Goliath!" (p. 195). David, biblical representative of the underdog, now represents the whites who had oppressed the natives. By this late point in the novel, Spirit's sense of identity and communal affiliation is complex and his response to victory ambivalent.

Realizing the privileges Reardan players enjoy, he feels shame at his celebration of a white team's victory at the rez.

At the conclusion to The *Absolutely True Diary of a Part-Time Indian,* Spirit strives to embrace the qualities of care, love, community, weirdness, and mourning that he takes to be the enduring legacy of his experience as a Native American that otherwise appears to him to be a dead end of alcoholism, depression, and early death. At the same time, he stretches the notion of "tribal" affiliation by engaging with what Benedict Anderson (2006) called a series of "imagined communities" that re-imagines the definition of "the tribe" to include aspects of Spirit's subject position that expand beyond his Indian heritage in a way that places his situation as an exile from the rez in the context of the Ellis Island immigrant narrative whose story involves a process of becoming a hyphenated American: "I realized that, sure, I was a Spokane Indian. I belonged to that tribe. But I also belonged to the tribe of American immigrants. And to the tribe of basketball players. And to the tribe of bookworms" (2007a, p. 217). The list expands to include over ten other "tribal" affiliations ranging from sexual practices, to fast food preferences, to familial relations.

Alexie's evolving relationship to American history is nowhere more apparent than in the final chapter of The *Absolutely True Diary,* "Talking about Turtles." We recall that the speaker's anger with the white woman in "On the Amtrak" stemmed from her myopic view of American history, and especially her sense that an 18th- or 19th-Century house on a hill near Boston was historically momentous. Comparing a pine tree on the Rez that he and newly reacquainted friend Rowdy climb, Arnold sees the beauty of the reservation and realizes its venerable qualities:

Older than the United States.
Some of them were alive when Abraham Lincoln was president.
Some of them were alive when George Washington was president.
... Some of them were alive when Benjamin Franklin was born.
I'm talking old.

(2007a, p. 220)

Like the *Time* essay, such a passage from *The Absolutely True Diary of a Part-Time Indian,* which frames a very old pine tree on the "rez" in terms of iconic U.S. statesmen, reads as if it were a post-9/11 rebuttal of Alexie's rejection of the "contact zone" in "On the Amtrak."

Flight

In the post-9/11 prose works I am treating in this chapter, Alexie positions himself as an American public intellectual, citizen, educator, and peace advocate who blurs lines defined in an identity politics model of selfhood. No longer donning the mantle of Angry Young Man evident in "On the Amtrak," Alexie now represents his liminal figure—the pockmarked Zits—as a shape-shifting, time-traveling, participatory witness to history who makes amends and seeks forgiveness. His dreamlike journey becomes a study in the narrator's—and, by extension, Alexie's—process of maturation. He challenges the relationship between violence, revenge, and citizenship.

In *Flight* (2007b), Alexie desublimates lingering anger that produces resentments. Implicitly critiquing, and distancing himself from, the reasoning that motivated the Native American speaker to dismiss a meaningful exchange about history, citizenship, and place with "the white woman" in "On the Amtrak," Alexie in *Flight* imagines his main character, "Zits"/Michael, as an orphaned juvenile delinquent from the Seattle area whose late mother was Irish and whose unavailable father was Indian. His ethnicity and subject position resist easy attempts at categorization via tribal affiliation:

> Yes, I am Irish and Indian, which would be the coolest blend in the world if my parents were around to teach me how to be Irish and Indian. But they're not here and haven't been for years, so I'm not really Irish *or* Indian. I'm a blank sky, a human solar eclipse.

> (2007b, p. 5)

By figuring himself as "a blank sky" Zits thinks of himself as open to the possibility of self-creation and transcendence—although it could also explain his early anger and potential for violence as he struggles to create a self.

In the first three chapters of *Flight*, Zits's antipathies towards white America resemble the speaker's views in "On the Amtrak." He is a dispossessed, shamed, physically disfigured (through acne, itself a sign of liminal transformation between boyhood and manhood), and often abused teen. Unlike the speaker in "On the Amtrak," however, Zits lacks a secure understanding of his identity in relation to other persons. Where insecurity led Alexie's speaker in "On the Amtrak" to dig in to his position as quintessential outsider and so to accentuate his differences from "the white woman," Zits's unstable self and mixed ethnic heritage, ironically, enable him in the novel's lengthy middle section (Chapters 4–18) to embody a compassionate perspective on U.S./Native American relationships. He imaginatively enters into the lives of persons, both white and Native American, across a wide swath of time and place. Reenacting nineteenth- and twentieth-century scenes of U.S./ Native American conflicts in all their brutality, and, on occasion, in their small-scale acts of caring for persons hailing from other national/tribal groups. Zits realizes that his bitterness has imperiled his survival. Deconstructing the hard-line view of Native American persons as always already victims and American whites as always already victimizers that motivated "On the Amtrak," Zits is repulsed by the immorality of violence in the name of upholding *or* challenging U.S. hegemony.

Zits will grow in stature and confidence by the end of the novel, when he is adopted by a caring, but firm, white foster parent couple named Mary and Robert. In the first three chapters, however, he appears as a shame-filled 15-year-old juvenile delinquent from Seattle whose anti-social behaviors culminate in an ill-fated attempt at an armed bank robbery. In a series of interlocking, dreamlike sequences that occupy Chapters 4–18 (of the 21-chapter novel), Zits experiences time travels that enable him to embody the subject positions of both white and Native American characters involved in mythic nineteenth-, twentieth-, and twenty-first-century events involving violent conflicts between U.S. officials and Native American persons.

In the visionary middle section of the novel, Zits embodies representatives of the U.S. government such as Hank Storm, a 1970s-era Federal Agent involved with murdering rebellious native persons in Idaho. He envisions Native American warriors involved with the June 1876 destruction of General Custer and the U.S. Seventh Cavalry at Little Big Horn. Zits thus pivots between spatial and temporal frames, and between telemediated histories and, through his imagination, direct witnessing and participation in events cast as vivid dreamscapes. Following the post-Freudian work of trauma theorist Dominick LaCapra, I would argue that through his time travels Zits acts out and eventually works through the personal resentments and political traumas that culminated in his ill-fated decision to carry out the white juvenile delinquent Justice's plans to commit an armed robbery on a Seattle bank.

Just as Zits's identity is inchoate, the situation of Alexie's storyteller in *Flight* is hybridic in relation to tribal, national, and individuated understandings of the narrative self. Zits's position as narrator differs from "On the Amtrak," but it is also unlike the position of the tribal storyteller venerated in Leslie Marmon Silko's *Storyteller*, for example, as knowing elder. *Flight* yokes together what critics have regarded as "Western" (White European) and "Native American" writings. The novel's "circular patterns of place and time" may be considered an homage to the "ceremonial legacies from which Alexie and other Native American writers draw" (Carroll, 2005, p. 74). Alexie's emphasis on an individual journey to self-knowledge through Zits's story, however, may be viewed as an aspect of Alexie's "westernized" approach to storytelling.

In a juvenile delinquent "kid jail" in Seattle, Zits in Chapter 2 meets Justice, a smart, bookish "white kid" who offers him "real kindness" and "care" (2007b, p. 21), including information on treatment for his disabling skin condition, and lectures on empowerment. A critic of organized religion and of U.S. genocide against native persons, the "white kid" is represented as a preacher who teaches Zits about the shameful history of U.S. treatment of native persons, including statements by Teddy Roosevelt who thought "the only good Indians are dead Indians" (p. 25). The young white preacher is an intellectual, but also a revolutionary activist: "The true revolutionary must set himself aflame" (p. 25). Zits dreams "about hurting people. About killing them" and about how he likes to "tear those black guys apart. I kill them and go cannibal" (p. 26). Justice is sympathetic to Zits, but a harmful character. He preaches revolutionary violence and dehumanization.

With the allegorical figure of "justice" as mentor, Zits transforms himself into an outlaw, terrorist, and sniper. He does so, ironically, to satisfy the aggressive nature of a white American. Zits says he feels "powerful" when "a big old white guy faints when I point a gun at him" (p. 33) during the botched bank heist that precedes the middle section of *Flight* in which Zits becomes a time-traveling participant witness in several centuries of Native American/U.S. conflict. Becoming a terrorist, Zits believes he "finally deserve[s]" Justice's "love" (p. 34). Engaging in terrorism, he enacts a contemporary version of a "ghost dance" ritual that will enable "my mother and father [to] return" (p. 35). But Chapter 3 ends with an illustration of Alexie's thesis that violent, terroristic actions are an inadequate response, even to true injustice: Zits spread out on the bank floor shot by a guard, a pawn in Justice's juvenile rebellion. Chapter 4 inaugurates the novel's shift from a contemporary realist mode into a surrealist time travel narrative. Insecure from the start, Zits's identity becomes radically destabilized, and also expanded in a manner Bakhtin would recognize as heteroglossic. Like Whitman, who boasted he could contain multitudes, Zits embodies the subject position of various white and native characters involved in the centuries-long conflict between Native Americans and U.S. persons.[3]

No longer a novice bank robber and angst-filled terrorist, Zits enters a twilight zone in which he incarnates, but cannot fully control, the actions of white and native personages. In Chapter 4,

---

[3] Justice inaugurates Zits's actions as a would-be terrorist keen on robbing a bank and shooting patrons, including a child. Through his rendering of the botched bank robbery that was masterminded by the white Justice, and in which Zits is wounded, Alexie defamiliarizes and critiques the television image of the Lone Ranger and Tonto. In *Flight*, Zits (Tonto) is drawn in to Justice's (the Lone Ranger's) plan for retributive violence, but Alexie's story rejects the association of Justice with violence and thus resists the telemediated image. Tribal identity (and, implicitly, Bush's War on Terror through regenerative violence) in the post-9/11 environment are also disrupted, and viewed as a form of antagonism to the U.S. polity that was threatened in 9/11. As opposed to the "fistfight" to overturn the Tonto stereotype that Alexie alluded to in the title of one of his most famous short stories, Flight replaces Fight. In this quintessential post-9/11 text, Alexie thus advocates a non-violent strategy of resistance that places faith in the therapeutic value of storytelling and that rejects what American Studies scholar Richard Slotkin termed "regeneration through violence."

for example, he personifies a 35-year-old white, muscular, and well-endowed FBI agent named Hank Storm, who hates Indians. As Storm, Zits finds himself in a motel on an Indian reservation in Idaho. It is 1975, and Storm and his partner Art have come to meet Horse and Elk, superficially anti-government activists who are double agents, "traitors to Iron," the radical Indian movement. As with his comments about Crazy Horse, an Indian who killed Indians, Zits's revisionary historical image of 1970s activists presents an ambivalent characterization of native persons as rebellious and cooperative with Federal agents. Elk and Horse produce from their trunk a gagged activist named Junior, tortured by the double agents in an interrogation. Junior refuses to talk, and so is murdered by Art. "You got blood on me," Elk says to Art. "We all got blood on us," Art says. Alexie presents torture as if the motivation was lawless aggression, not principled action. Zits identifies with Junior, but also with the racist Storm, instructed by Art to desecrate Junior's corpse. The Zits voice inside Hank's head at first resists Art's orders, but then he shoots Junior in a ritual enactment of regenerative violence. Because Zits links Junior's assassination to his own bank robbery, he questions his own gun-slinging that nearly costs him his life: "Justice made killing make sense. But it doesn't make sense, does it?" (p. 53). In Chapter 6, Zits adds: "Art and Justice fight on opposite sides of the war but they sound exactly like each other. How can you tell the difference between the good guys and the bad guys when they say the same things?" (p. 56). Here Alexie is working in an allegorical mode. "Art" (or aesthetic representation of violent subject matter) appears to have abandoned the ethical responsibility for art in favor of embodying a real politic in which "evil things"—torture, brutal murder—are justified once a culture imagines itself as at "war" with "art" produced by "soldiers." "Justice," like art, is another concept embodied by a character in *Flight*, the 17-year-old white juvenile delinquent and intellectual who encourages Zits to arm and terrorize citizens in a bank (an event that motivates Zits's time travels). The novel deconstructs the noble-sounding terms of "Art" and "Justice" by embodying these concepts in characters who mask aggression by enacting violence on different sides of a "war" involving the U.S. government (Storm to defend it against Indian rebellion) and two teenagers in a terrorist revolt against U.S. economic security (Justice and Zits in the bank hold-up). As much as Art and Justice, the two characters, and, one surmises, the two conceptions of value, appear on the surface to be on opposite sides of a debate, Zits realizes the two are merely identical figures of human aggression masked in idealistic terms: "they sound exactly like each other" (p. 56). By imagining Art and Justice as two aspects of a U.S. imaginary animated by regenerative violence, Alexie implicitly critiques America's Bush-era agents of the War on Terror. Zits interprets Art's comment that "In order to fight evil, sometimes we have to do evil things" as a rationalization that masks the aggression that produced the 9/11 attacks as well as its response. Hank, in other words, represents an ambivalent pawn in a game produced by the "Art" of propaganda disseminated by the Bush administration through spokespersons such as Dick Cheney and Donald Rumsfeld.

In Chapters 8 and 9, Zits experiences the narrative of Little Big Horn, the June 1876 battle with George Custer and his 700 white soldiers of the Seventh Cavalry who are "marching toward his slaughter" against "four or five thousand Indian warriors" (p. 69). A leading Indian warrior, Zits realizes, is, paradoxically, one "so white he gets sunburned," the "almost blond" Oglala Crazy Horse" (p. 67). In contrast to a scene in a primordial teepee made of buffalo skin in Chapter 7 in which Zits felt alienated and embraced by a "real" and "dark" Native American tribe, Zits realizes a more complex understanding of art and justice as he comes to see the "impure" (hybridic) roots of the greatest Indian warrior, who was himself partly white, "like me" (p. 68). The camp, Zits realizes, is a trap that will lead to what he, revising history, regards as the Indians' Last Stand in "the last real battle of the Indian Wars" (p. 71). As much as Zits, at least initially, identifies with the half-white Crazy Horse who sought revenge against the U.S. Calvary, which Zits acknowledges will lead to a history of pain and displacement for native persons, he also decries an excess of violence. He reads the "desecrating the bodies of the dead white soldiers" (p. 73) as foreshadowing Hank and Art's mistreatment of Junior's corpse in Idaho in the 1970s. Distraught over Junior's murder, Zits also feels "sick in my stomach and brain" as he witnesses Indian grandmothers cutting off the penises of dead soldiers (p. 72). Zits reminds himself that body desecration is part of "war" and thus may be viewed as "self-defense," but his revulsion to defilement leads him to question how murder is framed via idealist terms such as "war" and "self-defense" (p. 73). In a comment that reminds us of how "terrorists" were treated in Guantánamo Bay, Zits offers a new definition of what he witnesses: "They [the few surviving white soldiers] are being tortured" p. (74).

By the end of Chapter 9, Zits has thoroughly destabilized his relation to identity, tribal affiliation, time and space, and his ethical conception of violence, revenge, war, and relations between fathers and sons. Alexie interprets a cycle of historical violence in the context of Zits's contemporary reaction to being molested by "my new father" in a foster home near Seattle when he was 8 years old. Uncertain and ambivalent, he enters the rhetorical mode of self-interrogation and self-analysis:

> "Did I want revenge? Did I blame those strangers for my loneliness? Did they deserve to die because of my loneliness?// Does this little white soldier deserve to die because one of his fellow soldiers slashed my throat?//If I kill him, do I deserve to be killed by this white soldier's family and friends?//Is revenge a circle inside of a circle inside of a circle?
>
> (p. 77)

We may regard *Flight* as Alexie's traumatic verbal response to a political crisis that is quite literally written, in the form of a scar, onto Zits's emotionally wounded self. Zits feels love and security when embraced by his warrior father in the context of Custer's Last Stand, but he also regards his reenactment of the Battle of Little Big Horn as a traumatic repetition of a more personal crisis involving his relationship to his father, who abandoned him at birth. Cast as a young Indian warrior at Little Big Horn, Zits understands his father's request that he cut the throat of a white soldier as an act of revenge for having had his own throat cut in a prior conflict that resulted in "the huge scar on my neck" (p. 75). At the same time, Alexie associates the throat wound with Zits's inability to speak in protest to the scenes of inhumanity that he experiences in the bodies of perpetrators such as Hank.

Myriad scenes of intercultural hatred and upsetting violence characterize the middle section of *Flight*. Alexie does in Chapter 12, however, offer an example of paternal nurturance that warms Zits's hardened heart. He does so through the story of Old Gus who assists another white man, known as Small Saint, in rescuing a character named Bow Boy from the American "killer soldiers with rifles" (p. 99).

> The Indian boy has curled into the white soldier. Has his little arms wrapped around the soldier's neck. Bow Boy loves Small Saint like he was his father. Or his mother. Or both.//I remember I used to be like that little boy, holding tightly on to anybody who showed me even the tiniest bit of love. I haven't been like that in a long time.
>
> (p. 99)

Zits witnesses a scene from the historical past, but the image of a white authority figure cradling a young Indian boy—who had initially confronted soldiers with a bow and arrow as a would-be defender of his tribe—touches Zits on a personal level. Bow Boy's story reflects Zits's process of working through the trauma of his personal past and his resentment over how the U.S. government mistreated native peoples. Where Alexie's persona perceived Thoreau as a hypocrite in "On the Amtrak," Zits celebrates Gus and Small Saint's Thoreauvian action of "civil disobedience" as they "disobeyed orders" and so became "traitors" to save "an Indian kid" (p. 100). Gus agrees to be left behind as Small Saint and Bow Boy flee the approaching army. To enable Small Saint to escape with Bow Boy in his arms, Old Gus engages in what Zits perceives as a morally defensible use of force. Gus's repulsion of the charging cavalry reverses what Zits now sees as his own immoral acts of vengeance that "started when I shot a bunch of strangers in a bank" (p. 105), an action that Zits now regards as a "horrible, evil act" (p. 105).

We may read *Flight* as a moral Bildungsroman. Zits develops a nascent moral imagination characterized by compassion and self-scrutiny. He puts aside hasty judgments regarding such abstractions as heroism, courage, and justice:

> Is there really a difference between that killing and this killing? Does God approve of some killing and not other killing? If I kill these soldiers so that Small Saint and Bow Boy can escape, does that make me a hero?
>
> (p. 105)

Zits's comment suggests his moral compass extends beyond whether to engage in an act of terrorism or torture. Dramatizing the ideal of pacifism, he gets at the heart of whether there is such a thing as a just act of violence, or a just war. In "On the Amtrak," Alexie's persona accentuated his difference from the "white woman," a representative figure of the American imaginary. By contrast, *Flight*'s Chapter 12 ends with Zits's ambiguous blurring of relationships. Gus, the Irish "Indian killer," ends the chapter toting an "Indian warrior's rifle" (p. 100) at the onrushing cavalry, but what happens next is unclear:

> I take careful aim. I don't know if I have the heart to kill them. Isn't that odd? I once filled a room with bullets. I shot people who would never do me harm. And now I'm not sure I can shoot at the men who plan to kill me.//I hear screaming. I realize it is me screaming.//I hear weeping. I realize it is me weeping.//I close my eyes.
>
> (p. 106)

Who is the referent to the "I" who weeps, screams, and closes his eyes? Is it Gus? Zits? Is it Alexie? When and where is the killing happening? The speaker's extreme reactions suggest he is responding to an imagined historical past—the massacre of native peoples along the Colorado River near Kansas in the 19th Century. At the same time, the novel's contemporary act of violence—Zits's filling "a room with bullets" in the bank—occurs in the past tense, or prior to the historical events described in the present tense (p. 106). Alexie's blurring of self and other, participant and witness, U.S. and native, and victim and victimizer, as well as temporal and topographic sites, speaks to the author's desire to imagine himself as a proponent of a post-9/11 version of citizenship that privileges what Homi K. Bhaba has termed an "interstitial perspective" (Gray, 2011, p. 64). Alexie stresses forgiveness over lingering resentments concerning past misdeeds. He wants to end the process that American Studies scholar Richard Slotkin has described as the regeneration through violence that animated the Bush-era response to 9/11 via an endless War on Terror.

In the middle section of *Flight*'s circular narrative, Alexie imagines Zits as a witness-participant to scenes of retributive violence between Native American peoples and U.S. soldiers, as well as to a quasi-9/11 air attack narrative involving a Muslim terrorist named Abbas. The final, third section of the novel draws Zits closer still to his own personal history. Continuing to embody another character in Chapter 16, Zits, however, now finds him closer to home in the present day. In a primal scene of self-creation and identity, Zits personifies a 50-year-old, homeless, drunken Indian in Tacoma, who, it turns out, is the biological father who abandoned him at birth. After engaging with a white couple, Pam and Paul, who call 911 as he coughs up blood, the man flees, but not before playing the blame game: "It's all your fault" and "White people did this to Indians. You make us like this" (p. 136). Continuing on the cycle of dehumanization, Zits's father transforms Pam and Paul into metaphysical embodiments of a race rather than individuals acting on their conscience. As narrator, Zits resists his father's point of view and, implicitly, that of Alexie's persona in "On the Amtrak":

> I don't even know if I believe that. But I think this homeless body believes it. I think this fifty-year-old guy wants to blame somebody for his pain and his hunger. But what if it's his fault? What if he made all the decisions that led him to this sad-ass fate?
>
> (p. 136)

Zits is interrogating a liberal imagination that displaces responsibility for one's behavior from the individual and onto—arguably inescapable—historical traumas and socio-economic conditions as experienced by a racial, gender, or ethnic group. He tries on a conservative posture—opposite to the liberal perspective, but an equally simplistic assessment—that stresses individual answerability for one's actions.

Refusing help, Zits's father further alienates himself from the white couple by making sexually offensive remarks to Pam, leading Paul to punch him in the face. A "beaten bloody Indian" (p. 140), he asks for "respect" (p. 141) from people on the street, eventually finding a man willing to tell him a story about his own life and to share a photograph of his daughter. Embodying his homeless father, Zits takes from his pocket a photograph of himself as a

5-year-old. "Is that your son?" the man asks again. "No," I say. "It's me." (p. 150):

> I walk over to a delivery truck and turn the side-view mirror. I stare at my bloody reflection. I am older than I used to be. I am battered, bruised, and broken. But I know who I am. I am my father.

(p. 150)

In a figurative sense, Zits has been "delivered" through the truck's mirror because it reflects a scene of empathetic imagination. He identifies with his father, whom he had perceived as a figure of abandonment. He is admitting how he made his father's mistake of blaming all of his actions on a faceless oppression. In terms of literary forbears, Zits revisions *Hamlet*. Like *Flight*'s main character, Hamlet exhibits grief, rage, and, possibly, insanity. Apparitions that involve sequences of murderous vengeance drive Zits and Hamlet. Taking on *Hamlet*, Alexie revises the ending of Shakespeare's tragedy. By so doing, he revisions his relation to a father, whom he had viewed only in negative terms as a figure of shame and rage.

> It was father love and father shame and father rage that killed Hamlet. Imagine a new act. Imagine that Hamlet, after being poisoned by his own sword, wakes in the body of his father. Or worse, inside the body of his incestuous Uncle Claudius?
>   What would Hamlet do if he looked into the mirror and saw the face of the man who'd betrayed and murdered his father?
>   And what should I do now that I am looking into the mirror at the face of the man who betrayed and abandoned my mother and me?

(p. 151)

Zits wants, simultaneously, to kill his father, and himself, by plunging Hamlet's sword into his own body. As in prior chapters, however, Alexie's message is that forgiveness must trump vengeance to promote survival of the self and of the other, even if the other (in this case, the father) has injured the self in the past.

Chapter 18 encapsulates Alexie's attempt to engage in a productive fashion with Shakespeare, who signifies a human heritage that is futile to divide into Western and non-Western spheres. He rewrites the ending of Shakespeare's greatest play as a comedy, rather than as a revenge tragedy. Instead of a play that *begins* with a ghostly appearance of Hamlet's father, who calls for his son to murder Claudius to revenge the uncle's murder of himself, Alexie's ghostlike meeting with the estranged and maligned father occurs near the *end* of *Flight*. It is thus a culminating event in Zits's working through of his traumatic childhood. By way of the father, and, in a sense, the father through the son in an anti-Oedipal reversal, Zits returns to his own birth scene. Through this dream vision, Zits, via a memory within a memory, comprehends why his father abandoned him at the hospital when he was being born. Recovering his father's own deepest wounds, Zits, *as* his father, "remembers being eight years old, lying in bed while a man stands in the dark doorway" (p. 154). The "man" is Zits's paternal grandfather, who, drunk, had abused Zits's then child father by telling him he "ain't worth shit" because he failed at hunting (p. 156). As was the case in Alexie's extraordinary act of forgiveness of Lewis and Clark in the *Time* Sacagawea essay, Zits attempts to break a cycle of revenge, in this case by empathetically imagining the source of his father's decision to leave him. Defeated by his own father's denigrating words, Zits's father "cannot be a participant. He cannot be a witness. He cannot be a father" (p. 156) to the newly born Zits in the hospital: "And so he runs" (p. 156). Zits's act of becoming a "participant" and "witness" to his father's history enables him to challenge his own history of victimization. He symbolically gives birth to himself by surviving a psychic journey into the pain of others, which he views as inter-related to his own pain and loss.

In Chapter 19, Alexie returns to re-imagine the real-time scene in the bank from Chapter 3. "I have returned to my body. And my ugly face. And my anger. And my loneliness" (p. 158). Instead of shooting a little boy in the bank for "justice," he extends his empathetic imagination into how he will behave when returned to his own body. Instead of resenting the privileged white child in the bank, and destroying what he resents under the sign of "justice," Zits revises his own views on the life of the little boy, and of the privileged white bankers whom he had planned to terrorize:

They have better lives than I do.
 Or maybe they don't. Maybe we're all lonely. Maybe some of
them also hurtle through time and see war, war war, war. Maybe
we're all in this together.

(p. 158)

Zits's performance of a "what if" thought experiment turns a scene
of tragedy (for the white patrons in the bank as well as for Zits)
into a moment of insight in which Zits is able to "turn around,"
leave the bank, and start his life over again on "First Avenue"
(p. 158). In rainy Seattle, Zits, who used to "hate the rain," now
continues to construct his rebirth, in this case through baptismal
imagery, by stating, "I want it to pour" and "I want to be clean"
(p. 159).

As much as I have described the structure of *Flight* as occurring
in three segments and as one of a circular return in Part three to the
current scene of Zits in Seattle in Part one, the novel is also shaped
like a vortex. It drills inward, drawing Zits closer to the epicenter
of his own traumatic childhood wounds. Zits's self-analysis was
already evident, when he imagined why his father abandoned
him in the hospital. In Chapter 18, Zits embodied his father as
an 8-year-old who was verbally abused by his alcoholic father,
but in Chapter 19 Zits acknowledges his own story of physical,
sexual, and psychological abuse. He reveals that he was raped as
a 6-year-old by his Aunt Zooey's boyfriend. He was "shook" and
"slapped" by his aunt, and then verbally abused and silenced by the
man who raped him: "Don't tell anybody" and "Everybody knows
you're a liar" and "Nobody loves you anymore" (pp. 160–1). The
rape and the subsequent verbal messages amounted to a negative
education that Zits must willfully unlearn—a process undertaken
throughout the middle section of *Flight*. Zits states in a list format
that he "learned how to," among other signs of psychic distress,
"be cold and numb," an internal state that became manifest in self-
destructive and anti-social behaviors ranging from running away at
age 8, to trying to set the aunt's boyfriend on fire, to using drugs
and alcohol, to meeting "a kid named Justice who taught me how
to shoot guns" (p. 161).

Now, at the novel's end, Zits admits he needs "help" (p. 162). He
turns himself and his guns in to Officer Dave, who, in Chapter 20,

becomes a surrogate father, telling Zits, "You matter to me" (p. 168). In Chapter 21, he sets Zits up as a foster child with "Officer Dave's brother and sister-in-law" (p. 174). After placement in failed foster homes, Zits has finally found one that feels right to him.[4] Instead of greeting the breakfast table with silence, Zits replaces his "whatever" attitude with a mutual act of respect. He shakes hands with his foster father, Robert, enjoys a hearty breakfast, and agrees to attend a baseball game ("A baseball game! Jesus, how American," p. 176). Mary, his foster mother, blends for Zits winning aspects of Native American and U.S. cultures. He finds her "Indian cheekbones" (p. 175) appealing, vows to change from junk food to a wholesome diet, and promises to make the foster relationship "permanent" (p. 177). Her final act of helping Zits re-imagine his identity occurs through her statement that, "we need to start working on your skin" (p. 179), not in terms of racial or ethnic marking, but in changing Zits from pock-marked adolescent who feels shame over his appearance, to "handsome" (p. 179) mainstream middle-class American teenager. "A few months from now, you'll be brand-new," (p. 180) she tells Zits. Zits's final acts are to repeat the phrase "I'm sorry" and then, in a reversal of the opening of Melville's most famous novel, to recover his "real name" (p. 181); "Please, call me Michael" (p. 181).

Face

In the last section of this chapter, I return to Alexie's poetry by discussing lyrics from *Face* (2009). Extending his post-9/11 prose, *Face* demonstrates that Alexie has amended his earlier poetics, acknowledging the irreconcilable complexities of his mature subject position. In so doing, Alexie in *Face*, in effect, engages in a

---

[4]In "On the Amtrak" the speaker lumped all white Americans, including historical progressives and contemporary activists, as "the enemy." By contrast, Zits, exploited by most of his foster parents, experiences, and in the end embraces, the idea that at least *some* white Americans are sympathetic, some have even, at various points in history, helped native persons, often at their own peril. Chief among these supportive white officials in Zits's own life are Dave, a police officer, and Russell, a public defender in Seattle whom Zits characterizes as "yet another lifeguard who likes to save drowners like me" (p. 19).

lyric encounter with his prior self-makings. We may thus consider *Face* as a work of lyrical criticism. An effort in what American Studies scholar Donald Pease, in a Dartmouth College lecture on "The Work of the Humanities After Humanism," would refer to as "self-examination, self-criticism, and self-alteration," *Face* reflects Alexie's understanding as a postmodernist that the self is something made, rather than given, but also how, in the words of Pease, "what has been is open to change."

I can imagine readers questioning my decision to include such extensive commentary on Alexie's prose in a book otherwise devoted to lyric poetry. My response is that I consider Alexie's critique of binary thinking on identity and community to extend to his hybrid relation to literary genres. In this sense, *Face* is a fitting culmination to my Alexie chapter. In *Face*, Alexie defies neatly defined stylistic categories or literary affiliations. He cites with approval or riffs upon canonical white U.S. authors such as Edith Wharton, Richard Wilbur, F. Scott Fitzgerald, and Emily Dickinson. And yet he claims African-American comedian Richard Pryor as a major influence on his irreverent sensibility: "Well, poets and comics share a toolbox,//And their geniuses build the same fires,/So when you sing Shakespeare, I sing Pryor" (p. 128, "Unauthorized"). He regards Borscht-belt Jewish comic Henny Youngman's famous pauses when telling jokes such as "Take my wife, please" as an example of verbal art that "uses a caesura with some bite" (p. 129, "Unauthorized"). He praises alternative bands such as the Norman, Oklahoma, psychedelic group The Flaming Lips.

Face is a formalist *tour de force*. As rarely before, Alexie shows off his chops as a skilled practitioner of the traditional European poetic forms he learned at Gonzaga and Washington State. He crafts villanelles, sonnets, and rhymed quatrains, with the rhythm of most poems conforming to an iambic beat. Alexie is a prosodic formalist, but *Face* is a genre-busting experiment. As in Vladimir Nabokov's proto-hypertext *Pale Fire* (1962), *Face* includes footnotes that at once parody academic discourse and inform the reader as much about the poem under discussion as the subjective perspective of the footnote's author. In both ways, *Face* benefits from the hypertextual display of additional commentary. Comfortable working within the confines of a Western European poetics, Alexie situates his craft within a hybrid text thus upsetting associations between formalist poetics and conservative social views.

In *Face*, Alexie regards binary thinking about self and other as insensitive to his hybrid identity and often paradoxical situation within American society. A poor child who grew up on a reservation with an alcoholic father, he is represented in *Face* as a successful author who stays at five-star hotels. He casts himself as an upper-middle-class homeowner concerned about insect infestation, a middle-aged husband jealous of his spouse's former lovers, and a concerned parent of a frail child. Alexie in *Face* engages in deeply ambivalent ways with domestic versions of scapegoating and retributive violence. His destructive acts upon what he considers, at first glance, to be undesirable others, uncannily mirror—albeit on the smaller scale of home extermination of birds, insects, and rodents—the very acts of exclusion and terror upon a perceived, if in the end benign, threat to "homeland security" that characterized the Bush Administration's 2003 attack on Iraq in the aftermath of the 11 September 2001 attack upon the World Trade Center and the Pentagon.

Mourning deaths he has initiated in a manner suggesting the author is beginning to extend his perspective from humanistic to pan-species, Alexie in *Face* regards in sympathetic fashion the birds, ants, snakes, rats, mosquitoes, bees, orphaned baby geese, and spiders whose lives are snuffed out in the pages of his book. We may read his attention to animals that are typically viewed as pests or vermin and that he perceived as threatening human safety as expressing ecological concerns. His unleashing of Weapons of Mass Destruction against alien beings that inhabit his home may also be read metaphorically as Alexie's guilt-laden response to America's Global War on Terror following the 9/11 attacks. Instead of unselfconsciously administering violence upon a threat to home and family, Alexie examines the nature of revenge as an unsavory, even barbaric, but perhaps inevitable, aspect of life. In "Size Matters," he asks, "Why is the deadly reflex/That requires us to strike at our perceived enemies?/Revenge seems to be as basic as food, shelter, and sex" (p. 117, lines 38–40). Alexie's mixed response to the insects and other disparaged animals that he destroys, praises, and mourns in *Face*, I will argue, may be read metaphorically in relation to his bitterly mixed reaction to the "Terrorist Other" in a post-9/11 environment.

Alexie's perspective on animals in *Face* has the quality of what Pease calls "second sight." By "second sight" I mean that Alexie represents himself in relation to maligned parts of nature in two ways. On the one hand, he is cast as a typical U.S. middle-class homeowner, middle-aged family man, and professional author. A Native American storyteller, he self-mockingly refers to a Eugene, Oregon, poetry reading as an example of the "oral tradition." He interprets insects and birds as threatening property values, keeping a sick son up at night, and in general creating a nuisance that must be snuffed out. From this middle-class American homeowner perspective, little animals are not unlike the alien terrorists intruding upon what the Bush administration described as the American "homeland." Angry, frightened, and threatened by a strange life form invading the home, the homeowner reacts much as the American polity, under the Bush administration, reacted to the terrorist raid on American soil on 11 September 2001. Alexie creates a scapegoat to account for his vulnerability, and then he pays a member of a kind of professional army—an exterminator— to remove the perceived threat with extreme force. He then tries, unsuccessfully, to ignore the aftermath of the extermination. On the other hand, the speaker critiques homeowner Alexie. By metaphorical extension, homeowner Alexie is likened to the U.S. citizen who perceives homeland safety and comfort as built upon a dispossession of some type—of Middle Eastern rights for their oil, of Native Americans, of local animals seeking homes of their own.

The lead poem in *Face*, "Avian Nights," explores Alexie's actions as a privileged American homeowner with "second sight." Alexie signals his situation as a mainstream citizen through the adherence to established prosodic form. A narrative consisting of 20 quatrains, the lines follow an iambic beat, measure a pentameter length, and are rhymed AB/AB. Far from the alienated, would-be terrorist sullenly riding the rails on the East Coast in "On the Amtrak," Alexie is cast in the Pacific Northwest as a married man worried about a sick son in Seattle. A homeowner, he explains to the reader, as if trying to, in his own term, "rationalize" (line 26) why he hired an exterminator to kill a nest of "[s]tarlings [that] have invaded our home and filled/Our eaves with their shit-soaked nests" (p. 11, lines 1–2). The speaker's need to explain why he paid to exterminate the birds suggests he needs a forum to expiate guilt. The shift in tone, however, and especially how he describes the birds that survived extermination, speak to his regrets about his decision to hire a pest controller. He becomes, in his own word, a "witness" to the aftermath of violent actions he initiated.

Describing the starlings as vermin that carry disease, the homeowner persona sounds confident, and even self-righteous, about hiring the exterminator. As if trying to convince his audience of his decency, he disparages the birds, calling them "[r]ats with wings" (line 2) and "scavengers" (line 3). Setting up the "us" versus "them" scenario Alexie deconstructed in his post-9/11 prose, he speaks of "our home" (line 2). That the birds dwell within the speaker's home—in "the crawlspace above/Our son's bedroom" (lines 6–7)—justifies their removal. Along with their "shit" and "strange songs" (line 27), the starlings' "beating of wings/Through the long, avian nights" (lines 27 and 28) represent a threat to the symbol of home as a sanctuary invulnerable to disease, mystery, and death. Alexie's persona wants the bird noises to stop bothering his son's sleep, but he does not want to dirty his hands. A Spanish-speaking exterminator will do the ugly work. It is the professional killer who, without feeling or words, "uses a thumb//And finger to snap the birds' necks—*crack, crack,/crack*— then drops their bodies to the driveway/Below. For these deaths, I write him a check" (p. 11, lines 8–11). Here, Alexie's decision to write in formal, rhymed verse is especially effective. The off-rhyme of "crack" and "check" accents on a formal level Alexie's critique of the privileged homeowner who outsources his security.

Alexie's reaction to the extermination in "Avian Nights" can be suggestively contrasted to the controversial image of then-President George W. Bush in a flight suit landing in a fixed wing aircraft onto the *USS Abraham Lincoln* on 1 May 2003 with a "Mission Accomplished" banner affixed to it after the end of what turned out to be the first stage of a blistering invasion of Iraq.[5] Alexie does not celebrate the killings in his domestic "War on Terror." Instead of gloating prematurely over the destruction of an enemy, he acknowledges the birds are victims of his need to assuage his fear about his son's health.

"Avian Nights" is, at first, the kind of text that Richard Gray, in *After the Fall*, would critique for withdrawing "into the domestic

---

[5] "Commander in Chief lands on USS Lincoln." Friday 2 May, 2003. CNN.com/ InsidePolitics

and the security fortress of America" (2011, p. 17). The poem illustrates the binary thinking that Gray argued must be replaced with a perspective that privileges dialogue and hybridity, but Alexie also interprets the starlings as a family faced with a traumatic dissolution of their home. The father of a sick son, Alexie serves "to witness/The return of the father and mother/Starlings to their shared children, to their nest,//All of it gone, missing, absent, destroyed" (p. 11, lines 18–20). Rather than express relief after ridding his home of a threat, Alexie reduces the distance between self and other by identifying with the surviving starlings. They are members of a family in mourning for lost loved ones. No longer regarding starlings as diseased rodents hiding in the crawl-space, like terrorists waiting to pounce on his ill child, Alexie interrogates his attitudes, beliefs, and judgments. Choosing the interrogative mode, he steps down from his steep and icy peak of confident assertion. He also uses the interrogative mode to create an imaginative space that enables him to empathize with starlings as creatures more like than unlike him in terms of "family values" and spiritual yearnings. The baby starlings, he writes, "screamed to greet the morning light./What could they've been so excited about?/ What is starling joy? When a starling finds/A shiny button, does it dance and shout?//Do starlings celebrate their days of birth?/Do they lust and take each other to bed?/Are they birds of infinite jest, of mirth/And merriness? How do they bury their dead?" (p. 12, lines 29–36).

Unlike the younger Alexie persona in "On the Amtrak," the mature Alexie expresses vulnerability. He admits uncertainty about his righteousness by imaginatively entering into the emotional and ritual life of something he had perceived as alien, connecting his concern for his child to his imagination of the adult starlings' grief over their offspring: "We will never know how this winged mother/ And father would have buried their children" (p. 12, lines 37–8). Instead of hearing starling cries as "strange songs" (p. 11, line 27), he interprets their "scream and wail" (p. 12, line 42) as sounds of pain over grief that, far from barbarism, indicate paternal care: "We have never heard/Such pain from any human" (p.12, lines 43–4). No longer alien sounds threatening family security, the bird noises trigger Alexie's memory of how he reacted when "Our son almost died at birth. His mother/And I would have buried him in silence" (p. 12, lines 39–40). After describing how doctors used a machine to push blood through the son's frail body, Alexie in effect transforms the linguistic reactions of himself and his spouse into that of grieving starlings: "His mother and I sat/At his bedside eighteen hours a day. We cawed and cawed to bring him back" (p.13, lines 62–4). Early in the poem, "we" signified the speaker's difference from the starlings. Now, at the end, he expands referents to "we" to include non-human mourners. Rather than disparage birds as "Rats with wings," Alexie expresses fear and grief through the starling's "scree." He associates the starlings with noble human values: "How much love, hope, and faith//Do these birds possess?" (p. 13, lines 68–9). In the last three stanzas, Alexie unites the starlings with emotions less savory, but no less human, than the sweeter ones of "love, hope, and faith." Erasing significant emotional differences between human and bird, Alexie acknowledges the birds are victims of unwarranted human violence. It would make perfect sense for them to seek revenge: "if God gave them opposable thumbs,//I'm positive they would open the doors/ Of our house and come for us as we sleep./We killed their children. We started this war.//Tell me: What is the difference between//Birds and us, between their pain and our pain?" (p.13, lines 72–7).

Face replaces "us" versus "them" thinking with Alexie's comprehension of interconnectedness among all living things, and Alexie's burgeoning eco-consciousness. "In the Matter of Human v. Bee" begins with a quotation attributed to Albert Einstein: "If the bees die, man dies within four years" (p. 21). In "Cryptozoology," Alexie likens his citing of a crow "with a row of blue feathers" (p. 134, line 1) to his unique identity. Like the crow, he belongs to a tribe of one who defies categories. "I witnessed this odd glory// Of a crow that is the only one of its kind—/A bird that is the only member of its tribe" (p. 134, lines 16–18). In "Small Ceremonies," Alexie describes in serio-comic fashion how a spider rebuilds a web in the poet's mailbox after he tears it apart. As in "Avian Nights," the speaker compares his life and the "alien" creature that builds a home on his property. He likens his ritual of checking the mail with the spider's determination to craft its web as comparable parts of the "dumb instinct to survive" (p. 109, line 28). His clumsy quest for insignificant or annoyingly quotidian ephemera— "catalogs, postcards, ads, dead/Letters, bills, sweepstakes" (p. 109, lines 7–8)—leads him to bull in the china shop behavior in which "I destroy/What the spider creates" (p. 109, lines 10–11). The lyric turns from self-satire into religious confession. Crafting an impromptu prayer, he hopes to expiate guilt over his insensitivity to the spider dwelling: "I want to confess and atone//For the small sin of valuing my life/More than the life of this nameless spider/Who rebuilds his damn web for seven nights" (p. 109, lines 20–3).

An elegy, "The Sum of His Parts" shows the careless, often unknowing destruction caused by human dependence on powerful machinery. He casts the speaker after he accidentally drives his car over a snake. He spends most of the poem burying the snake that has been cut into three parts. In spite of theological doubt, Alexie entertains the possibility of a "Snake Heaven." He picks up pieces of the snake and buries them together to prevent the possibility that if "the snake's three pieces arrived//separately in Heaven,/ Would any of them be able to find the others?" (p. 52, lines 42–4).[6] "The Sum of His Parts" replaces tones of aggression, anger, and a desire for revenge with displays of vulnerability, humility, and an awareness of mortality.

"The Sum of His Parts" follows a five-part work entitled "The Blood Sonnets" in which Alexie recalls personal traumas such as the times "my father left me (and my mother/And siblings), to binge-drink for days and weeks" (p. 48, lines 1–2), as well as "[W]hen my mom called and said, 'Your father is dead" (p. 48, line 14). In part five of "The Blood Sonnets," the speaker recalls his grief when he and "six cousins bury/My father's coffin in gravel and mud" (p. 50, lines 57–8). Given that "The Sum of His Parts" follows the sonnet in which the son buries a father who was unavailable because of binge drinking, we can imagine connections between Alexie's grief for the father and mourning for the severed snake as elements of a holistic vision. Even if Alexie's father was something of a metaphorical "snake" because of his alcoholism, the mellowed, middle-aged Alexie offers a makeshift homage to him through sonnets typically associated with love. Similarly, "The Sum of His Parts" is a displaced

---

[6]In the third part of "The Blood Sonnets," Alexie anticipates his elegy for the snake in "The Sum of His Parts." He recalls his act of mourning for the starlings in "Avian Nights" when his speaker finds the fur of a dead mother rat in the crawlspace of his home. He proceeds to scoop up the dead rats he finds, and to bury them in the dirt. "Why do I mourn these rats? Why do I care?/Because even the vermin need our prayers" (p. 49, lines 41–2).

offering of care for the father. Born in trauma, Alexie extends his consciousness beyond humanism to include the snakes, rats, spiders, birds, all elegized in *Face*. Alexie performs acts of spiritual yearning that exist outside of established religious, ethnic, or tribal mandates.

In "Naked and Damp, with a Towel around My Head, I Noticed Movement on the Basement Carpet," Alexie riffs on William Carlos Williams's "Danse Russe" (1916) in which a lonely husband and father "dance[s] naked, grotesquely/before my mirror/waving my shirt round my head" and declares himself "the happy genius of my household" (Williams, 2008, p. 632). In "Naked and Damp," Alexie realizes he is, unlike the Williams persona, far from alone and far from in charge of his domain because "Ants invaded our home, our walls, ceilings, and floors" (p. 94, line 1). As in "Avian Nights," the speaker refers to the colonial perspective on Native Americans as his first impulse is to annihilate the perceived threat: "I killed the little red bastards by the dozens,/But they would not retreat or surrender" (p. 94, lines 2–3). As in "Avian Nights," Alexie's indeterminate position as both insider and outsider in relation to American society comes through loud and clear in "Naked and Damp." The bothered homeowner at war with "the little red bastards" is, symbolically, trying to rid himself of prior experiences as a poor "rez" Indian who lacked a father. The zany, self-parodying humor and pathos of the speaker's ambivalence towards the red ants animate his vitriolic stance towards his actions: "My war//With the ants was blasphemous. What kind of profane boor/Wants to genocide his sacred little cousins?" (p. 94, lines 9–11). Alexie is frustrated by his paradoxical situation as a bothered homeowner and a successful adult who nonetheless remembers life as a child on a reservation. Like the ants, he, too, scrounged for food and shelter and "shar[ed] the wormy government food" (p. 94, line 9). He interprets the battle with ants as a sign that he has lost his possibly illusory status as a privileged American homeowner. Unlike in "Avian Nights," he, not a paid exterminator, dirties his hands: "I felt poor/again, like a rez urchin, as if a dozen/Years of peace and joy had been destroyed by the war//With those terrorists" (p. 94, lines 13–16). By ridding his home of pests, he also, however ironically, engages in a figurative act of genocide against his own people and a murder of his prior identity.

I killed and killed and killed and killed my ant cousins.
I protected my home, walls, ceilings, and floors,
Because the rich must always make war on the poor.

(lines 17–19)

The passage seems to simultaneously refer to historical war—
Europeans against natives—and the "war" of the affluent middle
class who, often unknowingly, depend upon exploitation of
labor. The repetition of the phrase "and killed" suggests Alexie's
compulsion to destroy memories. The lines express shame. He has
internalized an American imaginary that associates wealth with
power and poverty and ethnicity with abjection. "Naked and
Damp" is bitter self-criticism. Instead of turning his rage outward
to critique a society he views as racist and classist, he disavows
the "red ants"—a trope for his poor, "rez" self of decades earlier.
He then subjects the figure of his otherness to violence. An attack
on his own success and middle-class status, "Naked and Damp"
Alexie affirms his social position by excluding his origins.

The final poem from *Face* that I will consider at some length,
"Mystery Train," takes us full circle back to "On the Amtrak."
Like the 1993 work, the poem from the 2009 collection imagines
Alexie on an Amtrak train in which he encounters another person,
who is, on the surface, very different. "Mystery Train," however, is
not set on the Eastern seaboard, but closer to the poet's birthplace
in the Pacific Northwest, as the author travels from Portland to his
home in Seattle (pp. 95–7). Itself a many-layered mystery, the title
illustrates Alexie's point that the American social text is an irrecon-
cilably complex tapestry composed of contradictory and contested
elements. The murky origins and subsequent history of musical
and filmic references to the phrase "Mystery Train" speak to the
hybridic, dialogic, and multicultural sense of identity that Alexie
explores in *Face*. "Mystery Train" references a classic American
blues lyric assigned to a leading African-American musician from
Memphis, Junior Parker. Parker, however, in part based his blues
on a folk song by the seminal Country and Western group, The
Carter Family. The title was subsequently made famous by Elvis
Presley in the 1950s, a fitting destination for the song given
Presley's heritage as a white, Southern, working-class performer
whose style was rooted in the African-American blues tradition.

Presley's best-selling recording of Big Mama Thornton's "Hound Dog" illustrates this observation. "Mystery Train" is also the title of a 1989 movie by independent filmmaker Jim Jarmusch involving culture intersections in Tennessee.[7]

By entering the "mystery train," Alexie in effect challenges his strictly oppositional subject position in relation to the "white woman" in "On the Amtrak." An outer journey as well as travel into the artist's interior, "Mystery Train" explores the enigmatic nature of the relation between self and other, or, better, the other within the self. The destination of the "Mystery Train" is homeward bound, to quote the New York Jewish American songwriter Paul Simon, but to a repressed part of the self. Alexie returns "home" to an uncanny (or unhomelike) sense of identity that challenges tribal thinking, unless one imagines such a thing as a tribe of one, or, in this case, two. As in "On the Amtrak," Alexie in "Mystery Train" at first seeks independence from other passengers to the point that he hopes for "an empty row" (p. 95, line 3). Symbolically, however, Alexie chooses "Coach Car C"— suggesting his seat will become a perch from which he can "C" (read: 'see') and a place in which he can "coach," that is, encourage and teach, himself and another passenger. Although he seeks privacy, mysteriously when he sees "a seat next to a teen" (line 4) he immediately grabs it. One senses the "teen" is simultaneously another passenger and a manifestation of the "teen" within Alexie. It is Alexie's persona, in this case, who engages in dialogue with the "teen," and it is the "teen" who is diffident. My sense that the "teen" represents a symbolic, but repressed, aspect of Alexie's identity is registered in the second stanza. He imagines the teen's

---

[7]From Moviefone website: http://www.moviefone.com/movie/mystery-train/2748/ synopsis [accessed 20 June 2012]

> Written and directed by the ever-unpredictable Jim Jarmusch, *Mystery Train* is comprised of three short anecdotes involving foreign tourists in Tennessee. Each story is set in a fleabag Memphis hotel which has been redressed as a "tribute" to Elvis Presley. Story one involves two Japanese tourists whose devotion to '50s American rock music blinds them to everything around them. Story two finds eternal victim Luisa (Nicoletta Braschi) sharing a room with stone-broke Dee Dee (Elizabeth Bracco) and having her problems solved by a spectral vision of the King. And story three offers the further misadventures of Dee Dee, her no-good boyfriend, and her dysfunctional family.

face as "blank," as if it were a *tabula rasa*, or a mirror into the unknown or unwritten. At first Alexie uses a clinical diagnosis—he assumes the teen has Asperger's syndrome—to categorize the young man's unusual affect. Labeling is convenient shorthand for Alexie to limit the mystery of a companion who lacks facial expression, seems unwilling to look directly at the poet, but who also remembers obscure facts, images, and figures with uncanny precision. The teen, however, simply describes himself as "weird" (line 7) as a "warn[ing]" to Alexie, the partner he has misread as a "straight." Defining oneself as "weird" is significant in terms of Alexie's emphasis in *Face* on defining the self as mysterious as well as outside mainstream, simplistic notions of identity. Alexie creates a tribe of two "others" by assuring the teen of his membership in the club of misfits on the American train: "I'm weird, too" (p. 95, line 8). Putting the teen in a position of hierarchy, he thanks him for his "kindness" (p. 95, line 9) for sharing a seat. The cordiality seems genuine and lighthearted. Alexie's offhand manner of putting his fellow passenger at ease contrasts with the phony courtesy that characterized the younger Alexie's politeness towards the "white woman" in "On the Amtrak." In many ways, the rapport between the two strangers doubles back upon and rewrites from a more empathetic perspective the relation between Alexie and the "white woman." Not only does Alexie initiate conversation, he learns from and is dazzled by how the teen describes the "landscape out the window"—the source of contestation and suppressed rage in "On the Amtrak." Instead of perceiving historical landmarks such as Walden Pond as signs of American Exceptionalism, as does the white woman, the teen has a "weird," that is, magical, ability to predict the location of quotidian places and anonymous things down to their color patterns. The teen notices a landscape that is far from exceptional in its historical significance. Instead, he points out aspects of the gritty working-class atmosphere that often accompanies railway corridors: "'Pretty soon,/There will be a yellow truck parked outside/A blue and red house.' Of course, he was right. As we traveled north, the kid always knew//What was coming next" (p. 96, lines 29–33). Noting that an upcoming junkyard used to house a dog, the teen expresses sadness when he ponders that it has died. In "On the Amtrak," Alexie felt the white woman misread the New England landscape because she had internalized misleading history books. By contrast, the "kid" is able, through his experience of riding the rails between Portland and Seattle 109 times over seven years in order to spend time with each of his divorced parents, to predict how the landscape will unfold. In "Avian Nights," Alexie's entrance into the life of starlings enabled him to recover traumatic memories of how his son nearly died at birth. In "Mystery Train," Alexie's knowledge of how the teen copes with divorced parents leads him to reflect on the nature of love between parents and children.

In the middle of "Mystery Train," Alexie refrains from a dialogue mode and turns inward for several of the poem's 21, roughly iambic pentameter quatrains. He invokes lyric's meditative qualities, but does so to imagine his way more deeply into the teen's peculiar situation in which he shuttles via interstate train between two parents who love him but despise each other. The teen's story resonates with Alexie's history as a product of a difficult marriage involving an estranged alcoholic father. In his meditation, Alexie reserves judgment about the teen and his parents. He refrains from the knee-jerk response of writing off the divorced parents as selfish and uncaring about their boy. Instead, he acknowledges the complexity of family relationships and celebrates the surprising lengths and creative solutions divorced parents will seek to maintain connections with their children: "was eager to disparage/His parents, but then I realized that//His folks must love him as obsessively/As he loves them ... It was lovely/And strange" (p. 96, lines 43–8). Far from perceiving the "weird" kid as a bother, Alexie regards him as a sage. He wishes to ask the teen "about pain" (line 48) and he wants "to be blessed" by him (line 51). The teen rarely speaks, but he intuits Alexie's acknowledgment of his emotional depth. In a manner uncharacteristically forthcoming about his vulnerability for a young male, he admits, "I have cried a lot of tears" (p. 96, line 56).

The teen narrates the meaning of mound formations that, he admits, "escape explanation" (p. 97, line 65). He reads the history and function of Mima Mounds, which consist of thousands of figurines "Created with gravel, rocks, dirt, and sticks" (p. 97, line 64), in such a way that it is impossible to determine whether they are of human, geologic, or animal origins, or some combination of the three. Not "Indian burial sites" (line 66) or "homes/For gophers or insects" (lines 66–7), and not a container of "bones/Or fossils or UFOs" (lines 67–8), the teen embraces the strangeness of 8-feet tall characters. "They're just odd//Geologic formations that will keep/Their secrets no matter how hard we try/To reveal them" (lines 68–71). We may read "odd/Geologic formations" as a multi-dimensional symbol for the teen himself, whose identity proves less stable and homogenous than usually assumed. Now, having embraced weirdness as a virtue, Alexie regards the "just odd" formation out the train window as a "secret" that is alluring *because* it defies categorization.

A remarkable act of literal and figurative revisioning of the contested American landscape, "Mystery Train" ends with a sweet scene that occurs after the Amtrak reaches Seattle. As Alexie leaves the station, he recites out loud the first lines of the poem we are reading, an act that the poet realizes makes him appear "crazy" to passers-by. He imagines he is perceived as "just another homeless schizophrenic" (p. 97, lines 80 and 82). Just as Alexie initially distanced himself from the gifted teen by casting him as a clinical type, the passers-by detach themselves from the oral poet by regarding him as an off-limits kind of person. But as with the poet's willingness to disrupt his first impression of the kid as "just" an example of an obsessive-compulsive type, Alexie uses poetry as satiric invective to overturn connotations of the terms "clarity" and "mystery." As in Emily Dickinson's "Much Madness is Divinest Sense" (1862), Alexie celebrates his oral poetry as a winning sign of indeterminacy: "Then fuck them for wanting clarity/And fuck them for fearing mystery" (p. 97, lines 83–4).

As with Alexie's recent novels, *Face* contests binary thinking on identity and community. In its surprisingly conservative form, the book also insists on the author's prerogative to move in and out of verse patterns such as the villanelle and sonnet typically associated with hegemonic Western European poetics without the need to identify himself as a formalist or free style experimentalist. U.S. poets in the 1950s and 1960s were neatly bracketed into the camps (or tribes) of formalist or free style through two influential anthologies. There was *New Poets of England and America*, the formalist anthology edited by Donald Hall and Robert Pack in 1957. It featured masters of boxy poems such as Richard Wilbur, John Hollander, and Anthony Hecht and an introduction by Robert Frost. And then there was *The New American Poetry: 1945–1960* (1960), an anthology self-consciously put together in the tradition of experimental modernists such as Ezra Pound, William Carlos

Williams, and Louis Zukofsky, and edited by Donald Allen. It included non-white authors such as LeRoi Jones (Amiri Baraka) and socially radical poets associated with Beat, Black Mountain, San Francisco Renaissance, and New York School poetics. A culminating point in his evolution, Alexie in *Face* creates a hybrid poetics that in effect turns a poetics of tribalism into a multiculture that at once touches essayistic, narrative, academic, stand-up comic, confessional, ecocritical, prayer-like, elegiac, and political strains. Alexie's poetics in *Face* is clearly one of the "both/and" rather than "either/or" variety. It is a poetics fitting for Alexie's uncertain, often paradoxical, and always mysterious subject position. He favors multiculturism over tribalism, and individual identity over either—or individual identity as incorporating, and transcending, simplistic nationalisms.

10

Coda: "Mending Wall" and Tikkun Olam: The Case for the Humanities Classroom

For the past 18 years I have served as a professor at Purdue, a large public land-grant Midwestern research university. Known for engineering, agriculture, business, and the sciences, it is most famous for the fact that 26 NASA astronauts, including Neil Armstrong and Guss Grissom, were Boilermakers. In this "real-world" context, I teach courses in the eccentric area of poetry analysis. Under the gun from financially-strapped parents and state legislators who demand concrete evidence of the economic value of a college degree, administrators want humanists to increase "efficiencies" and to provide scientific-style metrics to verify the value of what we do. How to quiet the chorus of criticisms that the humanities are simply a luxury that most students (except those at elite private colleges and the Ivy Leagues) can ill afford?

We sense that tenured faculty in the humanities are an endangered species, possibly the last of a dying breed. Even now, adjunct instructors and underpaid graduate assistants teach most courses in the humanities. Unfortunately, the guild these young teachers and scholars are making sacrifices to enter has less and less room to offer for them to enjoy the dignified career of their predecessors. Further, the ubiquitous presence of for-profit and on-line universities has put added pressure on brick and mortar universities to offer more options for students to take courses electronically. On-line "chat rooms" are replacing the face-to-face relationship fostered by a traditional classroom experience. A technophobic luddite whose most advanced classroom technologies remain the Xeroxed handout and syllabus, and the latest paperback copy of a reliable anthology of poems from Chaucer to Billy Collins, I find myself threatened by this brave new world. Has the time for what I do with love and passion, and what I believe to be of such fundamental cultural and pedagogic value, come to an end?

I'd like to make a case for the value of continuing to support, fund, and tenure experienced full-time humanities professors, whose work belongs in a classroom with a manageable degree of students. Given the *Tikkun* theme of "Tikkun Olam," I'd like to concentrate on how I teach "Mending Wall" (1914), a poem directly concerned with mending a broken world. One reason I teach this Robert Frost classic is because its meanings have been obscured by our sound-bite media culture. In class we notice the authoritative speaker of "Mending Wall" is *not* responsible for the oft-quoted proverb "Good fences make good neighbors," but rather this line is repeated twice by the dim-witted neighbor whom the speaker refers to as "an old-stone savage armed" who will "not go behind his father's saying." In the classroom we take the time to read and interpret the whole poem. We realize that the poem is a dialogue. Through attention to tone and perspective, we figure out that the main speaker—the character Frost clearly admires—contests what has become, ironically, the poem's best known phrase. Most importantly, I teach "Mending Wall" because the dialogue it records between the speaker and the neighbor reflects my sense of the value of a classroom teacher as a facilitator of a conversation, even if, as in Frost, there is a clear distinction between the knowledge base of the teacher and that of the student.

A Progressive might at first critique the speaker's act of calling the neighbor to mend the wall after the harsh New England winter has sent the stones tumbling to the ground. Such an act of wall building, the Progressive might argue, asserts borders that signify property ownership, and private rather than communal identity ("He is all pine and I am apple orchard./My apple trees will never get across/And eat the cones under his pines." But we need to consider the speaker's motivations for remaking that wall. The speaker challenges the neighbor's understanding that "spring mending time" merely asserts the Law of the Fathers to keep tradition going for tradition's sake. By reinterpreting wall building as "just another outdoor game," the speaker demystifies the aura of inevitability and grandeur of the tradition. The "savage" neighbor still adheres to tradition for its own sake, but the poem is a scene of instruction where the speaker, like a good classroom teacher, attempts to change the neighbor's (or students') mind by allowing the neighbor (or student), through dialogue and questioning, to arrive at a new definition of the meaning of the wall. "Spring is the mischief in me, and I wonder/If I could put a notion in his head:/Why do they make good neighbors?" The speaker challenges the congruence between mending the wall and reaffirming the "father's saying" that "good fences make good neighbors." Instead, the speaker's initiation of a return to the symbolic act of cultural construction through the demarcation of property lines is an invitation to the neighbor, and, implicitly, to the reader of the poem, to engage in an educational conversation about cultural making, tradition, and change. The speaker is something of a wicked school master. He is parodistic, witty, highly self-conscious, playfully mischievous, and contradictory. Wall building, from one perspective, is an enactment of a cultural hegemony as the neighbor mindlessly performs the act that conforms to the father's proverbial wisdom. The act of building the wall, however, can also be a mischievous scene of instruction, as the speaker initiates the neighbor in the performance of an event that the speaker as teacher does not perceive as valuable, except as a site on which he can question its traditional value.

"Mending Wall" is certainly set in a pedagogic space. It enacts a symbolic exchange that is an arena for a multiplicity of cultural struggles. Frost's language is marked by a plurality of value-laden perspectives that exist in challenging contact with one another. The symbolic gesture of rebuilding the wall after the winter's ravages and the hunter's violence means something different to the speaker and to the "savage" neighbor. As with Clifford Geertz's "thick" reading of the public meaning of a wink as, potentially, an involuntary tick, a secret code, a paranoid's belief in intrigue, or a parodist's mockery of paranoia, the speaker in Frost's poem perceives the symbolic event of wall-mending as multivalent. For him, rebuilding the wall is not a material necessity ("there where it is we do not need the wall"), but an excuse for the teacherly speaker to meet "and walk the line" on an annual basis with his student to discuss fundamental cultural values, such as putting up fences between persons where they may not be needed. Although the speaker initiates the neighbor in the ritual, an act one could argue reinforces dominant beliefs ("Good fences make good neighbors"), the speaker's analysis of his performance suggests that he is not merely rehearsing established codes of behavior that preserve the "father's saying." His analysis reaffirms cultural limits, but also suggests an experimentation with the meaning of cultural work such as teaching. The speaker challenges paternal lore—Greenblatt's "governing patterns of culture"—by way of the mindful enactment and playful attitude he brings to the ritual. In terms of finding resonance between the semantic meaning of the form of Frost's line (blank verse) and the speaker's ambivalent statement of cultural reconstruction within the poem, I will conclude with a prosodic analysis of "Mending Wall" that demonstrates how Frost acts out the conflicted meanings of culture making (wall building or line making) performed in the poem. As with the dialogic interpretation of wall building as a mindless return to the father's saying and as a witty gesture that subverts the highly restrained form, Frost troubles the regularity of the blank verse line through enjambment and metrical substitution. His relationship to an established measure allows for improvisation that challenges the conception of iambic pentameter as a hegemonic construct. Written as World War I approached, and in a period of profound aesthetic challenges to the maintenance of traditional formal constructs such as the poet's line of ten, Frost "mends" the fundamental sign of civic dwelling (the stone walls that designate where one person's place begins and another's ends), but does so in a way that suggests his openness to play, dialogue, and revision of these cultural acts.

Frost turns the reader's expectation for an established rhythm and meter into an opportunity to display prosodic surprises that disrupt the metrical regularity. His retention of an established line, the addition of formal restraint, enhances rather than constrains the possibilities for the creation of multiple meanings for his poem. The first syllable of the first word in the first foot of the first line of the poem, the "Some" of "Something there is that doesn't love a wall" rhymes with the meaning of the statement through the trochaic substitution and, on a syntactic level, with the inversion of the grammar of the sentence. The spondaic substitution in the fourth foot of line two – "frozen-ground-swell" – again rhymes on a prosodic level with the natural upheaval described in the first four lines. In his playful, witty, and improvisational display, Frost continually unsettles the reader's expectation of regularity in the blank verse line to enhance or to subvert the meaning of the "content" of the poem. The "feminine" ending (or silent eleventh syllable) in line eight: "but they would have the rabbit out of hiding" uses the unstressed syllable "ing" to suggest a visual pun, the invisible rabbit. The caesural pause midway in line nine: "To please the yelping dogs. The gaps I mean" uses another resource available to poet's working in a restricted measure to visualize content, in this case the "gaps" in the wall.

At other times, Frost creates "mischief" by visually displaying imagery that suggests a meaning opposed to the semantic content. An example occurs in lines 24 and 25 where the enjambment: "My apple trees will never get across/And eat the cones under his pines, I tell him" is contradicted by how the enjambed first line dips over into the second one. As the speaker is highly self-conscious about his wall-building activity, so too is Frost as a line builder who interprets his "Mending Wall" as a self-referential artifact. Lines such as "And on a day we meet to walk the line" and "We have to use a spell to make them balance" (with its eleven syllables, suggesting that the poet had to use a bit of technical magic to cram an extra syllable into a line that conformed to the five beat line) and the line "We wear our fingers rough with handling them" (poking fun at poets counting beats with their fingers) all suggest that Frost is enacting more than one form of cultural construction at the same time. He is rebuilding the wall in the poem and he is suggesting that the construction of linguistic artifacts based on traditional patterns can also leave room for disruptions that challenge cultural hegemonies by turning them into playful form. Mindfully enacted and understood as "just another kind of outdoor game," formal poetry in Frost's hands is taken outside the space and time of cultural legitimation (the classroom). It is given a recess, a lunch break, a chance to get outside and play.

In contemporary approaches to cultural studies, poetry as a genre has often been left out of discussions of culture because, unlike the novels and dramas that Stephen Greenblatt describes in his (1990) essay called "Culture," poetry is perceived as an obsolete form that expresses ahistorical (synchronic) perspectives on human action that ignores (diachronic) or historical accounts of human action. By using Robert Frost's "Mending Wall" (1914) as an example of a poem that recognizes the maker's place in culture as a negotiation with his specific time and place, I have tried to make a case for poetry in a cultural studies interpretive field by applying the interpretive theory of "culture" outlined by Greenblatt, Jackson Lears, and Clifford Geertz as a model of negotiation between movement and restraint though a dialogic critical practice to Frost's blank verse poem. I believe Frost's poem shows that it is in the face-to-face exchange between a knowing teacher and a student who is at least willing to show up to class to engage in a conversation about cultural values and traditions, that such a compelling approach to poetry can take place. I believe "Mending Wall" suggests why it is valuable to maintain the humanities, even at lunch bucket schools better known for exploration of the outer cosmos, than for probing the complex and often ambiguous contours of the inner cosmos of the human mind and heart.

BIBLIOGRAPHY

Adorno, Theodor (Fall 1975). "Culture Industry Reconsidered." Trans. Anson G. Rabinbach. *New German Critique*, 6, 12–19.

Agamben, Giorgio (2005). *State of Exception*. Trans. Kevin Attell. Chicago: University of Chicago Press.

Akavia, Naamah (2008). "Writing 'The Case of Ellen West': Clinical Knowledge and Historical Representation." *Science in Context*, 21 (1): 119–44.

Alexie, Sherman (1992a). "Evolution." In *The Business of Fancy Dancing*. New York: Hanging Loose Press.

—(1992b). "Reservation Love Song." In *The Business of Fancy Dancing*. New York: Hanging Loose Press.

—(1993). "On the Amtrak from Boston to New York City." In *First Indian on the Moon*. First published 1990. New York: Hanging Loose Press.

—(2002). "What Sacagawea Means To Me (and Perhaps to You)." *Time*, 8 July.

—(2005). "The Lone Ranger and Tonto Fistfight in Heaven" (1993). In *The Lone Ranger and Tonto Fistfight in Heaven*. New York: Grove Press.

—(2007a). *The Absolutely True Diary of a Part-Time Indian*. New York: Little, Brown and Company.

—(2007b). *Flight*. New York: Black Cat.

—(2009). *Face*. New York: Hanging Loose Press.

Allen, Paula Gunn (1993). "Kochinnenako in Academe: Three Approaches to Interpreting a Keres Indian Tale." In Melody Graulich (ed.), *Leslie Marmon Silko, "Yellow Woman."* New Brunswick, NJ: Rutgers University Press.

Anderson, Benedict (2006). *Imagined Communities: Reflections on the Origin and Spread of Nationalism*. London: Verso.

Anonymous (n.d.). "Allen Ginsberg." The Poetry Foundation website. Available at: http://www.poetryfoundation.org/bio/allen-ginsberg [accessed 20 December, 2012].

—(n.d.) "Frank Bidart." The Poetry Foundation website. Available at:

http://www.poetryfoundation.org/bio/frank-bidart [accessed 19 April 2012].

Axelrod, Steven Gould (2006). "Between Modernism and Postmodernism: The Cold War Poetics of Bishop, Lowell, and Ginsberg." PAMLA Presidential Address. *Pacific Coast Philology*, 42: 1–23.

Bakhtin, Mikhail (1982). *The Dialogic Imagination: Four Essays*. Trans. Michael Holquist, Vadim Liapunov and Kenneth Brostrom. Austin: University of Texas Press.

Barnes, Kim (1993). "A Leslie Marmon Silko Interview." In Melody Graulich (ed.), *Leslie Marmon Silko, "Yellow Woman."* New Brunswick, NJ: Rutgers University Press.

Barron, Jonathan and Selinger, Eric (2000). "Introduction." In *Jewish American Poetry: Poems, Commentary, and Reflections*. Hanover, MA: Brandeis University Press.

Belasco, Susan and Johnson, Linck (eds) (2008). On "Dear John, Dear Coltrane." In *The Bedford Anthology of American Literature: Volume Two*. Boston: Bedford/St. Martin's Press.

Bhaba, Homi ([1994] 2004). *The Location of Culture*. London: Routledge.

Bidart, Frank (1990). *In the Western Night: Collected Poems: 1965–1990*. New York: Farrar, Straus & Giroux.

—(1999). *Desire*. New York: Farrar, Straus & Giroux.

—(2002). "Introduction." In Frank Bidart and David Gewanter (eds), *The Collected Poems of Robert Lowell*. London: Faber & Faber.

Binswanger, Lionel (1958). "The Case of Ellen West." Trans. Werner M. Mendel and Joseph Lyons. In Rollo May, Ernest Angel, and Henri F. Ellenberger (eds). *Existence: A New Dimension in Psychiatry and Psychology* (pp. 237–364). New York: Basic Books.

Bishop, Elizabeth (1979). *The Complete Poems: 1927–1979*. New York: Farrar, Straus and Giroux.

Bleich, David (2000). "Learning, Learning, Learning: Jewish Poetry in America." In Jonathan Barron, and Eric Selinger (eds), *Jewish American Poetry: Poems, Commentary, and Reflections*. Hanover, MA: Brandeis University Press.

Bloom, Harold (1973). *The Anxiety of Influence: A Theory of Poetry*. Oxford: Oxford University Press.

—(1999). *Shakespeare: The Invention of the Human*. New York: Riverhead Trade.

Bordo, Susan ([1993] 2004). *Unbearable Weight: Feminism, Western Culture, and the Body*. Tenth anniversary edn. Berkeley: University of California Press.

Breslin, James (1985). Review of "Howl" and "Kaddish." In Lewis Hyde (ed.), *On the Poetry of Allen Ginsberg (Under Discussion)*. Ann Arbor: University of Michigan Press.

Breslin, Paul (1987). *The Psycho-Political Muse: American Poetry Since the Fifties*. Chicago: University of Chicago Press.

Brown, Joseph A. (1986). "Their Long Scars Touch Ours: A Reflection on the Poetry of Michael Harper." *Callaloo*, 9 (1): 209–220.

Butler, Judith (2005). *Giving an Account of Oneself*. New York: Fordham University Press.

Byrne, Edward. (2008). "John Coltrane, Michael S. Harper, and Amiri Baraka: Jazz Music and Poetry." Available online: http://edwardbyrne. blogspot.com/2008/09/john-coltrane-michael-s-harper-and.html [accessed 21 March 2012].

Carby, Hazel (1998). *Race Men*. Cambridge, MA: Harvard University Press.

Carroll, Kathleen L. (Spring 2005). "Ceremonial Tradition as Form and Theme in Sherman Alexie's *The Lone Ranger and Tonto Fistfight in Heaven*: A Performance-Based Approach to Native American Literature." *The Journal of the Midwest Modern Language Association*, 38 (1), 74–84.

Caruth, Cathy (1996). *Unclaimed Experience: Trauma, Narrative and History*. Baltimore, MD: Johns Hopkins University Press.

Cavitch, Max (2006). "Emma Lazarus and the Golem of Liberty." *American Literary History* 18 (1), 1–28.

Chauncey, George (1994). *Gay New York: Gender, Urban Culture, and the Making of the Gay Male World, 1890–1940*. New York: Basic Books.

Chiasson, Dan (2007). "Presence: Frank Bidart." In *On Frank Bidart: Fastening the Voice to the Page* (pp. 48–67). Ann Arbor: University of Michigan Press.

Cofer, Judith Ortiz (2005). "The Latin Deli: An Ars Poetica." In R. S. Gwynn and April Lindner (eds), *Contemporary American Poetry*. New York: Penguin.

Coltrane, John (1964). "Dear Listener." Liner notes for *A Love Supreme*. Impulse Records.

Davidson, Michael (1997). *Ghostlier Demarcations: Modern Poetry and the Material Word*. Berkeley: University of California Press. Available online: http://www.english.illinois.edu/maps/poets/m_r/reznikoff/ davidson.htm [accessed 1 June 2012].

DeShazer, Mary K. (1994). *A Poetics of Resistance: Women Writing in El Salvador, South Africa, and the United States*. Ann Arbor: University of Michigan Press.

Dickstein, Morris (1991). "Allen Ginsberg." In John A. Garraty and Eric Foner (eds), *The Reader's Companion to American History*. Boston: Houghton Mifflin Company. Available online: http:// www.answers.com/library/American+History+Companion-letter-1G#ixzz1fWA0XXy8 [accessed 3 January 2012].

Doty, Mark (2004). "Human Seraphim: 'Howl,' Sex, and Holiness." *Poets.org*. Available online: http://www.poets.org/printmedia.php/ prmMedialD/2190 [accessed 10 June 2012].

Dunick, Lisa (2004). "On Dear John, Dear Coltrane." *Modern American Poetry*. Available online: http://www.english.illinois.edu/maps/ poets/g_l/harper/dearjohn.htm [accessed 15 July 2012].

Eliot. T. S. ([1922] 1971). *The Waste Land*. San Diego: Harcourt Mifflin Harcourt.

—(1975a). "Tradition and the Individual Talent." In Frank Kermode (ed.), *Selected Prose of T.S. Eliot*. New York: Harcourt Brace Jovanovich.

—(1975b). "*Ulysses*, Order, and Myth." In Frank Kermode (ed.), *Selected Prose of T.S. Eliot*. New York: Harcourt Brace Jovanovich.

Elliott, Emory (ed.) (1991). *American Literature: A Prentice Hall Anthology*, vol. Two. Englewood Cliffs, NJ: Prentice Hall.

Emanuel, James A. (1967). *Langston Hughes*. New York: Twayne.

Farrell, Barry (1966). "The Guru Comes to Kansas." *Life Magazine*. 27 May, 78–90.

Ferrell, Tracy J. Prince. (1995). "'Theme for English B' and the Dreams of Langston Hughes." *English Review*, September, 36–7.

Fink, Thomas & Halden-Sullivan, Judy (2013). "Introduction." In *Reading the Difficulties*. Tuscaloosa: University of Alabama Press.

Flanzbaum, Hilene. (1999). "The Imaginary Jew and the American Poet." In Hilene Flanzbaum (ed.), *The Americanization of the Holocaust* (pp. 18–32). Baltimore, MD: Johns Hopkins University Press.

Fontenot, Chester J., Jr. (1981). "Angelic Dance or Tug of War? The Humanistic Implications of Cultural Formalism." In R. Baxter Miller (ed.), *Black American Literature and Humanism* (pp. 33–49). Lexington: University of Kentucky Press.

Forché, Carolyn (ed.). (1993). *Against Forgetting: Twentieth-Century Poetry of Witness*. New York: W. W. Norton.

Fredman, Stephen (2010). *Contextual Practice: Assemblage and the Erotic in Postwar Poetry and Art*. Stanford, CA: Stanford University Press.

Freud, Sigmund (1917). "Mourning and Melancholia." In *The Standard Edition of the Complete Psychological Works of Sigmund Freud*. (Vol. 14, pp. 239–60). London: Hogarth Press.

Frost, Robert (1995). *Collected Poems, Prose, and Plays*. New York: Library of America.

Geertz, Clifford (1973). *The Interpretation of Cultures*. New York: Basic Books.

Gilman, Sander (1991). *The Jew's Body*. New York: Routledge.

Ginsberg, Allen (1995). *Collected Poems, 1947–1985.* London: Penguin.

Gish, Nancy K. (1988). *The Waste Land: A Poem of Memory and Desire.* New York: Twayne.

Graulich, Melody (ed.). (1993). *Leslie Marmon Silko, "Yellow Woman."* New Brunswick, NJ: Rutgers University Press.

Gray, Richard (2011). *After the Fall: American Literature Since 9/11.* Chichester: John Wiley & Sons.

Greenblatt, Stephen (1990). "Culture." In Frank Lentricchia and Thomas McLaughlin (eds), *Critical Terms for Literary Study.* Chicago: University of Chicago Press.

Grossman, Allen R. (1989). "Orpheus/Philomela: Subjection and Mastery in the Founding Stories of Poetic Production and in the Logic of Our Practice." *Triquarterly* Winter 77: 229–48.

—(1992). *The Sighted Singer: Two Works on Poetry for Readers and Writers.* Baltimore, MD: Johns Hopkins University Press.

Guimond, James (1968). *The Art of William Carlos Williams: A Discovery and Possession of America.* Urbana: University of Illinois Press.

Hage, Ghassan (1998). *White Nation: Fantasies of White Supremacy in a Multicultural Society.* Sydney: Pluto Press.

Halliday, Mark (1990). "Interview with Frank Bidart." In *In the Western Night: Collected Poems: 1965–1990.* New York: Farrar, Straus & Giroux.

Halter, Peter (1994). *Revolution in the Visual Arts and the Poetry of William Carlos Williams.* New York: Cambridge University Press.

Harlow, Barbara (1987). *Resistance Literature.* New York: Routledge.

Harper, Michael S. (2005). "Dear John, Dear Coltrane." In R. S. Gwynn and April Lindner (eds), *Contemporary American Poetry.* New York: Pearson Longman. Originally published in book form in *Dear John, Dear Coltrane,* University of Pittsburgh Press (Pittsburgh, PA), 1970, reprinted, University of Illinois Press (Urbana, IL), 1985.

Harrowitz, Nancy A. and Hymans, Barbara (eds). (1995). *Jews & Gender: Responses to Otto Weininger.* Philadelphia, PA: Temple University Press.

Hartman, Anne (2005). "Confessional Counterpublics in Frank O'Hara and Allen Ginsberg." *Journal of Modern Literature,* 28 (4), 40–56.

Hartman, Stephanie (1999). "All Systems Go: Muriel Rukeyser's 'The Book of the Dead' and the Reinvention of Modernist Poetics." In Anne F. Herzog and Janet E. Kaufman (eds), *"How Shall We Tell Each Other of the Poet?": The Life and Writing of Muriel Rukeyser.* New York: St. Martin's Press.

Hejinian, Lyn (1991). "The Person and Description," *Poetics Journal 9*; "The Poetics of Everyday Life, Symposium." (ed.) Barrett Watten and Lyn Hejinian, 170.

Hennessy, Rosemary (Summer 1993). "Queer Theory: A Review of the *differences* Special Issue and Wittig's *The Straight Mind.*" *Signs*, *18*, 964–973.

Hogan, William (Spring 2004). "Roots, Routes, and Langston Hughes's Hybrid Sense of Place." *The Langston Hughes Review*, *18*: 3–23.

Hughes, Langston (1940). *The Big Sea*. New York: Knopf.

—([1949] 1994). "Theme for English B." In Arnold Rampersad (ed.), *The Collected Poems of Langston Hughes*. New York: Knopf.

Hyde, Lewis (ed.) (1985) *On the Poetry of Allen Ginsberg (Under Discussion)*. Ann Arbor: University of Michigan Press.

Jahner, Elaine A. (1994). "Leslie Marmon Silko." In Andrew Wiget (ed.), *Dictionary of Native American Literature*. New York: Garland.

Jarraway, David (2003). *Going the Distance: Dissident Subjectivity in Modernist American Literature*. Baton Rouge: Louisiana State University Press.

Jeffreys, Mark (1995). "The Ideologies of Lyric: A Problem of Genre in Contemporary Anglophone Poetics." *PMLA*, *110–12*, 197.

Jemie, Onwuchekwa (1989). "Jazz, Jive, and Jam." In Harold Bloom (ed.), *Langston Hughes* (pp. 61–92). New York: Chelsea House.

Johnson, E. Patrick and Henderson, Mae G. (eds). (2005). *Black Queer Studies: A Critical Anthology*. Durham, NC: Duke University Press.

Johnson, James Weldon (1960). *The Autobiography of an Ex-Coloured Man*. New York: Hill and Wang.

Kahn, Ashley (2002). *A Love Supreme: The Story of John Coltrane's Signature Album*. New York: Viking.

Kellner, Bruce (2004). "'Refined Racism': White Patronage in the Harlem Renaissance." In Harold Bloom (ed.), *The Harlem Renaissance* (pp. 53–66). New York: Chelsea House.

Kennedy, X. J. and Gioia, Dana (2009). *An Introduction to Poetry*. Boston: Longman.

LaCapra, Dominick (2000). *Writing History, Writing Trauma*. Baltimore, MD: Johns Hopkins University Press.

Lakoff, George (2006). *Thinking Points: Communicating Our American Values and Vision*. New York: Farrar, Straus & Giroux.

Lamb, Robert Paul (Spring 2008). "'A Little Yellow Bastard Boy': Paternal Rejection, Filial Insistence, and the Triumph of African American Cultural Aesthetics in Langston Hughes's 'Mulatto.'" *College Literature*, *35* (2), 126–153.

Lazarus, Emma (2007). "The New Colossus." In J. Paul Hunter (ed.), *The Norton Introduction to Poetry*. New York: W. W. Norton.

Lears, T. J. Jackson (1983). "From Salvation to Self-Realization." In Richard Wightman Fox and T. J. Jackson Lears (eds), *The Culture of Consumption*. New York: Pantheon.

Leitch, Vincent B. (1988). *American Literary Criticism from the Thirties to the Eighties*. New York: Columbia University Press.

Lenz, Gunter H. (1984). "Black Poetry and Black Music: History and Tradition in Michael Harper and John Coltrane." In *History and Tradition in Afro-American Culture* (pp. 277–319). Berlin: Campus Press.

Leonard, Keith (1997). "Michael S. Harper." In William L. Andrews, Frances Foster Smith & Trudier Harris (eds), *The Oxford Companion to African American Literature*. New York: Oxford University Press.

—(n.d.). "Michael S. Harper's Life and Career." *Modern American Poetry*. Available online: http://www.english.illinois.edu/maps/ poets/g_l/harper/ [accessed 19 June 2012].

Liberman, M. M. and Foster, Edward E. (1968). *A Modern Lexicon of Literary Terms*. Glenview, IL: Scott Foresman.

Lowell, Robert (1956). *Life Studies and For the Union Dead*. New York: Farrar, Straus & Giroux.

Mack, Michael (2003). *German Idealism and the Jew: The Inner Anti-Semitism of Philosophy and German Jewish Responses*. Chicago: University of Chicago Press.

MacLeish, Archibald (2007). "Ars Poetica." In J. Paul Hunter (ed.), *The Norton Introduction to Poetry*. New York: W. W. Norton.

McBride, Dwight A. (2005) "Straight Black Studies: On African American Studies, James Baldwin, and Black Queer Studies." In Patrick E. Johnson and Mae G. Henderson (eds), *Black Queer Studies: A Critical Anthology* (pp. 68–89). Durham, NC: Duke University Press.

Mikics, David (2007). *A New Handbook of Literary Terms*. New Haven, CT: Yale University Press.

Miles, Barry (1989). *Ginsberg: A Biography*. New York: Simon & Schuster.

Miller, Arthur ([1947] 2000). *All My Sons*. London: Penguin.

Mitchell, W. J. T. (1994). *Picture Theory*. Chicago: University of Chicago Press.

Moore, Walter (2011). "Postmodern *Howl*: A Cultural Clash and Censorship, 1957 to Today." Unpublished essay.

Morgan, Bill (2006). *I Celebrate Myself: The Somewhat Private Life of Allen Ginsberg*. New York: Viking.

Myles, Eileen. "Repeating Allen." *Poets.org*. Available online: http://www.poets.org/printmedia.php/prmMedialD/21914 [accessed 13 May 2012].

Nadel, Alan (1995). *Containment Culture: American Narratives, Postmodernism, and the Atomic Age*. Durham, NC: Duke University Press.

Nealon. Jeffrey T. (1997). "The Ethics of Dialogue: Bakhtin and Levinas." *College English*, 59 (2), 129–48.

Nelson, Cary (ed.) (2000). "On Dear John/Dear Coltrane." In *Anthology of Modern American Poetry*. New York: Oxford University Press.

Nisenson, Eric (2001). *The Making of Kind of Blue: Miles Davis and His Masterpiece*. New York: St. Martin's Press.

Omer-Sherman, Ranen (2002). "Emma Lazarus, Jewish American Poetics, and the Challenge of Modernity." *Legacy: A Journal of American Women Writers*, 19 (2), 170–91.

Pease, Donald. (2009a) "August Wilson: The Work of the Humanities After Humanism." Annual Presidential Lecture at Dartmouth College, February 18, 2009. [Accessed via YouTube. 1 December 2012].

—(2009b). *The New American Exceptionalism*. Minneapolis: University of Minnesota Press.

Peddle, Ian (Spring 2004). "'There's No Way Not to Lose': Langston Hughes and Intraracial Class Antagonism." *The Langston Hughes Review*, 18, 38–55.

Peterson, Nancy J. (ed.) (2009). *Conversations with Sherman Alexie*. Jackson: University of Mississippi Press.

Pinsky, Robert (1978). *The Situation of Poetry: Contemporary Poetry and Its Traditions*. Princeton, NJ: Princeton University Press.

Porter, Lewis (1999). *John Coltrane: His Life and Music*. Ann Arbor: University of Michigan Press.

Pratt, Mary Louise (1991). "Arts of the Contact Zone." In *Profession 91* (pp. 33–41). New York: Modern Language Association.

Quinn, Justin (2003). "Coteries, Landscape and the Sublime in Allen Ginsberg." *Journal of Modern Literature*, 27 (1), 193–206.

Rampersad, Arnold (1988). *The Life of Langston Hughes: Volume I: 1902–1941, I, Too, Sing America*. New York: Oxford University Press.

—(2002). *The Life of Langston Hughes: Volume II: 1914–1967, I Dream a World*. New York: Oxford University Press.

Randall, James (1984). "Interview with Michael S. Harper." In Joe David Bellamy (ed.), *American Poetry Observed* (pp. 88–100). Urbana: University of Illinois Press.

Rector, Liam and Swenson, Tree (eds). (2007). *On Frank Bidart: Fastening the Voice to the Page*. Ann Arbor: University of Michigan Press.

Reznikoff, Charles (1978). *Testimony: The United States (1885–1915)*, vol. 1. Santa Rosa, CA: Black Sparrow Press.

Roach, Joseph (2010). "Performance: The Blunders of Orpheus." *PMLA*, 125 (4), 1078–86.

Rosenthal, M. L. (1991). Article from *The Nation*, 19 September 1959.

In *Our Life in Poetry: Selected Essays and Reviews* (pp. 109–12). New York: Persea Books.

Rowell, Charles H. (1990) "'Down Don't Worry Me': An Interview with Michael S. Harper." *Callaloo*, *13*, 780–800.

Rubin, Steven (2000). "Poets of the Promised Land, 1800–1920." In Jonathan Barron and Eric Selinger (eds), *Jewish American Poetry: Poems, Commentary, and Reflections*. Hanover, MA: Brandeis University Press.

Rukeyser, Muriel (2005). *The Collected Poems of Muriel Rukeyser*. Janet Kaufman and Anne Herzog (eds). Pittsburgh, PA: University of Pittsburgh Press.

Sanders, Ed. (2000). *The Poetry and Life of Allen Ginsberg: A Narrative Poem*. New York: Overlook Press.

Schmidt, Peter (1988). *William Carlos Williams, the Arts, and Literary Tradition*. Baton Rouge: Louisiana State University Press.

Scott, Jonathan (Spring 2006). "Advanced, Repressed, and Popular: Langston Hughes During the Cold War." *College Literature*, *33* (2), 30–51.

Seidel, Frederick (Winter–Spring 1961). "Robert Lowell: The Art of Poetry No. 3" *Paris Review 25*. Available at: http://www.theparisreview.org/interviews/4664/the-art-of-poetry-no-3-robert-lowell [accessed 5 December 2012].

Shakespeare, William (2000). "My Mistress' Eyes Are Nothing Like the Sun" (Sonnet 130). In Joseph DeRoche (ed.), *The Heath Introduction to Poetry*. Boston: Houghton-Mifflin.

Sheppard, R. Z. (1985). "Mainstreaming Allen Ginsberg." *Time*, February.

Silko, Leslie Marmon (1977). *Ceremony*. New York: Viking.

—(1981). "Language and Literature from a Pueblo Indian Perspective." In Leslie Fiedler & Houston A. Baker (eds), *English Literature: Opening Up the Canon*. (pp. 54–72). Baltimore, MD: Johns Hopkins University Press.

—(1989). *Storyteller*. New York: Arcade Publishing.

—(1996a). "Fences Against Freedom." In *Yellow Woman and a Beauty of the Spirit: Essays on Native American Life Today*. New York: Simon & Schuster.

—(1996b). "Interior and Exterior Landscapes." In *Yellow Woman and a Beauty of the Spirit: Essays on Native American Life Today*. New York: Simon & Schuster.

—(1996c). "On Nonfiction Prose." In *Yellow Woman and a Beauty of the Spirit: Essays on Native American Life Today*. New York: Simon & Schuster.

—(1996d). "The People and the Land ARE Inseparable." In *Yellow*

Woman and a Beauty of the Spirit: Essays on Native American Life Today. New York: Simon & Schuster.

—(1996e). "Yellow Woman and a Beauty of the Spirit." In *Yellow Woman and a Beauty of the Spirit: Essays on Native American Life Today.* New York: Simon & Schuster.

Silko, Leslie Marmon & Wright, James (1986). *The Delicacy and Strength of Lace.* Anne Wright (ed.). Minneapolis: Graywolf Press.

Slotkin, Richard (1973). *Regeneration Through Violence: The Mythology of the American Frontier, 1600–1860.* Middletown, CT: Wesleyan University Press.

Smith, Raymond (2004). "Langston Hughes: Evolution of the Poetic Persona." In Harold Bloom (ed.), *The Harlem Renaissance* (pp. 35–51). New York: Chelsea House.

Sollors, Werner (1986). *Beyond Ethnicity: Consent and Descent in American Culture.* New York: Oxford University Press.

Stepto, Robert B. (1990). "Let's Call Your Mama and Other Lies about Michael S. Harper." *Callaloo, 13,* 801–4.

Stewart, Susan (2002). *Poetry and the Fate of the Senses.* Chicago: University of Chicago Press.

Stitt, Peter (1990). "Introduction." In Peter Stitt and Frank Graziano (eds), *James Wright: The Heart of the Light.* Ann Arbor: Michigan University Press.

Svonkin, Craig (Fall 2010). "Manishevitz and Sake, the Kaddish and Sutras: Allen Ginsberg's Spiritual Self-Othering." *College Literature, 37* (4), 166–93.

Tashjian, Dickran (1978). *William Carlos Williams and the American Scene, 1920–1940.* Berkeley: University of California Press.

Thoreau, Henry David (2000). *Walden and Other Writings.* New York: Modern Library.

Turner, Daniel C. (Fall/Spring 2002). "Montage of a Simplicity Deferred: Langston Hughes's Art of Sophistication and Racial Intersubjectivity in *Montage of a Dream Deferred.*" *The Langston Hughes Review, 17,* 22–33.

TV.Com. *The Phil Donahue Show.* Available at: http://www.tv.com/shows/the-phil-donahue-show [accessed 9 July 2012].

Vendler, Helen (1977). Review of *The Book of the Body. Yale Review, Autumn,* 78–9.

—(1997). *Poems, Poets, Poetry: An Introduction and Anthology.* Boston: Bedford Books.

Waters, William (2003). *Poetry's Touch: On Lyric Address.* Ithaca, NY: Cornell University Press.

Watten, Barrett and Hejinian, Lyn (ds.). (1991) "The Poetics of Everyday Life, Symposium," *Poetics Journal 9*: 170.

Weinberg, Jonathan (1995). *Speaking for Vice: Homosexuality in the Art of Charles Demuth, Marsden Hartley, and the First American Avant-Garde*. New Haven, CT: Yale University Press.

West, Cornel (1994). *Race Matters*. New York: Vintage Books.

Weston, Jessie ([1920] 1957). *From Ritual to Romance*. New York: Doubleday.

White, Edmund (2007). "On Ellen West." In *On Frank Bidart: Fastening the Voice to the Page* (pp. 110–11). Ann Arbor: University of Michigan Press.

Whitman, Walt (1855). "Preface." In *Leaves of Grass*. In *The Complete Poems*. New York: Penguin Classics. Reprint edition 2005.

Williams, William Carlos (1951). *The Autobiography of William Carlos Williams*. New York: New Directions Press.

—(1991). *The Collected Poems of William Carlos Williams*, vol. 1: 1909–1939. Christopher MacGowan and Walton Litz (eds). New York: New Directions Press.

—(2007). "This is Just to Say." In J. Paul Hunter (ed.), *The Norton Introduction to Poetry*. New York: W. W. Norton.

—(2008). "Danse Russe." In Susan Belasco and Linck Johnson (eds), *The Bedford Anthology of American Literature*, vol. 2. Boston: Bedford Books.

Williamson, Alan (1984). *Introspection and Contemporary Poetry*. Cambridge, MA: Harvard University Press.

Wright, James (1990). *Above the River: The Complete Poems*. Middletown, CN: Wesleyan University Press.

INDEX